Hatteras Blues

A STORY FROM THE EDGE OF AMERICA

Tom Carlson

The University of North Carolina Press | Chapel Hill

Designed by April Leidig-Higgins
Set in Minion by Copperline Book Services, Inc.
Manufactured in the United States of America

This book was published with the assistance of
the Blythe Family Fund of the University of North
Carolina Press.

Excerpt from *Murder in the Cathedral* by T. S. Eliot,
copyright 1935 by Harcourt, Inc., and renewed
1963 by T. S. Eliot, reprinted by permission of the
publisher.

Excerpt from "Landscape with the Fall of Icarus"
by William Carlos Williams, from *Collected Poems
1939–1962, Volume II*, copyright © 1953 by William
Carlos Williams. Reprinted by permission of New
Directions Publishing Corp.

The paper in this book meets the guidelines for
permanence and durability of the Committee on
Production Guidelines for Book Longevity of the
Council on Library Resources.

Library of Congress Cataloging-in-Publication Data
Carlson, Tom, 1944–
Hatteras blues: a story from the edge of America /
by Tom Carlson.
      p. cm.
Includes bibliographical references.
ISBN 0-8078-2975-7 (cloth: alk. paper)
      1. Charter boat fishing—North Carolina—Outer
Banks.   2. Foster family—North Carolina—Outer
Banks.   3. Outer Banks (N.C.)—Description and
travel.   I. Title.
SH531.C37   2006
799.16'09163'48—dc22   2005010245

09 08 07 06   5 4 3 2

Mo
whose presence, whose absence,
illuminates this book

Ernie and Lynne Foster
and Tall Bill Van Druten
teachers and friends

Al, Doc, Ed, Flo, Jake, Stan, and Bart
The old-timers on the benches at
Carlson's Corner

The First Families of the Outer Banks,
living and otherwise, who shaped their
lives with their backs and hearts, in
equal measure.

And a tiny, forgotten shoot of one old
family tree, a little girl whose storm-worn
tombstone struggles by itself above a tangle
of greenbrier, cedar, lichen, and vine:
Midgett, Cinderella
15 September 1914 – 30 September 1914

Contents

Maps and Illustrations

Preface

It was the heart of the Great Depression, and for Ernal Foster it had turned into fish-or-cut-bait time. He'd decided to fish—which was appropriate since that's what he did for a living out of tiny Hatteras Village on the Outer Banks of North Carolina. Ernal Foster, age twenty-five, had few prospects, $800 to his name, and an idea. He talked about his idea obsessively with his younger brother, Bill, and now he was going to see if it worked. Like almost everyone else in Hatteras Village, the Foster family made its living commercial fishing. The waters of the vast Albemarle and Pamlico sounds separating the Banks from the mainland teemed with spot, menhaden, croaker, sea trout, flounder, and many other species. When the weather was good, you could leave the sound and head out the inlets to the ocean, where you could set your nets just offshore. Even haul seining off the beaches helped to pay the bills. All of it was honest, backbreaking, mind-numbing, and often dangerous work.

When Ernal was a kid and had time off from helping his father fish, he'd sometimes borrow a boat and ferry customers from the mainland across the sound and out to the Atlantic beaches. In the afternoons he'd bring them back. Sometimes he and a friend would offer to take some of the beach passengers out fishing in the boat. They always had takers. Other times, Ernal would be sitting with his brother Bill and friends along the docks and they would see the fancy private sportfishing boats coming up from Miami or down from Montauk or Ocean City. The boats were sleek and shiny, and their owners often tan and dashing and full of exotic stories and bravado. These men were here because they knew what the boys knew: that the inshore waters off the Outer Banks were alive with fish—bull redfish, slammer blue-fish, mackerel, and countless bottom fish (jacks, tautog, sea bass, shark)—around the numerous wrecks. And further offshore, some twenty miles or so out, near the warm waters of the Gulf Stream, there were dolphin, tuna, wahoo, king mackerel, and then some really big gamefish, including the king of the pelagics—the blue marlin. They hadn't heard of anyone catching one yet, but they were there, as sure as the tides.

In addition to the visiting yachtsmen, other fishermen sometimes made their way down the Outer Banks to Hatteras Village by hitching rides on the mail boat or in jalopies with half-deflated tires so they could drive on the soft beach sand. They would try to get the commercial fishermen in the village to take them out gamefishing, but, more often than not, the locals chose not to give up a good day's commercial haul.

Here's where Ernal Foster's idea came in. Like many great ideas it was quite simple: what if you built a boat first and foremost for sportfishing and you made a living taking parties out for gamefish? Oh, you could convert the boat for commercial fishing if you had to, but the point was to get people to come down to Hatteras Village (even if there were no road and no bridge out to Hatteras Island) and pay you to take them out fishing for fun. Was it possible to make a living at it? Skeptics among the village elders were legion, but Ernal was willing to bet his stake on it. Ernal gathered up the wood—mostly juniper—cured it himself, and took it around to four boatyards be-fore one down in Marshallberg agreed to build it exactly the way he wanted it. In April 1937, the *Albatross* was in the water. It cost $805. Ernal took it home to Hatteras Village. His mother was so upset at her son's harebrained scheme she wouldn't even go look at the boat he had spent his last dime on. The first summer, Ernal and Bill made four fishing trips, $25 a trip, all day. The next few years weren't much better. Then the war came, and Ernal and Bill were in the service. Then they were back home and back in the charter fishing business. And then their luck changed.

I first encountered the *Albatross* fleet in 1984 when I was vacationing on the Outer Banks with my family. We were headed to Ocracoke Island, just a ferry ride across the narrow inlet from Hatteras Village. We had stopped

The *Albatross* fleet, Hatteras Village, North Carolina (Courtesy of Ernie Foster)

at the Hatteras Harbor Marina for lunch, and there, a stone's throw from our table, was the picket fence of aluminum outriggers angling up from the line of sleek fishing boats rimming the marina. Except at one spot: here six red-and-white-striped cane poles snaked up arthritically amid the orderly aluminum fence. I walked over toward the barber-pole outriggers to a tiny portion of the marina that said "Foster's Quay," probably less than a hundred feet long. There side by side in three slips sat the *Albatross*, the *Albatross II*, and the *Albatross III*, white hulled with aqua trim and very nearly triplets. They were graceful and bygone and beautiful with their high, flared bows, their open, no-frills cabins, each with bench seats and brass-and-wood-spoked wheels. Behind the cabins were wood-slatted fighting chairs and distinctive, rounded sterns. Except for the rounded sterns, they reminded me of the boats I'd grown up with on the Jersey Shore in the 1950s.

The *Albatross* fleet stayed firmly moored in my mind over the years. Fifteen years later I found myself booking a summer charter from my home in Memphis. I'd just finished teaching summer school at the university, and I was ready for a break. Since I often switched from academic to freelance writing in the summer, I thought I might do a story on Ernie Foster and his boats, and there seemed ample reason. Ernie's father, Ernal, had taken that chance in 1937, and the result was a thriving, multimillion-dollar charter

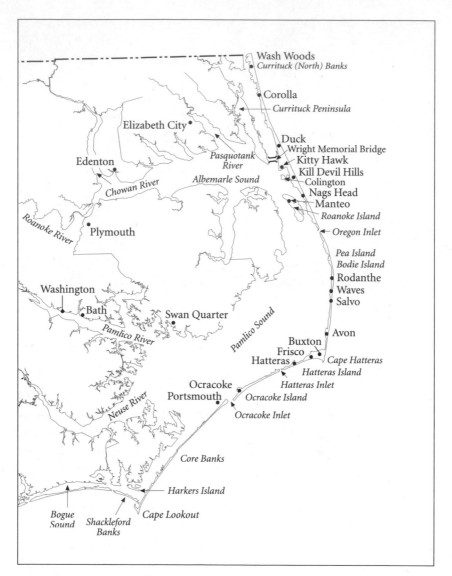

The Outer Banks of North Carolina

fishing industry on the Outer Banks. Anyone who knew acknowledged that Ernal had started the whole thing. And the string of "firsts" for the fleet was impressive too. Ernal and Bill caught the first blue marlin for a paying customer off the Outer Banks. They also caught the first white marlin and the first sailfish, and recorded the first "Grand Slam": a blue marlin, a white marlin, and a sailfish, all in the same day. And then they caught the world-record marlin, and Hatteras Village was suddenly known as the "Billfish Capital of the World." It still is. The first tarpon, the first striped bass on a rod and reel (they had been harvested commercially only up until that point). The first catch-and-release marlin on the East Coast, the first woman to catch a marlin. And on and on. And then their luck changed again.

In the more than five years I spent traveling back and forth to Hatteras Village, however, the story grew into something more than a fishing story. It became a larger, more complex narrative of family and community, of fierce independence and communal strength, of love and loss. The *Albatross* fleet was struggling now to compete with the myriad larger, faster boats underwritten by big corporations as tax write-offs and captained by off-islanders. Captain Ernie wasn't getting any younger, and his children turned their backs on the business and left Hatteras Island for opportunities on the mainland. Hatteras Village in general was threatened by an exodus of its young. And then there were the developers. Huge, twenty-room McMansions were going up on the Atlantic beaches east of town and on the sound side as well. One of the last untouched fishing villages along the North Carolina coast now had a line of ragged, nonindigenous palm trees planted along the road in its very center, an advertisement for Hatteras-by-the-Sea, a new condo complex with all the amenities. And, at the northern edge of town, Slash Creek was going up along a pristine estuary. Developers and politicians were in bed together on Slash Creek. The town was angry. The developer said publicly, "F——'em! If I want to build a miniature golf course and have fireworks and giant clowns with flames shooting out their asses, I will!" So the battle was joined. A family's traditions and a community's identity in one corner and rough-and-tumble American Progress in the other—if *Hatteras Blues* was about triumphant beginnings, it was also going to be about tragic endings.

And, I discovered, it was not going to be a dispassionate account. Soon enough, the Foster family and the people of Hatteras Village stopped being subjects of a story and turned into humans who touched me deeply and compromised me journalistically. I had grown up with people like them on the Jersey Shore, had served them meals and coffee and listened to their stories for years at my family's boardwalk restaurant on Manasquan Beach. The Fosters and their friends reanimated a part of my past, but more than that, their imminent loss, the elegiac note that sounded in the background of their lives, was a note I was hearing myself. I gradually realized that I had been drawn deeply into this story because of my own impending loss. My lovely wife of more than three decades was dying of a slow, degenerative disease. I was the primary caregiver, had been for years, and it was finally exacting a toll. In hindsight, one of the reasons I began this writing project was as a kind of professional distraction. But the story didn't distract me at all. If anything, it directed me; it walked up to me and took my hand and showed me precisely what I should not neglect. It turned out to be a lesson for me, this story I was witnessing, in how to prepare for absence and loss, and then how to grieve with some measure of grace and dignity. No wonder I had been drawn to it, to these people. I have tried to keep my presence in the story to a minimum, but I am in it because it would be dishonest to pass myself off as an objective, disinterested observer. I wasn't. The story of these people unexpectedly but indelibly became my story. I believe too that the story of the Foster family and the people of Hatteras Village is, in many ways, the story of us all.

Acknowledgments

For much of the historical background of the Outer Banks, I, like everyone else, owe a major debt to David Stick, the dean of Outer Banks historians, whose lifetime of research and numerous books and articles paved the way for all subsequent commentators on this special part of the world (just as his passion for ecological and cultural preservation was instrumental in creating the Cape Hatteras National Seashore). Other subsequent commentators I found especially lucid and useful include Ben Dixon MacNeill, Alton Ballance, Rodney Barfield, and Anthony Bailey.

I also wish to express my thanks to the numerous oral historians, both professional and amateur, who took the time to interview citizens and to transcribe and archive the results so that local history and myth, truth and tall tale, might be preserved forever. Among their number are Glen Carlin, Dale Farrow, Michael Tiedt, Len Belarco, Don Wharton, Elizabeth Leland, David Wright, David Zoby, Mark Taylor, Vera A. Evans, and of course the staff of the *Hatteras Monitor* and the *Island Breeze,* who do such recording of the passing parade for a living and who have been doing it for years. A special thanks to Buddy Swain of Hatteras Village for his impeccable memory, technical skills with visual material, and what we all have so little of— time.

Institutional help came from the Outer Banks History Center in Manteo, the Dare County Library, and the Hatteras Village Library. I would also like to thank the Hatteras Village Civic Association, whose hard work recently resulted in a magnificent virtual historic tour of the village, www.Hatteras OnMyMind.com. And because history's richest shapes are formed in the half-light of graying memories—where headless horsemen and ghost ships appear—I would like to thank the many local citizens I interviewed and rode out fishing with over the past few years. They reminded me once again that the line between history and myth is drawn in water. I reserve a special nod to writer Jan DeBlieu; her *Hatteras Journal* and *Wind* capture the poetry of a people who enjoy a spare clarity of being, and whose lives ignore the confining concepts of beginnings and endings.

For my crash course in the geology and ecology of the Outer Banks, I wish to express my debt in part to Orrin H. Pilkey Jr. and William J. Neal, editors of the Duke University Press series *Living with the Shore*; and to John Alexander and James Lazell, on the one hand, and to Dirk Frankenberg, on the other, for their informative and wonderfully readable texts.

Yet another debt of gratitude is extended to the University of Memphis for once again providing me with the time and resources to complete this project. The university did the same with my first book twenty-five years ago. If consistency is the hobgoblin of little minds, it is often a virtue in large, sometimes impersonal institutions.

My thanks to Susan Westmoreland, whose editorial skills, patience, and moral support cannot be repaid.

To colleagues David Lyons, Tom Graves, Jim Newcomb, and Gordon Osing, for their good humor, suggestions, and technical assistance; to Leonid and Friderika Saharovici for their linguistic advice; to Alan Albright for his help with matters of sailing and the sea.

For the visual dimension of the book, I have, first and foremost, to thank Lynne Foster, whose enthusiasm, historical sleuthing, and talented eye and ability to tame the fickle Cape Hatteras light resulted in many of the photographs in this narrative. Thanks too to James C. Anderson at the Photographic Archives of the Ekstrom Library at the University of Louisville and to photographers Steve Earley of the *Virginian-Pilot* and Mike Halmanski of the *Island Breeze.*

And to the Fosters themselves, each and all, who generously shared stories, family albums, old film footage, heirlooms, and ordinary information, and who opened their homes and their lives to an eager listener. And to John M. Cleveland, whose little pamphlet on the family, *The Albatross Fleet,* was so wonderfully up close. Tall Bill: I include you in the *Albatross* family, of course.

And finally, profound thanks to my editor, David Perry, whose initial enthusiasm never flagged once and whose love of fishing—and a good story— it turns out was equal to mine.

Hatteras Blues

At length did cross an Albatross,
Thorough the fog it came;
As if it had been a Christian soul,
We hailed it in God's name.

—Samuel Taylor Coleridge,
The Rime of the Ancient Mariner

I became aware of the old island . . .
a fresh, green breast of the new world.
—F. Scott Fitzgerald, *The Great Gatsby*

CHAPTER ONE

Loomings

It was mid-September of 1933, and the Foster men were doing what they always did, as long as the weather allowed. They were haul seining in the Pamlico Sound for trout, menhaden, spot, and croaker. Far to the west across the sound from their two small boats was the mainland of North Carolina. A half mile to their east was tiny Hatteras Village, where they lived. Their hometown was on a thin ribbon of sand that started out at the Virginia line some 120 miles to the north, curved gradually out into the Atlantic, and then hooked back in and continued south to Cape Lookout. The Outer Banks was 175 miles long, give or take, and looked in silhouette like a hawk's beak. Hatteras Village was at the tip of the beak, forty miles out into the Atlantic Ocean. Hatteras Village was tiny (all its residents could easily fit in half a high school gymnasium) and infamous for its storms.

Storms were very much on the mind of Charles Foster that cold fall day. His sons, Ernal and Bill, were busy with their nets. They were absolutely killing the fish. When they weren't bent to the nets, they were clowning around with each other. A storm had been predicted—forecasting was an inexact science in those days—but the skies didn't lie, and it looked ominous. Charles Foster couldn't get his boys off the fish. Ernal had inherited the Foster pigheadedness, and his father knew it, so he told the boys he was taking his boat back to Hatteras Village and made them promise they would soon follow. The boys fished through the night. By morning it was clear their father's worries had been justified. At first light the wind was howling, quickly headed up to 100 miles per hour, and the storm surge was alarming. Ernal and Bill decided not to risk the short run north to the village; it would take them across the treacherous mouth of Hatteras Inlet. They decided instead to take their catch and head straight in from where they were, to the sound side of Ocracoke Island. They made it ashore, barely, their fish-heavy boat wallowing in the swells on the sound. The wind snapped their clothes and pulled at their legs as they struggled to the Green Island Club, a private hunting lodge on the backside the island. The club manager and four hunters were already huddled there.

That night the full fury of the storm was unleashed. Even though the lodge was on reasonably high ground, the storm waters swirled around the building. Soon waves were crashing against it. A loose barge shouldered into the lodge and tore part of it away. At that point the manager decided to take everyone to the nearby generator house, but when they looked, it was gone. They'd have to stay put and take their chances. Their only amusement was sitting halfway up the main staircase and watching the lodge's big bird dog floating around downstairs aboard the dining room table.

What was left of the lodge was vibrating sickeningly under the constant pounding of the surf. Something had to be done. Young Ernal figured their only hope of survival was to get up under the roof on the lee side of the structure. Against the protests of the manager, Ernal smashed out a window, and they made their way across the pantry ceiling to the shelter. As Ernal brought up the rear, the pantry began ripping away from the rest of the building and he was forced to leap across the growing breach with a bird dog in his arms. The night was harrowing, and later each man admitted that he hadn't expected to see the morning. But they did, and it greeted them with blue skies and sun and calm seas. Ernal made a run for his boat, now sunk in a nearby marsh. As he worked to bail it out and get the motor running, he looked up to see a darkening sky and a wind rising ominously, this time from the northwest. The eye of the hurricane had passed, but its backside fury was on its way, along with a four-foot wall of water heading east across the sound right at Ernal. Ernal threw down his tools and ran. By the time he made it back to the remains of the lodge, the water was up to his chest.

Through the night they ate what canned goods they could find and drank water from the toilet tank high up on the wall. Sunday morning showed that the storm had left. It also showed the eaves of most of the lodge even

Ernal Foster, Hazel Foster, and young Ernie (Courtesy of Ernie Foster)

with the ground and the devastation nearly complete around them. The Foster boat was long gone, but Ernal and Bill scouted up a fishing punt and, after considerable coaxing, got the one-cylinder engine to come to life. The trip across the inlet to Hatteras Village and home was a sobering experience. The sound was full of debris, and all the fish houses out on stilts were gone or crazily afloat. As they neared the village, things weren't much better, but when the Foster family saw the boys, given up for lost in the violent storm, thoughts of things material quickly disappeared.

Some years later, Ernal Foster would tell his young son Ernie to prepare himself now—every life on the Outer Banks, he said, has one big storm in it.

Captain Ernie Foster donated his bathroom door to a museum. I was looking at it right then, on the second floor of the Chicamacomico Lifesaving Station Museum in Rodanthe, North Carolina. It was a pretty door — smallish, double-paneled, richly varnished, and highlighted with hand-painted pinstriping, some of which ended in delicate sprays of flowers. The small card beside the door said it came from the wreck of the *Priscilla* in 1899. Later Ernie would tell me how he came by it and about the bathroom part.

Captain Ernie Foster was the person I had flown all the way from Memphis to meet. Captain Foster, Ernal's son and the last of the breed. He ran the old *Albatross* charter fishing fleet now, and now more than ever, moored amid a seemingly endless line of muscular BMWs, stylish Cadillacs, and buxom Bentleys, the three wood-hulled boats seemed like a set of graceful Model T's.

I wanted to meet Ernie Foster and the Foster clan because his late father, Ernal, had invented the big gamefishing business on the Outer Banks of North Carolina in the 1930s. The son of a commercial fisherman out of Beaufort, and the grandson of no one knows who, young Ernal designed the boat himself, a hybrid commercial fisher and a charter fishing boat for sportsmen. With no windshield or wheelhouse, and with deep decks, the *Albatross* was capable of carrying 12,000 pounds of fish. Just as important, and more revolutionary, there were two wooden swivel fighting chairs in the stern that would accommodate big gamefishermen. Ernal fitted the boat with an old flathead-six car engine he found in a junkyard, and the maiden voyage of the *Albatross* was homeward bound, up the narrow Core Sound, then into the bigger Pamlico Sound behind Hatteras Village.

The second reason that brought me to Hatteras Village and the Fosters had less to do with beginnings than endings. There were only a handful of second- and third-generation fishing families left on the lower Banks, a few over on Ocracoke Island and just two in Hatteras Village, the Fosters — Ernie and his cousin Willy — and Spurgeon Stowe. Ernie fished with the old boats built by his father. Willy, who these days found himself fishing weekends more and more because of his job as an administrator at Hatteras Middle School, ran the *Ol' Salt* out of Teach's Lair Marina, just down from the *Albatross* slips. Willy's boat was a slick, custom forty-six-footer with twin 420-horse Caterpillar diesels. Spurgeon Stowe had chosen to run a couple of bottom-fishing boats with names like *Miss Hatteras* and *Miss Clam*. He catered to city slickers and their kids.

Ernie Foster and his captain partner of nearly twenty years, Tall Bill Van Druten, were the only ones sticking to the old ways — charter fishing mainly from May through September (but more and more now with king mackerel and bluefin charters in the fall and winter), then commercial fishing in the off season in the same *Albatrosses*, just as his father had done. It seemed clear that when the *Albatross* fleet went, when Ernie quit and took to whittling on the dock benches as his father had done, an era would end. And more than that: when these original families, whether or not they fished for a living, families whose names were still everywhere—Whidbee, O'Neal, Rollinson, Burrus, Farrow, Midgett, Ballance, Austin—when these people retired, or when they died, or when the younger among them married off-islanders and moved away, or when the off-islanders moved in and took their places, and then these mainlanders were joined by retirees who built their overblown sand castles because their lawyers got town councils to loosen up the zoning laws, when the affluenza bug drifted south down the Banks from cluttered Kitty Hawk and Kill Devil Hills and Nags Head— when all of this happened, and it was happening fast, an entire way of life would disappear, a commercial system of values based on the sea and a system of community values as old as the Mayflower Compact.

There were no real villains in any of this. Certainly there were the usual characters: ethically challenged politicians, greedy developers, hard-headed locals who wouldn't know self-interest if it spilled into their boots. But these were standard-issue players, as ordinary as gulls huddled on the beach in winter. No, what was happening to Hatteras Village was simply commercial Darwinism at its unsurprising and banal best. It was, it seemed, the inevitable fate of any small community unlucky enough to find that the value of the ground under its feet has suddenly gone through the roof. What was happening was progress, pure and simple, American as apple pie, sometimes as garish as the Las Vegas strip, sometimes as sanitized as Hilton Head, and Disney's happy town, Celebration—but progress nonetheless. Americans love instant gratification—we save little money—and that same impulse is true of American progress. In the blink of an eye, the slabs have been poured and the framers are there with their leather tool belts and boom boxes, shirtless and whistling in the sun, ready to change the skyline.

What was equally typical was that much of what was being lost in Hatteras Village was intangible—a manner of being, a way of living day-to-day —and what was tangibly being lost was being lost so quickly that it almost seemed a trick of the eye. The W. H. Gaskins House, circa 1860—the oldest house in the village—here today, then, overnight, gone. Bulldozed for someone's septic system. The momentum of money and wants. Soon all we'd have to marvel at were the trace remains of the way it used to be—a rotting sharpie in the weeds behind a boatyard, a cluster of live oaks shading an empty foundation. History for pell-mell Americans is often not a living narrative so much as an elegy, stunning in its empty frames and righteous rationales. Tourist-besieged Hatteras Village was losing its natural patina to designer pastels. And the last-of-the-breed *Albatross* boats were succumbing to the most primitive of Darwinist imperatives; the parasites were consuming the host. The great alpha male who had spawned all these diesel-powered sons was being driven off by them. An old culture was under siege; it could not last.

And for me, apparently, the door to this drama once belonged to Ernie Foster's bathroom. It was a door I had decided I would open very slowly. I had grown up with commercial and charter and head boat captains in Manasquan, New Jersey, a small beach resort town sixty miles south of New York City. Our house faced the ocean on the east, and on the south side, twenty-five yards away, was the Manasquan River. The Manasquan River was the beginning of the Intracoastal Waterway to Florida. The water route continued down the Chesapeake Bay, the Albemarle Sound, and the Pamlico Sound, whose waters lapped the shores of Hatteras Village. Connections. In fact, in 1941 Ernal Foster the Elder would deliver a boat from North Carolina to Jones Beach, New York, on Long Island, and in the process cruise out the Manasquan River and right by the oceanfront house I grew up in.

The myriad docks and marinas were further up the Manasquan River on the Manasquan and Brielle sides and across on the Point Pleasant side as well. I knew skippering boats for a living spawned a closed society. Captains by nature were suspicious, cantankerous, busy, and stubborn. They very likely distrusted state and federal governments that year after year tied their calloused hands with quotas and byzantine regulations, and so they surely wouldn't cotton to someone thrusting a business card in their faces, telling them he was going to write a book about them.

No, I would go slowly. I'd arranged a charter with the *Albatross* fleet two days from now. It was mid-May, and there would be billfish around, wahoo, bull dorado, some yellowfin—but that wasn't the point. I was hoping I'd catch some of the skippers before high season started in early June when the schools let out and there would be charters seven days a week. I was hoping an all-day charter fish-and-talk aboard the *Albatross* would open a few bathroom doors. I had decided to stay over on Ocracoke Island, a forty-minute car-ferry ride south from Hatteras Village and the *Albatross* fleet. My wife, Mo, and I and our children, Winnie and Dan, had loved it over there when we'd first come down more than twenty years ago. I could explore Ocracoke Village, the charter fleet that ringed Silver Lake Harbor, and also I wouldn't run the risk of being seen snooping around Hatteras Village. The village, population just over 600, could be a very small place. All things in good time.

Before heading for the ferry less than a mile ahead at the south end of Hatteras Village, I couldn't resist pulling off Highway 12 onto the expanse of gravel behind Hatteras Harbor Marina and the tiny slice of it called Foster's Quay. There were the three sets of red-and-white cane outriggers, the little building that announced "The *Albatross* Fleet." It was late afternoon, and there was no one around. I got out and looked at the fleet, three gleaming white boats with aquamarine decks neatly in a row separated by white-streaked pilings topped by sleepy sea gulls and pelicans. The sea gulls stirred first. Then the pelicans heaved themselves into motion, like old athletes, creaked forward, their worn wings sculling the hot air. The high, flared bows of each *Albatross* offered the classic silhouette of the old Hatteras commercial fishing boats, and the rounded stern gave each its final fillip. Here was the signature look of the classic Hatteras fisher. And it was functional. If the boats were gamefishing and had to reverse engines toward a big fish, the rounded sterns kept the anglers in the fighting chairs from drowning in the slosh kicked up by the maneuver. And with a wide, flat rear apron curving around the stern, commercial fishing from these old boats was made easier by giving those retrieving the nets a higher place to stand. And the rounded sterns kept the nets from getting snagged on the corners. The fighting chairs were removable, and, with a little reconfiguring, bins could be installed to hold the commercial catch. The flying bridges had been installed later, but they managed to keep the purity of line of the original design. Down in the far slip was the original *Albatross,* smaller and slimmer than her children, as graceful and dignified as an aging duchess in a Henry James novel.

· I took the free, state-owned ferry across Hatteras Inlet to Ocracoke Island and drove the sixteen undeveloped miles south to the village gathered around Silver Lake. In 1953 the state had taken all of Ocracoke Island except the 700-odd acres of the village itself and added it to the Cape Hatteras National Seashore. At the time, it had angered many of the locals, but it no doubt saved the island from massive development.

I checked into the Boyette House, a tidy and cheerful little motel within walking distance of the lake. I walked the few sidewalkless blocks to the busy perimeter of Silver Lake Harbor. It was a horseshoe hodgepodge of old and new, local and tourist: old cottages tucked in among gnarled live oak and red cedar trees next to kite stores and kayak rentals and Pirate's Den pubs, surrounding ratty commercial fishing boats next to sleek Bayliners and Bertrams. It was much more touristy than Hatteras Village. The upscale, out-of-scale Anchorage Inn complex down the far end of the harbor road toward the Coast Guard Station and the Portsmouth Island ferry was clearly the wave of the future. On the way back, my eye fixed on a peeling general store wedged sideways between the sandy road and the water. It looked like a country store in a hundred small towns outside Memphis, where I lived. On the marina side of the store was an empty slip advertising the "*Miss Kathleen*, Captain Ronnie O'Neal, Inshore Charters." O'Neal was one of those ubiquitous Hatteras and Ocracoke Island names. I went into the store and into a thick nimbus of lunch meat, pickle, old fish, and cigarette smells. The woman behind the counter had a friendly face that looked as though it had been fashioned from hand-tooled leather. She was busy making sandwiches for the fishing parties the next day. I asked her about Ronnie O'Neal. "Oh, he's a good one," she said. "Been fishing here for years. He'll put you on 'em." I had a day to kill, and an inshore trip with an O'Neal seemed like the perfect warm-up for my *Albatross* adventure. An O'Neal, in fact, had years ago captained one of the *Albatross* boats. Besides, I was itching to fish.

I sat in the sun on the bench outside the store, and it wasn't long before the *Miss Kathleen* was backing into her slip. Ronnie and his young mate came up in yellow waders toward the store. Ronnie appeared to be in his forties, wiry and lean and weather lined, with thick brown hair, gap toothed, and a big walrus mustache. He had an easy manner and a sly, friendly smile. I introduced myself and said I'd like to go out tomorrow. We walked into the store. Ronnie and his mate grabbed a cold drink, and we made arrangements. The usual: meet at the boat at 6:00 A.M. He said if I wanted to, I could walk down a few blocks and turn right and there was a little gift boutique his wife ran. It was in the house he grew up in. She made her own jewelry and stuff like that. Most people said she was pretty talented.

The next morning we loaded our gear aboard the thirty-three-foot *Miss Kathleen*. It had clearly been converted from a strictly commercial fishing boat to one that would accommodate sports fishermen. We headed out to some structure Ronnie knew held some fish. It was an old railroad bridge and a bunch of boxcars that had been dumped offshore in the 1970s. Just outside Silver Lake Harbor, Ronnie pointed over my shoulder. "Over there is Teach's Hole. That's where Blackbeard raided ships from."

I'd done my homework. In the early eighteenth century, Edward Teach, his crew, and his ship *Adventure* hid out in a slough and plundered ships coming into Ocracoke Inlet. But in November 1718 Blackbeard was bested by his nemesis, one Lieutenant Robert Maynard. After a spirited battle, Maynard captured Blackbeard's sloop and Blackbeard along with it. He cut off the pirate's head and stuck it on a pike. Legend has it that when Maynard threw Teach's headless carcass overboard, it swam around the boat three times.

About four miles out, Ronnie found it with no trouble. We were in eighty-three feet of water, and Ronnie's fish-finder showed fish stacked up like planes over O'Hare. The rods and reels aboard the *Miss Kathleen* had seen better days. The rods were banged up, some ferrule wrappings fluttered like telltales in the wind, and most of the bailers on the old spinning reels were in need of new springs, so you had to close them manually. The line and leader probably needed changing too. A lot of fish broke us off. Ronnie seemed unconcerned by it all, and so was I. The young mate, just up from Miami, was quick to re-rig us. We were catching big blues. When we ran out of frozen ballyhoo, Ronnie just reached in the fish box and cut up some of the blues into chunks, and we were back in business. Ronnie kept moving the boat back over the structure and the column of blips on the screen above it, and each time we'd get tight. We caught three fat sea bass to go with the blues. We were hoping for some amberjack, but none showed up.

Just before we quit, I hooked into something huge. It took the bait and began moving off slowly, crackling and creaking monofilament line off the spool. I was using a medium-weight spinning rod and twenty-pound-test line. I told Ronnie I couldn't turn whatever it was. It felt like a big grouper or a lemon shark or some such. No big runs, no angry tugging. It was in no hurry and was clearly used to getting its own way. Ronnie backed the boat over it and I took up what line I could. Nothing doing. Finally, it must have gotten down into the structure, under the sunken railroad bridge, maybe, like Billy Goat Gruff, and he broke me off. I staggered backward from the quick change in physics and found my balance on the fighting chair. It's always a strange feeling to lose something like this, something in your own weight class and stronger, with a sudden parting, a snap calculated perhaps in the dark by a thing whose ancient instincts have found the means to free itself, and by so doing to celebrate its size, its strength, its longevity, and thereby to disappoint the thing up there in the light connected to its mouth. I sat in the fighting chair to rest my aching arms. There was that poem "The Fish" by Elizabeth Bishop, who raised a similar fish to the boat and saw in its lower lip five old fish hooks and four pieces of line and a crimped wire leader, still with its swivel:

Like medals with their ribbons
Frayed and wavering,
A five-haired beard of wisdom
Trailing from his aching jaw.

She released it, of course, this Old Testament prophet of a fish.

Earlier this same summer I had fished out of Venice, Louisiana, at the mouth of the Mississippi River. The marina was tucked in among oil and gas refineries a quarter mile from a sign that read: "Stop! This is the Southernmost Point of the State of Louisiana!" We went out in one of the sleek center-console Glacier Bay boats owned by Peace Marvel, whose name apparently came from a dramatic conversion experience in which he switched from Jim Beam to the Lord. Captain Marvel greeted us but had been booked with another group, so he handed us off to a young, handsome kid named Steve. Steve was on the LSU swim team and looked it. He was as sleek as the boat he drove—very fast—and at the shoulders seemed very nearly as wide. Here was the mouth of the Big Muddy, and the waters were surprisingly blue—aching, cerulean blue twenty miles out. And Steve knew this water literally from top to bottom. He explained that he scuba-dove many of the offshore rigs and knew which held which species of fish in abundance.

On the way out, we trolled and caught dolphin and albacore and blackfin tuna and even successfully did sight-casting for the tuna with big, top-water poppers. But I wanted my friend Gordon—a colleague at the university and a well-published and world-traveled poet, but a neophyte fisherman whose largest catch to date was a slab crappie the size of his hand—to experience the dark weight and mystery of that other world now beneath his feet. I had explained this secretly to Steve. Steve knew just where to go. It was a natural gas rig in about 300 feet of water. He backed the boat right up to the massive metal legs of the rig. Far above us, a group of curious hardhats leaned over a walkway and watched. Two live pinfish, two heavy sinkers, and as soon as they touched the bottom, both boat poles doubled over. Mine broke me off immediately. Gordon fought his gamely, but it apparently got into the maze of rig braces and cut his line too.

"Plan B," Steve announced, unfazed. Two more pinfish, but this time the poles were put in the rear holders by the transom. Steve started the twin 125-horse outboards, and instructed us: "Free spool them to the bottom again, and as soon as they hit bottom, lock the reels down. Don't touch the rods." We did what he said as he stood at the console, his hand on the throttle. When the lead hit the bottom, we locked the reels down and the poles immediately doubled over. Steve gunned the engines and, as though raising water-skiers up, he flew out fifty yards from the gas rigs and quickly cut the engines. The poles were still doubled over. We had earlier put on fighting belts around our waists. Steve yelled, "Go to work, guys!" We grabbed the rods and stuck their butts in the belt cups. After fifteen minutes I got my fish up. A thirty-pound amberjack. Gordon was still wrestling his. Twenty minutes later he was still wrestling his. It was a very hot day, and Gordon was sweating and carrying on. We were giggling at him, and he, as always, was laughing at himself too. "Damn," he grunted at one point, "I haven't made noises like this since my wedding night!" We doubled over. Ten minutes later, he wheezed, "I think I've got him now." Steve said, "Trouble is, there's a fish two hundred feet down there who's thinking the same thing." Finally, Steve looked over the side and said, "We got some color," and a silver shape appeared far down in the clear water. Then it was in the boat. A huge amberjack, bigger than mine. "This rig's got the biggest ones," Steve said, as the fish and Gordon lay together in the bottom of the boat like spent new-lyweds. "Which one goes in the cooler?" Steve asked, and we got to laughing again. Gordon managed a grin and an obscenity.

We water-skied for amberjack three or four more times until we were just too tired to fight them anymore. We went further inshore to another rig and caught some blues, gag grouper, and red snapper and then called it a day. Gordon and I sat in beanbag chairs near the transom and drank cold beer as Steve hit warp speed even through the narrow, reed-lined maze of channels and cuts making up the Mississippi River delta, even through the wakes kicked up by the massive oil tankers and huge, steel-hulled work boats shuttling back and forth to the rigs. Steve had told us to hang on and not to worry. He knew what the boat could do, and besides, when the time came, he said, he could stop the boat on a dime and give us nine cents change. So we relaxed. Gordon couldn't stop talking—not just about the size of the fish he'd caught, but that feeling like no other—like the one I'd had many times before and would have again out with Ronnie O'Neal off Ocracoke Island.

————————

On the way back to Silver Lake Marina, Ronnie and I talked. I knew that back in the 1950s and 60s one of the captains of one of the *Albatross* boats was a fellow named Captain Oliver O'Neal. I asked Ronnie if he was any relation. "I don't know," he said, with an odd indifference. It seemed curious to me because in the South where I now lived, even in a metropolitan area of more than a million people, an inordinate number of conversations between strangers started with "Now, who is your family?" Or "Was your Daddy a cotton factor for the Hohenberg Company in the 1930s?" Or "Are you the Purifoys from Twist, Arkansas?" Family and family roots and family trees were a fascinating prefatory obsession where I lived. Not so on the Outer Banks, apparently, for Ronnie wasn't the only one I would encounter out here whose interests in subjects genealogical were oddly lukewarm at best.

Finally, just to fill the silence, Ronnie added, "My father washed up here, married some Indian woman, and stayed. At least that's the way the family story goes." And then he turned back to his affairs. He was much more animated by the here and now, about the boat business. It was easy to get him going on the new, big "plastic" boats. "These big boat captains," he said with contempt, "they're just hired by owners who buy these boats as tax write-offs. They pay the captains whatever." He was far from finished. "A lot of these boats that go out from the big marina hotels"—he gestured up the way toward the Anchorage Inn complex, where I'd had a beer yesterday —"they're just money machines. If a captain of one of those big rigs hears on the radio that they're into tuna twenty-five miles north of Ocracoke Inlet, say—well, hell, he can just run up there wide open. The price of fuel isn't coming out of his pockets. I can't afford to do that. Plus those boats have to kick back 7 percent or whatever to the Anchorage. That's the way this business is going."

––––––––––––––––––––

I was up at 3:30 the next morning. Outside it felt like a wet army blanket. It was going to be a hot day again, but at least we'd be out on the water, the blue water this time, out in the Gulf Stream. The first ferry for Hatteras Island was at 5:00 A.M. The twenty-minute drive from Ocracoke Village to the ferry pickup was punctuated by feinting possums, numerous rabbits crisscrossing in my headlights, and white herons stock still in the occasional water flanking the road. There was a rosy blush just starting in the east as I pulled up to the front of the wait line for the ferry. I was the first car. After a while a truck and then another pulled up behind me and killed their engines. When we left on the ferry, we were two trucks and two cars and a lot of empty deck space.

At Foster's Quay less than a mile from the ferry landing, Tall Bill Van Druten was already fussing around aboard the *Albatross II* getting things

Captain Tall Bill Van Druten
(Courtesy of Ernie Foster)

ready. He was checking the oil in the twin diesels under the floor inside the open cabin. When he stood up, I could see why the name on his *Albatross* shirt said Tall Bill. Captain Van Druten was about six feet six inches and thin as a bulrush, which made him seem taller, but sinewy strong, weathered, and tanned. Tall Bill had passed sixty a few miles back, his thinning brown hair and hawkish features resting comfortably above a quick, shy smile. He seemed perfectly suited to be in a Thomas Hart Benton mural, one of those Depression-era "March of American History" narratives that wrapped around the dome of a state capitol somewhere. The figures were always types, impossibly elongated and seemingly with extra joints. Tall Bill would be at the tiller of his boat in the section called "The Story of American Fishing," just down from "The American Frontier" and "The Age of Industry."

Tall Bill wiped his hands with an engine rag, and we introduced ourselves. They say if you have a dog long enough, you'll end up looking like it. Just now, it struck me that the same seemed true of boats. Tall Bill had been running the *Albatross* fleet for more than fifteen years (the *Albatross II* was his favorite), and they—Captain Bill and his boat—seemed, even at first glance, built from the same specs: long, lean, nicely aged, and unadorned, both designed to cut through the elements cleanly, both gracefully reduced to the essential infinitive: to fish. All else was beside the point. Bill excused himself and headed up to the bridge. The interior of the boat had the same spare personality: four fighting chairs, a simple open cabin with two long, white-cushioned benches running along each side and a four-paned windshield at the far end. No televisions, no carpets, no nothing except what was required to bring a fish to the fish box.

The mate came up from down below with the last two of the seven rods we'd be trolling. She put them in their holders and came over and introduced herself. Dita Young seemed somewhere in her thirties and had been chiseled from marble. Everything about her was large and square; her face, her jaw, her shoulders, her stocky trunk, her massive calves, even her tattooed ankles. She was less shy on the uptake than Bill, and we sat and talked while she had a quick breakfast: a bagel, black coffee, and three Marlboros. Her smile was easy and genuine and her voice chronically basso and rough as a cheese grater, the latter no doubt from her smoking, but also, she explained, from having to yell all day over two wide-open diesels. She lived with a roommate-boyfriend who was a mate also — we'd wave to him on the way out. At home, she said, she couldn't stand to have conversations with him between rooms. She didn't want to raise her perpetually hoarse voice. She'd been in Hatteras Village ten years and loved her work. I could see Dita was wondering where the rest of the fishing party was. Without going into detail, I explained to her what I was up to, writing a book and so on, and she seemed satisfied. "Cool" was all she said.

Tall Bill came down from the bridge. We talked briefly about what kind of fishing we wanted to do. I'd caught my share of dolphin, I told him, and yellowfin and wahoo, and they were fun, but I added I hadn't ever caught a billfish of any kind. We agreed to fish a smorgasbord spread — daisy chains of different colored rubber squid on metal spreader bars, some trailing green monsters for tuna, other artificials for billfish. We'd also troll ballyhoo, both naked and skirted. Ballyhoo are baitfish nine to twelve inches long with a little sword for a lower lip. They are the bait of choice for sailfish, marlin, wahoo, and just about anything else. After they're put on the hook their noses are run up the shank and wired to it. Some are trolled as is — "naked" — while others are fitted with a brightly colored rubber skirt over their heads. Before Dita rigged up our ballyhoo, she took them over to a water bucket and squeezed the shit out of them, literally. I asked why she did that. "It makes them more flexible, gives them better action in the water."

We were out of Hatteras Inlet now, and with the *Albatross II* topping out at around twenty knots, it would be an hour and a half out to the Gulf Stream. The Gulf Stream was closer to shore at Cape Hatteras than anywhere else north of Miami, but the *Albatross* was no speedster. Bill explained that we'd set the spread—the arrangement of trolled baits—before we reached the Gulf Stream, but, he added, fishing the changes in water color and temperature at the edges of the Gulf Stream was usually where the real action was. The water changed color as the warm, northward-moving Gulf Stream met a cooler, southbound current. Add underwater structure that eddied up the water, and the mix became a powerful cocktail of churning nutrients and baitfish, the lighter water especially. When we reached the Gulf Stream this day, it would be seventy-three degrees, some five degrees warmer than the southbound Labrador Current. Dita set out the spread using the outriggers, the flat line rods in the holders to the left and right of the fighting chairs, and finally the shotgun rod up on the bridge behind Tall Bill. You always trolled the shotgun furthest back. Some of the other baits were so close they bounced around in the prop wash.

At 8:30 one of the flat line poles went off. A nice-sized wahoo. I wanted to release it, but Dita had gaffed it and swung it aboard before I could say anything. She said she had a special recipe for wahoo salad and wanted to serve it to her boyfriend tonight. Would I mind? A few minutes later we boated another. Wahoos are beautiful fish, not for their delicacy of detail or subtlety of color, but for the single-minded ruthlessness of their design. Like barracuda and their freshwater cousins—the pickerel, the northern pike, and the muskie—wahoos are long-snouted torpedoes with a bad attitude. They will hit trolled bait at fifty miles per hour, and if you get tight to a large one, it might well extend your sleeve length. Like all fish, the wahoo has a distinct personality. Most fishermen boating a fish check size; they don't study expression. But it's there. Bottom fish—sea bass, tautog, grouper, snapper—seem shocked, gaspingly so, that something has lifted them out of their comfortable library darkness. In the boat they quickly become thumpingly disoriented, afraid, then compliant. But the pelagics are a different matter, those fish who live near the surface, who swim alone or in packs through the blue-green spokes of the sun or the dark, heaving anger of storms, and who can visit, with a mere leap, the environment of another world altogether. When these fish are removed from their medium so close at hand and dumped onto a harder surface than they've ever imagined, they're angry, violent to the point of psychosis. All billfish, wahoo, dorado, tarpon, permit, bonefish, barracuda, and family: you can see it in their furious, steely faces, in the fight they're willing to engage in both in the water and in the boat. They will not go gently into that fish cooler; they will not become a triangular flag on the outrigger without a struggle.

Later, when I've met Captain Ernie Foster and we've become friends, he will tell me a story about a fish, a marlin, at the end of which there are tears in his eyes and a catch in his throat. It's the story of a long-ago charter aboard the original *Albatross*, of a father and son, out in the blue water for marlin. They hooked one, the son in the chair. It was a good-sized marlin, around 500 pounds, but not a record by any means. "We fought that fish for seven hours—seven hours," Ernie says. "I tried every trick in the book and that fish countered it perfectly. It was like a chess match, and I was losing." Finally, they got the fish leadered beside the boat. "And after seven hours of fighting, do you know what that fish did?" Ernie asked rhetorically. "It made not one but two full leaps completely out of the water, right beside the boat! If I had grabbed its tail as it went up, it would have lifted me off the deck." The boy in the fighting chair was understandably thrilled and wanted to keep the fish. Ernie recalls what happened next. "I turned around and told the father and his son, 'We are not keeping this marlin.'" There was stunned silence as Ernie turned back around and released the fish. And there was a good deal of silence on the way home. Ernie had declared earlier to me that "a blue marlin is the fastest, most powerful, awe-inspiring thing I've ever seen in nature." And this marlin on this trip was best in show. This is where tears came to Ernie's eyes and his voice quavered. To him it had been obvious. "That fish, that amazing fish, deserved to live!" He couldn't say any more, didn't feel the need to. Finally he added the coda. Years later he received a letter. It began: "You may not remember me, but a long time ago you took me and my son out fishing for marlin . . ." The father did not regret what Ernie had done: "I want you to know you taught my son a lesson that day, and it's made him a better man."

We made it to the Gulf Stream. Thirty miles out, the depth drops off to 450 fathoms (a fathom is a unit of nautical measure based on the distance between an average man's outstretched arms—about six feet). We were in prime billfish water now. I went up the wood ladder to the bridge and joined Bill. From years of practice with strangers on charters, he was easy to talk to. We listened to the squawking radio for a while. Five boats were tight to white marlin, but none got them to the boat. Huge container ships lumbered by us at intervals, their decks piled high with huge pastel boxes. Bill was not used to a party of one, he said with a smile. This time of year, and especially during June, July, and August, the parties were usually family groups of four to six. Sometimes they would be make-up parties, that is, groups of one, two, or three people paired up with others so as to share the charter fee. Bill laughed and said, "You know, when we get back to the dock, you often get fights, even among family groups, as to who caught what and who gets to keep what after they're cleaned." (For a fee, the mate and often the captain will clean the fish right there at the dock.) Bill whined in mockery: "I want the tuna!" "We want that big dorado!" He added, "You'd be surprised how ugly it can get." Families would walk off not speaking to one another. Strangers would end up squaring off. It could even get nasty aboard the boat. Usually the issue was whose turn it was to bring in the next fish. Bill said he had designed a system of each person choosing a number before leaving the dock to avoid these annoying fights.

While he talked, something was trying to connect in me. Then it hit me. "You're from New Jersey," I said, not as a question. He admitted it. It turned out he grew up in Point Pleasant Beach, New Jersey, the next town over from Manasquan where I lived as a boy. In fact, if you were good enough, you could cast from the Manasquan side of the Manasquan Inlet and land your sinker in Point Pleasant Beach. I saw it done once. Bill had that nice Central Jersey accent, somewhere between the Philly patois and the New Joisey cabbie-speak, which began thirty miles to the north of where we grew up. Then he said my name to himself, ruminating. Now his synapses were firing. "Are you the Axel Carlsons from Carlson's Fishery or the Carlsons from Carlson's Corner?" he asked. "Carlson's Corner," I said. "My parents owned it. I worked there from the time I was seven all the way through college." He smiled, and we figured out that I had probably served him coffee and cooked him a hamburger forty-plus years ago. When he was growing up there, he worked on the boats in various Manasquan River basins, wrapped rods for the MV Tackle Shop in Brielle.

Tall Bill's memories were amazingly detailed. In tandem we carefully pieced together an era gone by, a Jersey Shore that no longer existed. He had loved growing up there as much as I did, had loved the sea as much. We found ourselves arranging matchboxes, hooks, pocketknives, odd nuts and bolts between us on the bench we were sharing up on the bridge as we trolled so as to get just right the arrangement of stores on Arnold Avenue in Point Pleasant and Main Street in Manasquan, or the order of commercial fisheries and marinas on both sides of the river. Clark's Landing, Bogan's Basin, the Brielle Yacht Club, the Marlin Tuna Camp. And the myriad boats, each with its story: *Kingfisher, Tambo II, E-Z, Frisco, Catch-a-Lot, Magdalena, Sea Witch*. And so many more. We knew a lot of the same people, remembered much of the same gossip and lore, the same watering holes four decades old. "Did you know Captain Frank Stires? Bill Zuber . . . ?" "Remember that band at the the Osprey?" The Ved Elva, the Sand Bar, Buddy's Blinker Inn, the Student Prince, the Red Barn, Jenkinson's up on the Point boardwalk? Resnick's? Do you remember that accident on the river bridge in 1958 . . . ? So many things I'd forgotten. So many things I remembered. It's true: memory so often hoards the banal and casually tosses away the gravest events, the most fanciful. I can remember exactly what that brand new 1958 Olds that hit the counterweight on the gates at the top of the Manasquan River Bridge looked like afterward. I went to see it. Four young men killed. You could walk from the front of the car to the back seat, down the middle of it. And yet I can't remember what I gave my wife for our anniversary three years ago. The ancient mundane litters the ground around our feet while memory drags love and our loved ones out of sight to its secret cave, pure and deep. I told Bill why I'd come here, the story I wanted to write. He nodded. He understood. And I knew he'd tell Ernie about it if I missed meeting him when we got back to the dock, and it would be okay. After a long silence, I told him about my wife, at home with multiple sclerosis, and failing, it seemed. How coming down here helped with that too. He turned and looked at me steadily, his *Albatross* hat shading his eyes, and then turned back toward the bow. He seemed to understand that also.

Our reminiscing eventually picked back up, and as we talked, Bill evidently had one eye cocked on the spread we were trailing. He suddenly yelled down below, "Dita! Something just boiled on the shotgun!" It was the ballyhoo furthest back in the spread, trailing from the elevated rod up on the bridge where we were sitting. A sailfish slashing at the bait, but not taking it. We watched to see if it made a second pass. Nothing doing. The afternoon floated quietly by. Dita took a nap up in the forward bunk. I stretched out on the cushioned bench below a brace of rods rocking in their holders from the ceiling above me. After a while I went back up on the bridge. I sat in easy silence with Bill, mesmerized by the calm seas, by the bow of the *Albatross* nosing like an iron across the back of a bright blue shirt. On the way in we caught a few small dolphin. But we'd had our trip. We'd covered a lot of water.

Back at the dock, the *Albatross III* was already in. As we swung into our adjacent slip I saw Ernie Foster talking to his party. Ernie was a stocky man, in his late fifties, his thick limbs and sloped shoulders shaped by his work. A slow grin often bloomed beneath his thick eyeglasses and thick head of yellow-gray hair. He was red, far too fair-skinned ever to really tan, even well into the wheelhouse of August. He walked slowly and wide legged, with a sure, muscular roll. The brief length of Foster's Quay, four, maybe five boat-widths across, including its little single-car-garage-sized office, was the natural habitat of Captain Ernie Foster. There was no question he belonged here, that he commanded this place, yet his movements in this little diorama were not those of an alpha male—sly, alert, and yawningly dangerous. Beneath the hard work his body did, even at the dock, there was a gentleness in Ernie's manner. He leaned in, listened hard, a hand lay lightly on a customer's shoulder when his reply came. Ernie was one of those people you see at a distance whose choreography would identify him long before his face did.

We cleaned our wahoo, hosed down the boat, and Bill and I went into the little *Albatross* office to settle up and cool off. I hoped to talk to Ernie, but he was busy with customers, the boats. As I was about to leave, Ernie was alone at the cleaning table for a moment. I walked over and introduced myself, said I'd been Bill's party-of-one. He glanced over at our few fish Dita had tossed up on the plank walkway behind the boat. She was already dragging the two stiff wahoo over to her truck. They trailed at either side of her like two pressure-treated fence posts. Ernie'd clearly had a long day too, so I decided not to bother him with my plans. He'd find out.

———————————

AUGUST 10. On this trip back to Hatteras Village, the desk clerk at the Village Marina Motel assigned me a room with a kitchenette, a ka-thunking air conditioner, and a rusty tub. I was a hundred feet from the *Albatross* office and the boats. The heat was oppressive, even at dockside, where there should have been that steady southwest breeze, but there wasn't, where the water should have cooled things off, but it didn't, where 4:30 P.M. should have helped out, but it didn't lift a finger. The whole Midwest and eastern seaboard had been in the throes of a heat wave for weeks. The Outer Banks hadn't gotten a pass this time. It was hot, get-under-the-eaves-of-the-little-*Albatross*-Fleet-charter-shack hot, as the *Albatross II* came in between the small marina jetties and into the glassy waters of the small harbor. Tall Bill swung the *II* around in a perfect arc and backed into the slip right next to the shack. The diesels barely changed rpm's, and Tall Bill didn't touch a

Captain Ernie Foster
(Courtesy of Lynne Foster)

thing, a piling, the wharf, the wood walkways along each side. Justin, the good-looking young mate with blonde-streaked hair, secured the ropes. The party, six in number, a family it appeared, certainly related, looked happy, sunburned, and exhausted. Two of the young men in the group were still drinking beer and laughing. They climbed up onto the dock, while the others passed up the coolers, the loose clothing, and backpacks, and stood to watch Justin perform the ritual emptying of the fish box in the stern. A small crowd had gathered to see how the *Albatross II* had done today. Groups always wandered up and down the marina walkways at this time of day to compare the catches of the different boats. This time of year they were looking for the occasional big yellowfin tuna, or wahoo, or Citation-sized dolphin (though June was the best time for them).

Justin tossed up dolphin after dolphin, their electric colors, yellow and blue, gone to dull pastels now, and stiff like warped planking. They were all bailers with an occasional hoister here and there. Bailers were small ones that you simply lifted into the boat without assistance—no gaff, no net. Hoisters were a little bigger, and as Justin explained, "With hoisters, you have to decide pretty fast whether to lift them in or gaff them. If you lift them for the party you aim toward the fish box so if the dolphin comes off in mid-air it continues on right into the fish box." He smiled and made the basketball ref signal for two points. "Count it. Bingo!" Above the bailers were gaffers, the Citation-sized fish—thirty-five pounds and up—bulls if male and cows if female, but none had showed up in the weed lines today. Most of the trophy fish had been caught already or had packed their bags. The total catch today was thirty dolphin (state regulations allowed sixty per boat: ten per person).

Tall Bill came down from the bridge and onto the dock, the ever-present Winston tweezered in his long fingers. He was worn out too, but pleased about the catch. "This sure beats yesterday," he said. "Yesterday we got nothing. Zero. Today we could have limited out I bet, but these folks said they'd had enough." He smiled and the party did too, and they began using their hands, signing rapidly to one another. Three of the six in the party were deaf-mutes. The others knew how to sign, so it was all signing. They were happy as could be. When they left, Bill and Justin got to laughing about it. "Man, I'm seeing fish back there behind the boat, and I'm yelling from up on the bridge for them to do this, get over here, move your rod under this one, over that one, and no one's doing anything! They can't hear me!" Bill was laughing hard. Justin was too, in that quiet Brad Pitt way he had. "Geez, they'd get a fish on, and I'd have to turn them around facing me—away from the fish!—to try to tell them what to do. Then I'd take them by the shoulders and turn them back around toward the fish! Man, it was full charades out there!"

Justin put the fish in a big plastic garbage can and dragged the bouquet of dry tails over to Tall Bill at the cleaning table in front of the charter shack. He lined up about twelve of the dolphin on the table, heads facing him, and with a very sharp filet knife, made four quick cuts: one diagonally behind the head, one along the spine, one along the belly, and a little one across the base of the tail. Same on the other side. Fast and smooth, all the while talking to someone at the end of the cleaning table about the goddamned bureaucracy involved in helping someone get a captain's license. The knife continued moving, slicing. "You fill all these damn papers out, attest to the hours he's ridden with you, driven with you, he fills out all his parts, and they reject it because he sent in his fingerprints with blue ink instead of black! Can you believe that? And he got his fingerprints done at the police station here!" Tall Bill paused in his tirade to swing all the fish around so that they were tail toward him. As he started up his rant again, he caught the point of skin up high on each dolphin's shoulder between his thumb and a fish scaler, and he peeled it down to the tail cut where he let it hang by an epidermal thread off the end of the table. Over, and the other side the same. By this time he was done with his red-tape editorial, and had moved on to greenhorn tourists who, when told they'd be going out dolphin fishing, would often say, "Oh no, we don't want to catch Flipper." Now twenty-four skins were hanging from twelve fish off the end of the table. It looked like a ragged awning in the breeze. He then made one continuous slice under the exposed meat on each side of the fish, and two fat filets came loose and dropped into the party's cooler at his feet, its ice water turning rosier with each filet. The fish carcass went into a garbage can (the skin was left hanging so the carcass could be dispensed with in one head-spine-tail-and-skin motion). The carcasses would be dumped offshore on the next trip out.

For captaining an *Albatross* charter, Tall Bill made $175 a trip. He also made another $40 or $50 for cleaning the fish. And maybe a tip. The mate, Justin, made $85 a day salary plus tips, which averaged a little over $100 per party. It was a long day's work, often twelve hours, and it was demanding, especially if you had greenhorns aboard, or drunks, or just nasty people used to giving their own orders and getting their own way, and always expecting to catch fish. "Fishing's like anything else," said Bill; "you have good days and bad. I feel bad too when I work my butt off looking 'til my eyes ache for fish — for birds, bait, debris, temperature changes, weed lines — anything that might hold a fish — and we come home empty handed. Most people understand that can happen, but some don't. I tell them, 'You have to remember, this is Hatteras. The water that was here today won't be here tomorrow. We'll have brand new water tomorrow.'" He offered the moral of the story: "In this business there are no guarantees for them — or us."

AUGUST 12. Sunday, and it was steel gray to the east and worse to the west. It was a blowday, and few boats had ventured out, especially with the forecast of lightning and rain. Tall Bill was hanging around the little office shack, hoping to snag some walk-up business for later in the week. He was sitting out on the shack's back porch, which was just wide enough for a bench seat and a hanging canvas chair. Bill was in the latter, his long, thin legs coiled around themselves. He was also wrapped up in a book and a cigarette when I came along. A huge pampas grass bush crowded over the railing at him, its tassels sprinkling gold dust on his light blue "*Albatross* Fleet" cap and knit shirt. His reading had made him pensive, or maybe it was something else.

Just inside the door to the porch was *Albatross* Business Central, a room maybe ten by fifteen with two walls of photos under Plexiglas, dating back to the 1940s. Family, fishermen, old cars running down two planks from an old ferry, hanging billfish with their weights written across them in white paint, men and women, many surely long dead, kneeling behind a fat spray of tuna or picket fence of huge wahoo. Here and there were more recent technicolor photos. Another wall had shelves full of *Albatross* T-shirts and hats for sale. A couple of chairs were occupied by huge gold Penn conventional reels in various states of repair. A wood-and-glass-fronted counter jutted out five feet from one wall. A telephone, a calendar with upcoming charters penciled in, a cup full of pencils and pens. Hanging tavern-wise from the ceiling behind the counter were a small TV and a VCR.

Out on the porch, Tall Bill was talking to a young couple about a charter. They were from Maryland shores, had their own boat. The young man knew a lot about bay and sound fishing, but not the blue-water variety. After exchanging basic charter information, Bill and the young man got into a discussion about the cyclical appearance and disappearance of striped bass and weakfish populations. Bill took over, very gently, like the skilled teacher who asks a question he's been pondering for years. What emerged was a mini-ecology/ichthyology lesson on stripers. "They blame it on the commercial fishermen all the time. But so many factors go into the life cycle of a striper—who knows what causes the cycle to be interrupted? When stripers go up to spawn in the brackish water, it's a very delicate thing. If there's too much salinity, the eggs float and birds get them or they blow away. If the water's too fresh, the eggs sink, get covered over with silt. If it rains too hard, it flushes the eggs out of the rivers, or nitrate levels go up too high from wash-off in farmers' fields. Nitrates cause algae blooms in the slow water, and these deoxygenate the water and kill the eggs." Bill lit another cigarette, took his time exhaling. He knew he had the floor. He continued. "If there's not enough rain, the water gets too salty or dries up the spawning places. Then if the eggs actually hatch, it has to coincide with the correct hatches of brine shrimp, and when the baby stripers get bigger, silverside hatches. It's their food source. So it's very complicated. To say the problem is commercial fishermen or whatever—that's just too easy." The lecture hovered gracefully above our heads like a gull holding motionless on a plank of air. Some small talk ensued, thank-yous were given, and the couple wandered off down the line of boats.

"Nice people," Bill said. Then there was a long, comfortable silence. Bill was obviously still in an introspective mood. "You know," he began, lighting yet another cigarette, "people are leaving here earlier and earlier each summer." I had no way of noticing of course. Why is that? "Well, it's a couple of things, really. The schools are starting earlier and earlier. When you and I went to school in the fall, and we grew up in resort towns too, we always started after Labor Day, right? Nowadays, they start a week or two earlier, so they have to get back home earlier. Their schools have all these teachers' in-service training days, a fall break in October, in addition to Thanksgiving, and so on." One of the odd coincidences of the *Albatross* captains—Ernie, Tall Bill, and even nephew Willy Foster—was that they'd all been teachers. Ernie had gone to North Carolina State University and had taught at several high schools, the last time at the Dare County seat up in Manteo on Roanoke Island. Tall Bill had graduated from Glassboro State and had taught high school science. Willy got out of East Carolina University and had taught PE and was now an administrator at the Hatteras Middle School just up Highway 12.

The other reason for an earlier end to the summer season on the Outer Banks? "People are getting more scared of the hurricane season, so they hedge their bets by renting earlier and leaving earlier. It's really dumb," he says. "People see a hurricane forming in the southern Caribbean, and they think it's going to be in Hatteras tomorrow. So off they go. It's probably because Hatteras is always used as a reference point by weathermen for all hurricanes coming up the East Coast. So it scares people." It seemed that charter fishing cycles, like fish-breeding cycles were equally complicated and delicate.

More talk got at what was probably the source of Tall Bill's introspective mood today. He'd been thinking about his family, his two grown children (a son soon to be married and a daughter), but mostly about his wife who had died just last year—unexpectedly, and as fate would have it, in Bill's arms as he was helping her into bed after she had complained of dizzy spells. Thirty-three years of marriage. There wasn't much downtime in the charter fishing business, which may be a merciful stay against grief, but when there is, the mind sheds its leash, wanders freely. Life is hard here, unpredictable. Out on this sand strip, huge storms make huge things disappear, just like that. Outer Bankers have learned to accept this suddenness of loss in their outdoor lives, in their fishing, are quietly proud that they have done so, like their fathers and grandfathers, their mothers and grandmothers before them. But when fate steals inside your home and makes someone disappear, just like that, these people are like the rest of us. It's hard to accept. And in the sweet, salt-scented light of a late afternoon like this one, after a good day on beautiful water, the thought of going home to an empty house, of not being able to say, "What's for dinner?"—well, even for these weathered and calloused and caring men like Tall Bill Van Druten, it was probably even a little harder for the heart to accept an indoor tragedy rather than an outdoor one that sinks boats, one in which nature exacts its time-old toll.

————————

AUGUST 15. Same damp room at the same motel. The same thunking air conditioner. It was still hot, Memphis hot—in the 90s and humid, and it had been for the better part of a week now. Before I'd finished unpacking, the phone rang. It was Ernie Foster, telling me to come over the hundred feet to the *Albatross* office. I still hadn't gotten beyond introductions with him. When I got over to the *Albatross* office, Ernie was sitting in the hanging sling chair on the little back deck, the same one Tall Bill had been lecturing from a few days earlier. The two doors to the little shack were open for ventilation. Ernie had to be here—Tall Bill did it yesterday—to answer the phone from people wanting charter information, or to deal with walk-up customers seeking charters or wishing to join others in a make-up charter. Both kinds of business would appear in the course of our conversation.

Ernie got up athletically and began talking as if we had known each other an entire lifetime and had been in mid-sentence until I'd wandered off. "Come here," he said as he went into the little office; "I want to show you something." He went in behind the counter, disappeared beneath it for a second and came to the surface with a videocassette in his hand. "It's been awhile since I've seen these myself," he allowed as he slipped the cassette into the VCR under the TV hanging behind the counter. What appeared and ran on and on —jumpily, jump-cutting, grainily in black and white with people and boats and even fish moving a little faster than in real time, as though in a dream or a silent movie—and then suddenly cut to color footage with a big-band musical score and silly subtitles and men aboard the two *Albatrosses* with pleated pants, pencil-thin mustaches, women in Betty Grable swimsuits and big straw hats and men's shirts knotted at the bare waist, smoking cigarettes and waving shyly, then back to jalopies racing among the sand dunes, and long-ago public fish fries, then cut to men with pomaded hair next to big-billed, hanging fish—what was running on and on was Hatteras Village more than a half century ago, the *Albatross* fleet in its adolescent bloom, and a gone generation of Fosters, men and their wives, Bill and Ernie's father, Ernal, and Ernal's wife, Hazel, and then knee-high Ernie and Willy, and

Captain Oliver O'Neal, and family whose names Ernie recited like a catechism. Kinflicks. And more than that.

"We took a lot of these films——," Ernie said as he hit the Pause button to sign up a customer for a charter, "eight millimeter, some sixteen, but over the years, customers would also send copies of films they'd made of their trips out on our boats to Bill and my father." Eventually Ernie had them spliced all together and put in video format.

Then when the customers left the office, he once again reached up over his head and started up the past. He was clearly enjoying seeing these things he'd gotten out for me, knowing by the press of a single button, he could part a curtain no one else in the village could. He frequently would hit Pause and freeze the image of a person to explain who it was, which relative, which village official and what noble or scurrilous or stupid or funny incident their lives had been reduced to in the collective memory of the village. Sometimes it was to get straight exactly which marlin that was—the one that got tail-wrapped and sank like a car, or that one, "Yeah, see that one?" —holding steady on a huge fish bowed half in, half out of the *Albatross* far offshore. "That's Uncle Bill on the *Albatross II*, and that's the world-record marlin they're hauling aboard. That's it. We shot the film from the other *Albatross.* 810 pounds. June of 1962. Maybe you've seen it when you come into the village; it's in a glass case in front of the public library." I had. The fish seemed unreal to me, the way when I stood next to some of my football linemen students at the university, they seemed unreal. It was a matter of scale.

The footage moved on to what was clearly a village festival of some sort. The Pirates' Jamboree held every April up by the Hatteras Lighthouse. Started having them in the mid-1950s and quit around 1970. A tourist gimmick to kick off the summer season. And there it all was, shaky visual vestiges of a long-gone "Can-do" civic spirit. It rolled by us like clouds—the jittery parade of floats, the dune buggy races on the beach (Stocky Midgett, in his stripped-down '55 Cadillac, and Leon Jennette were the best. "Man, look at them tearin' up the dunes and everything! This was National Park Service land and no one said a thing. Can you imagine today?"). And there were the sea dory races out through the surf and back, even the crab races for the kids—and then the races and tricks along the beach with the famous Banker ponies (they're supposedly descended from old Spanish stock that swam ashore from shipwrecks). They had to be brought over from Ocracoke Island on Frazier Peele's boat. There weren't any more ponies on Hatteras Island. And there was the fish fry for 2,000 people—Spanish

Boating the world-record blue marlin aboard the *Albatross II*, June 1962 (Courtesy of Ernie Foster)

mackerel, sea trout, bluefish. Hush puppies and cole slaw being ladled out to lines of people with paper plates. And the Blackbeard look-alike contest (Edison Meekins, manager of the Hatteras Marlin Club, was the best), and the Queens of the Jamboree ("There's Winona Peele and Bette Rollinson Gray from Buxton"). And the grand finale, the Jolly Roger Ball with the great pirate costumes. All the kids wanted to wear eye patches.

And then back to barer landscapes and the boats. An old eight millimeter panned down the narrow harbor right behind us. It was riding aboard the original *Albatross*. The channel was uncrowded, but as the camera lingered on a boat, a commercial fisher, an old lapstrake cruiser of some sort, Ernie would name the boat and often the captain too. Sometimes he paused the film to tell a story about one of the captains. Or about himself, about how, when he was very young, he caught a 300-pound bull shark inside the narrow entrance to the channel and harbor. He took me over to the office door. We could see the breakwater, the entrance about 200 yards away. "Right there." He and his friends had seen a couple of sharks fin their way inside the breakwater, and so they got a big hook and a bloody bonito. They wore it out, but were afraid to have it in the rowboat with them, so they dragged it up on the beach and beat it to death. "So much for the Great White Hunters," Ernie smiled. And there was footage of the drift whale washed up on the beach, huge, with people milling around it, looking at it and back at the camera. Some people were standing on it, hands on hips, like loggers on a redwood in the Pacific Northwest. The whale stayed there a week, for gawkers. "Can you imagine that thing there today? The people in those million-dollar oceanfront homes would be screaming bloody murder for some civic action. The smell! The unsightliness!"

Finally, cut to old footage of a couple of the *Albatross* boats trolling together, with the big, red Diamond Shoals Lightship behind them. Did they often troll together? "Oh sure. We did it all the time." There was a long silence as the boats circled the lightship, exhaust wisping up from their sterns, people moving around aboard, raising drinks, waving. "I guess I kind of miss that," Ernie said softly. It was said not to me but to himself. In fact, I realized that as Captain Ernie's narrative went on, it became more and more private, more hermetic. As the footage unrolled, it took Ernie somewhere else, to a place and time long gone. A family business, uncrowded fishing grounds, virgin weed lines hiding countless fish, customers who wrote them Christmas cards, a fraternal bond awaiting them, when there was finally time, in the village's sand-and-paint winter months.

We watched the remainder of the video in silence. When it was over, and as though to confirm the elegiac turn his mind had taken for the way things had been, Ernie began a story about a charter a year or so back. The doctors who had performed his wife's mastectomy up at Norfolk General wanted to charter the *Albatross*. They were shocked at the price, Ernie said, incredulous. "I mean these people charged us around $3,500 each an hour for two hours of work. It would take me two weeks of twelve-to-fifteen hour days out on the water to make that kind of money. I'm not begrudging their charges to us, but when they want a boat, a captain, a mate, all the equipment, and the know-how—all this for a few bucks. . . ." He turned and looked out the window facing a line of shining charter boats. *Citation* was the closest one. It was getting hot in the office. Back out on the back porch, at least there was a whisper of a breeze. Looking for wind was a foreign activity on the Outer Banks —kind of like trying to cool off in Alaska. More typical were the signs you saw along Highway 12 on the way to Hatteras. "Why let the wind ruin your vacation?" They wanted to rent you canvas windbreaks for the beach. But here we sat, sweating and fanning as though we were at a tent revival in Alabama. The two doors to the little shack were open for ventilation. Things were definitely slowing down. The fishing too had slowed with the heat and the season, down to modest-sized dolphin and an occasional tuna outside and Spanish mackerel and small blues inshore.

What was happening on Hatteras Island was a subtle seasonal transition, when the tourists began to leave, and the locals, catching their breath, began to make their repairs to house and boat, car, themselves, and got ready for the next influx, this time of "the real fishermen," as Ernie called them, the men and women who came down beginning in mid-September, but even more so in October and after for the running of the big drum and stripers along the beaches and the herds of their brethren gathered in Hatteras Inlet. Such people also came for the king mackerel in October, peaking near Thanksgiving and lasting until around Christmas. Ernie clearly liked going out for kings, especially in November when the competition had been thinned out by the start of hunting season. He liked it too because the tactics for these tackle-busters had changed. "A lot of us have switched to live bait and lighter tackle," said Ernie. Instead of trolling the usual spread of baits and teasers up, baits and teasers down, the new tactic was to catch live menhaden on the way out and then to slow-troll or drift live bait on smaller hooks and lighter rods and reels. Running a couple of triple rigs—two or three treble hooks rigged tandem-style, each with a live bait (sometimes topped off with a colored plastic skirt)—often brought up the big smoker mackerel, the thirty- to forty-pound shimmering torpedoes that would peel off 200 yards of line if the fisherman was caught flat-footed—or even if he wasn't. "It sure gets the angler more involved," Ernie chuckled. "The switch," he added, "has been one of the nicer developments around here in the last fifteen years."

We talked more about the fall fishing season on Hatteras. I wanted to hear Ernie on the season down here that was so wonderfully mythologized for me almost a half century ago at the Jersey Shore by those old-timers making plans to head down to Hatteras for striper and drum just as the tourists were packing up and the fishing was picking up. It had always been my favorite fishing season too, in New Jersey, and now here. Fall striper fishing had been good now for about fifteen years. They came back to the Outer Banks in 1987 after years of prolonged absence up and down the East Coast. When the water temperatures started dropping in the fall, the stripers, or rockfish as they're often called down here, began their southern migration from the Chesapeake Bay and points north. "It really starts in earnest in November," said Ernie, "but the peak months are December and early January." The colder the winter the further south the fish headed, sometimes huddling up at Cape Lookout further down the coast. Water temperatures around forty to fifty degrees often triggered the best bites. In the early fall, diving gannets and laughing gulls and herring gulls and blackback gulls meant schools of baitfish—menhaden, croakers, herring, weakfish—along the beach, and probably stripers underneath them. The gulls would hover, waiting to pick up what the stripers stunned and mangled in their frenzied feeding.

Oregon Inlet, Wimble Shoals, Cape Point at Hatteras, Hatteras Inlet, Ocracoke Inlet: these were the prime spots. Inlet fishing on an ebb tide when the baitfish and eels flood out to the warmer water of the Atlantic could be exciting fishing. It could also be extremely dangerous, especially in a small boat. The stripers were usually in the shallow, choppy side of the inlets — that would be the southern or Ocracoke Island side of Hatteras Inlet — and getting a thirty-seven-foot boat over to them, even if it drew only two-and-a-half feet of water, could be a tricky business. The secret was to hold the boat just outside the chop and cast into it using big surf rods for distance. For the deeper fish, it was deep-jigging bucktails. But if the fish were working the surface, artificials of choice included surface plugs like Atom Poppers or Cordell Pencil Poppers or metal spoons or Hopkinses. Live eels worked too. Bigger boats like the *Albatross* preferred to troll just on the outskirts of the inlet sandbars using bucktails, spoons, or eels. Laws allowed fishermen to keep two stripers over twenty-eight inches long.

It was time to close up shop. Ernie had to stop by the old net house and do some odds and ends before he went home. He wanted me to meet his wife, Lynne. "You'll like her. She's an interesting woman," he said. Plans weren't made firmly this time of year; couldn't be. In a village well under a thousand in population (not counting the renters), friends and families — those involved with the tourists — might well not see each other until after Labor Day. I'd grown up with it myself, in New Jersey.

Ernie locked the *Albatross* office and drove south toward the net house. After a while, I got up and walked down three slips to the original *Albatross*. I climbed down and sat in the fighting chair. No one was around. The fishing was done for the day, the strollers were back in their rental units, and it was too early for the dinner crowd at the Breakwater just to my left at Oden's Dock.

Ernie and Tall Bill were fascinating, complex characters and decent, hardworking human beings. They would be fun to watch. It made me think of teaching in the early 1980s in Communist Romania, at the University of Bucharest. I'd gone there as a Fulbright professor, but had come home a student. I was the one who'd gotten the education — about life, about culture, about courage, about how belief, and art, and patience and love could ultimately defeat any circumstance. Not just me. My wife, Mo, and our children, Winnie and Dan — we'd all gotten the same education, experienced the same shift in values concerning what was important and what was not. I had the feeling, sitting amid the gathering shadows on the *Albatross*, watching the sun sink into the Pamlico Sound, that I was about to learn more than I could ever teach in a book. This time, though, I'd be the only student in the class. The children were grown and gone, inventing their lives, Winnie in the fashion industry in New York, Dan in the travel business in San Francisco. And Mo was home, in a wheelchair now, down to one good arm (her left), her indomitable will, and her unflagging midwestern cheerfulness. Her nurses loved her. We had met in graduate school at Rutgers in the late 1960s. She came from Minnesota and privilege and went east to boarding schools and then to Wellesley. I grew up in the hot dog business and went to public high school. When I was small, my family took in boarders. My grandparents spoke with accents from the old country. I think we fell in love in the library on College Avenue. Her name then was Maureen Donoghue. In a police lineup looking for Irish suspects, she wouldn't have stood a chance. Eileen Ford—slim, with gray-blue eyes that changed like the sea, translucent skin, a face Giacometti-long and thin. Her hair was not that wispy, Irish barmaid flax. It was rich and thick, Irish sweater–thick, champagne and ash with darker hints, hair that would easily ignore a stiff wind across Galway Bay, all worked into a magnificent braid that came down over her shoulder almost to the small of her back. It was the kind of golden rope it would have been an honor and sensual privilege to climb slowly down from a burning building. I said poetic stuff like that to her back then. She would shake her head and smile.

Mo was diagnosed with MS right after Winnie was born in 1973. Her doctors told us it wasn't wise to have more children since a pregnancy would likely exacerbate her symptoms. Daniel was born in 1975. Mo made it through fine. We were very happy. But gradually the illness progressed, and as it did, it strained our marriage—and then it strengthened it into a fine fortress. We were seldom apart. Mo found my passion for fishing amusing, but back then she almost always came along anyway and read books. There was an empty fighting chair next to the one I was in just now; I was trying to train myself not to wish for things I couldn't have, but I wasn't very good at it.

The waves fold thunder on the sand . . .
—Hart Crane, "Voyages: I"

CHAPTER TWO

These Restless Banks

"The Outer Banks" refers to a slender chain of barrier islands and sandbars that parallels the North Carolina mainland from its northern border with Virginia to Cape Lookout, some 175 miles to the south. The term "Banks" was used at least as early as 1725 when the North Carolina Council ordered island settlers from Europe to allow Poteskeet Indians to hunt on "any of the said Banks land." From north to south, the Outer Banks trace a graceful, sloping arc southeast for about seventy-five miles to the village of Rodanthe, the easternmost point in North Carolina. From Rodanthe, the thin ribbon of land then swings ever so gently south and west for about twenty miles to famous Cape Hatteras and its notorious Diamond Shoals, often referred to as the "Graveyard of the Atlantic."

At this point the Outer Banks look like the silhouette of a graceful, eastward-billowing sail. At Cape Hatteras, the land widens out to a thirty-square-mile mass of marshes, tangled scrub, and Buxton Woods. Here, again from an aerial perspective, it's as though Cape Hatteras has become the boom of the sail bellied out above it. Below the boom, the sand spit shrinks back down to a finger, sometimes only a tenth of a mile wide, and veers southwest where, in close to fifteen miles or so, it reaches Hatteras Village, and, just below that, Hatteras Inlet. Continuing south and west across Hatteras Inlet is Ocracoke

Island which runs for approximately sixteen miles until it reaches Ocracoke Inlet. Across this second inlet is yet another pair of thin sand fingers called Portsmouth Island and the Core Banks. These terminate at another point of land, Cape Lookout. From Ocracoke Island to Cape Lookout is approximately seventy-five miles. Below Cape Lookout, the islands make an even more dramatic westward turn and run for another thirty miles to Bogue Sound near Beaufort and Morehead City. The Bogue and Shackleford banks do not normally share the Outer Banks designation, but, in fact, they display the same barrier island features, as does the series of islands that continues south of the Bogue and Shackleford banks all the way to famous Cape Fear, nearly at the border of South Carolina.

From north to south, the Outer Banks are separated from the North Carolina mainland first by the thin Currituck Sound, which ends around Kitty Hawk to the south. Then three great bays take over, pushing the Banks even further offshore. The northernmost of these bodies of water is the Albemarle Sound, an east-west bay that receives waters principally from the Chowan and Roanoke rivers. Below Albemarle Sound is Pamlico Sound, the largest of the three sounds. Pamlico Sound stretches from Roanoke Island to the north all the way past Cape Hatteras, Hatteras Village, and Ocracoke Island to Portsmouth Island. The southernmost of the three bays is Core Sound, and like the Currituck Sound to the north, it tapers to a candle-thinness on the map, ending at Cape Lookout.

The Outer Banks of North Carolina are unique in both their parabolic shape and the distance they extend (up to forty miles) from the mainland. And in terms of moody, even violent weather, they have only one possible earthly peer—the eastern coast of Australia. Along the continental United States, the Outer Banks have no rival in their vulnerability to damaging weather —hurricanes, northeasters, winter storms. As Tall Bill Van Druten rightly complained, Cape Hatteras is used by weathermen as a geographical point of reference for almost every eastern seaboard hurricane or storm regardless of whether or not it's tracking toward North Carolina. But it's equally true that for millennia North Carolina's outermost, thin rind of land has stuck its fragile chin out into the Atlantic and dared anything coming by to take its best shot. And many have. Records kept by the National Weather Service show that since 1900 North Carolina has experienced a major hurricane every two to three years. Hurricane season begins on June 1, but typically the killer hurricanes show up later in the season (August, September, October). Hurricanes that devastate the east coast of the United States develop in the subtropical waters of the Caribbean or off the west coast of Africa where the ocean waters heat up faster than the Atlantic Ocean. As these weather anomalies track northward, they pick up intensity and wind, and storm-surging seas often head for the thread-thin land and vulnerable communities of the Outer Banks. Winds and seas precede hurricanes by days on the Outer Banks. If the hurricane spirals onto the Banks themselves, the tenuous land and its tenuous communities are struck by violent counterclockwise winds. Then comes the calm "eye" of the hurricane, when an eerie stillness prevails. And then the second act begins, an equally violent back half of the hurricane, this time with its clockwise winds. The result is a quick left-right punch that first drives sand and water up through the inlets along the Banks (or through new ones created by the storm) into the sounds behind them, and then after a pause, drives the water east or seaward, out of the sounds again. In the fall of 1933, Ernal Foster was very nearly killed by this stuttering violence.

The history of the Outer Banks is rife with legendary hurricanes: the hurricane of September 1857, which sank the passenger ship ss *Central America* with the loss of more than 400 lives; the "Terrible Storm" of August 1769, which state governor William Tryon attributed to a "blazing star" recently seen in the heavens, but which some residents saw as the wrath of God for their having danced on Sunday night. In fact, old hurricanes may well have profoundly altered the early demographics of the United States. In the summer of 1585, ships sent out by Sir Walter Raleigh landed near present-day Kitty Hawk and settled their passengers on Roanoke Island behind and slightly south of the place the Wright brothers would make famous. Ships frequently resupplied the small band of English settlers. Then, in June 1586, Sir Francis Drake, the great military hero and explorer, arrived at Roanoke Island to reinforce its English settlers and to bring supplies. Unfortunately a hurricane arrived at the same time as Drake. According to the journals of Ralph Lane, leader of the colonists, in that storm which produced "thunder . . . and raigne with hailstones as Bigge at hennes eggs," and "greate Spowtes at the seas as thoughe heaven & [Earth] would have met," Captain Drake "sustained more perill of wracke then in all his former most honourable actions against the Spaniards." Given the sunk ships and lost men and supplies, Lane and his group decided they'd had enough; they left with Drake. Had the hurricane not struck, and had Lane's men remained, they would have found that more supplies and reinforcements were on the way in a group of ships dispatched by Sir Walter Raleigh. Raleigh's ships arrived soon after

Lane and Drake and their group had departed. As a result, Jamestown on Chesapeake Bay to the north, not Roanoke Island and the Outer Banks, became the site of the first permanent English settlement in the New World.

Before Jamestown in 1607, however, there was one more attempt to colonize the Outer Banks: this was the more mythic, yet equally doomed, attempt by John White and his band of 116 men, women, and children to settle once again on Roanoke Island, this time in July 1587. White was forced to return to England, leaving behind over 100 people, including his daughter and his granddaughter, Virginia Dare, the first European to be born in America. White's return to the New World colony was delayed by England's mobilization of shipping against an impending invasion by the Spanish Armada. When White was finally able to return in the summer of 1590, the colony had vanished. All efforts to find the settlers proved futile. Had they succumbed to disease and starvation? Had they been slaughtered by the Indians? Had they drifted off and joined up with the Indian community? The mystery remains. They truly had forever become the "Lost Colony" of American lore.

Hurricanes on the Outer Banks, most without names and chroniclers, have shaped and punctuated history ever since. But even as dramatic and destructive as hurricanes can be, Outer Bankers know that their lives and certainly their property are more likely to be threatened by the more frequent northeaster storms that haunt the Banks. Northeasters are larger and longer lasting than hurricanes. They are usually formed as low-pressure cells over coastal areas where air temperatures differ dramatically — colder over the land, warmer over the water. The area off the coast of North Carolina is ideal for these lumbering bulls because of its proximity to the winter track of the polar jet stream. Northeasters gradually develop dangerous counterclockwise winds that typically cover a thousand or more miles and can batter a coast from the northeast for days on end. Compare this to the typical hurricane, which is 300 to 400 miles in diameter, with the greatest winds concentrated in a compact center of that mass. The anger of a hurricane is usually measured in hours. Northeasters often rampage for days.

Probably the most destructive coastal northeaster experienced by North Carolina and most of the eastern seaboard was the Ash Wednesday storm in early March 1962. A Class 5 storm, it struck the coast during spring tides, resulting in tremendous storm surges. It lasted through five high tides and damaged or destroyed hundreds of structures, created new inlets, tore up groins and sea walls, and ran numerous ships aground. While the Ash Wednesday storm did tremendous damage, it also proved an effective schoolmaster, finally bringing home to stubborn seasonal residents and engineers alike a fundamental truth that had been evolving slowly: simply put, the lesson was that trying to stabilize the Outer Banks, to attempt to hold the land in place, was doing infinitely more harm than good. So-called "hard" engineering, building inflexible man-made structures or even erecting artificial sand dunes was, in fact, raising havoc and accelerating the destabilization of this dynamic ecosystem. It was the age-old story of human arrogance in fooling with Mother Nature. She had been managing the Outer Banks since they appeared in the Sangamon Interglacial Period more than 100,000 years ago; and in a mere 100 years of contemporary engineering, humans had succeeded in upsetting the delicate dance of forces that kept the Outer Banks unique and beautiful. As late as 1971, Congress appropriated more than $4 million in seed money toward an estimated $50 million tab that would in effect finally and permanently "stabilize" the Outer Banks. It would be accomplished by building one long sand dune 20 feet high and 500 feet wide its entire length, almost 200 miles—the Great Wall of China made of sand, wire grass, and sea oats.

Enlightened engineers, geologists, and naturalists were outraged. They went to work, and they won. Congress was persuaded. The National Park Service was persuaded. Its superintendent, Robert Barbee, finally announced the new collective wisdom: "We're not God. We can't hold back the sea forever." This was on the national news. Implied in the superintendent's terse announcement was a truth many enlightened islanders and engineers and naturalists already knew: that the Outer Banks constituted a dynamic ecosystem, that the system had a mind of its own, that it was going to do what it chose, to go where it wanted to go, and that the best its puny recent inhabitants could do was to acknowledge and to respect the will and decisions of this delicate place and stay out of its way.

While the principle ingredient in the Outer Banks is sand, the recipe is far more complex. Barrier islands like the Outer Banks contain varieties of peats made of roots and stems and mud, marls formed from clay and shell and pebbles, loams born of the humus in the high hammocks and old-growth live oak and red cedar forests, and myriad oozes and slimes on the sound side of the landform. A barrier island is a delicate stew, a subtle swirl of ingredients, textures, and colors. And it's a stew that will not sit still on the table. The primary reason a system of barrier islands will not stay put is the vagabond nature of the sand that it comprises. Sand loves to roam, not whimsically, but on the fixed rails of an ancient and complex system of physics —the physics of wind, of water, of varied storm systems—even the physics of its own unique physical geometry. Siliceous sand is made of oxides and silicons derived from pulverized rock. Calcareous sand comes from calcium-based seashells. Sand of the seashell variety comes in cubed shapes or spheres. Sand from pulverized rock comes in flat, thin flakes. The siliceous sand has more hobo in it. It travels more frequently, further, and faster. Thanks to millennia of glacial grinding and retreat, this rock-based racing sand is the predominant type on North Carolina's Outer Banks. For example, scientists figure that each year from Oregon Inlet to Cape Hatteras alone, between one-half to one million cubic meters of sand are transported laterally along the shore. If you realize that an average dump truck holds fifteen cubic yards of sand, the volume of transit is truly staggering. A single wave, slightly longer than a football field would weigh about 2,500 tons. It would contain almost a million pounds or nearly 15,000 cubic feet of sand.

Many more tons of sand are hurled not laterally along the beaches but due west, right up onto the beaches themselves. During storms this direct beachward movement is done with such force that the water with its sand suspension hurdles over the first line of dunes or in the low areas between their peaks. This so-called overwash seawater ends up in the low swales between the first and second or second and third line of sand dunes, where much of the sand settles out as the wave water becomes stationary or retreats slowly back to the shoreline. The evidence is clear: contrary to common belief, storms more often than not increase the volume of sand and therefore landmass. The problem is that the increased deposits always move the central mass of the islands further south and west, much to the dismay of beachfront residents and random others further inland where the gypsy sand comes to rest. (A Putt-Putt golf course now lies buried under the western slope of Jockey's Ridge, the largest sand dune on the Outer Banks.)

And to exacerbate its restlessness, scientists discovered, the sand of the Outer Banks sits on its own slippery self. That is, core samples taken almost a half century ago disproved the widespread scientific assumption that the Outer Banks rested atop an ancient coral reef. One-hundred-foot-deep core samples taken the length of the Banks showed that the Outer Banks were all sand: the first thirty feet or so was Holocene sand, dating to a maximum of 5,000 years ago; under that was simply older sand, dating to the Pleistocene Era. Not only were the Outer Banks a relatively new structure; they lacked a fixed foundation. It's no wonder then that, given the relentless physics and the lack of a geological anchor, the Outer Banks are wandering south and west at a good clip. North of Cape Hatteras the average rate of shoreline migration is five feet per year. Up around Oregon Inlet the rate of retreat is fifteen feet a year. In addition, Oregon Inlet itself is moving south at the astounding rate of nearly a hundred feet per year. That is, since it opened in 1846, Oregon Inlet has moved more than two miles south and almost 1,800 feet toward the mainland. The huge Herbert C. Bonner Bridge, opened over the inlet in 1963, may well end up spanning nothing but sand. Much of it does already.

Probably the most publicized example of the restless nature of the Outer Banks landmass involves the famous Cape Hatteras Lighthouse. For years the rate of shoreline retreat in the area of the lighthouse was twenty feet per year. Groins, rock, and sandbagging did little to slow the inevitable. The lighthouse that was erected in 1870 a full 1,600 feet from the sea was going to be claimed by it. Finally, during the course of June and July 1999, engineers from the International Chimney Corporation of New York laid down tracks, jacked up the structure, and moved it 1,600 feet back into Buxton Woods. The sea is still moving toward it.

While "hard" engineering against the forces of the sea has long since been discredited, even some attempts at softer engineering have had deleterious effects. In the 1930s, for example, when the National Park Service took over management of the Outer Banks as a national seashore, they called in the WPA's Civil Conservation Corps to build three parallel lines of oceanfront sand dunes from the Virginia–North Carolina border to the north to Ocracoke Inlet to the south. The new dunes were planted with cordgrass, sea oats, American beach grass, and wire grass, all of which propagated through rhizomes —creeping stems that grew underground and anchored themselves in loose, shifting soil. The dunes continued to grow after they were built, many to a height of fifteen feet, and the project seemed a rousing success. The only trouble was that as the dunes rose, the shoreline receded. The gently sloped beaches, once 150 yards wide, had narrowed to half that. The reason was simple physics. Storm waves and storm surge, no longer able to overwash dunes or to shoot between them and thereby dissipate their energy and deposit their sand inland, found themselves crashing into a high wall of sand. The wave energy was then hurled backward and downward onto the beaches in front of the artificial dune wall. Such massive energy thus directed had the effect of gouging the beach, deepening its profile and narrowing it as the sea crowded into the excavated area. The digging process would eventually take on its own momentum, and the beaches would be scooped out by the sea and disappear beneath it. Then, of course, so would the artificial dunes, and nature would finally prevail yet again and rearrange her furniture in its normal configuration.

The human history of the Outer Banks is the history of America writ narrow. Like the geological history of the Banks, its human counterpart also follows a unique yet familiar physics: Native Americans, settled or nomadic, wrest a living from the land and sea; exploratory forays are sent out from Europe, in this case the first ones by Italian explorer Giovanni de Verrazano, in the employ of the French, in 1524. Worlds collide: explorers, indigenous peoples. Accommodation is sought: Verrazano's men swam into the beach somewhere near Hatteras Village and gave the Native Americans beads and looking glasses. Verrazano was convinced the Outer Banks were an isthmus with a vast sea behind them, which led to India and China. He dubbed it "Verrazano's Isthmus" and sailed back to Europe. Settlements were attempted, at first tentative and unsuccessful. Then, more successful immigration followed. Native Americans had to choose now between fight or flight. On the Outer Banks, it was evidently flight or assimilation (recall Captain Ronnie O'Neal's family lore about his ancestor washing up on Ocracoke and marrying an Indian). As Europeans increased in numbers on the Outer Banks, the Native Americans decreased until almost all the tribes were missing in action: the Croatans, the Corees, the Roanokes, the Hatorasks, the Poteskeets, the Muchapungas or Mattamuskeets. And others. And with them the poetry of their place names: Hatterask, Cococon, Mattamuskeet, Chicamacomico, Kinnakeet. Anglicized, bastardized, then eliminated altogether, mostly by the tongue-tied U.S. Postal Service. In the 1870s and 1880s, Chicamacomico and Kinnakeet became the present-day villages of Salvo, Rodanthe, Waves, and Avon.

In the seventeenth century, most of the life on the Outer Banks was concentrated in the northern half, thanks to Currituck Inlet at the Virginia boundary and Roanoke Inlet further south opposite Roanoke Island. In the eighteenth and early nineteenth centuries, the northern banks around the present-day towns of Kitty Hawk, Kill Devil Hills, and Nags Head slowly became beach resorts (for vacationers and those fleeing malaria outbreaks on the mainland) as well as a sportsman's fishing and hunting paradise. Little or no fishing pressure presented eager visitors with mackerel-crowded seas, and for gunning enthusiasts the Currituck Sound, which from the 1790s to the Civil War had experienced a steady drop in salinity, provided the huge quantities of brackish-water grasses necessary to attract ducks, geese, swan, and more than 300 other species of fowl. For some visitors, tourists, and sportsmen, the problem was neither fish nor fowl. It was another species:

human. Greeting these off-islanders was a mix of corncob-rough stockmen, whalers, part-time fishermen, and, according to some official complaints, "Pyrats & runaway Servants."

The Outer Banks have never been for the faint of heart or the dry of feet. Early on, especially, it seems, the inhabitants of the Outer Banks didn't merely adapt to their environment; they became indistinguishable from it —its moody, impetuous weather, its restless land, its willfulness, its stubborn insistence on beating the odds.

the whole pageantry

of the year was
awake tingling
near

the edge of the sea

—William Carlos Williams,
"Landscape with the Fall of Icarus"

CHAPTER THREE

This Working Village

NOVEMBER. "And, let's see," said the portly master of ceremonies, squinting over the top of his glasses to read the raffle card, "the six-inch, extra-wide boner"—everyone's howling—"goes to Karen Whidbee!" The laughing and whistling increased as an attractive young woman, smiling good-naturedly and shaking her head, went up to the podium to get her fish-cleaning knife. It was the Captains' Banquet, one of the biggest social affairs served up by Hatteras Village. This year it was being held at the Channel Bass ("The Restaurant with a Reputation!") at the north end of town next to the little bridge over the Slash.

Tall Bill and Ernie had been fretting all week about how everyone was going to manage to fit in there, it was such a small place, and when we arrived, it was very crowded; but we got our raffle tickets and a table easily. Above the bobbing heads of the crowd, you could see the festooning fish-nets, the frozen wooden sea gulls, the old blown-up maritime photos, and the huge taxidermied fish—channel bass, of course, but also wahoo, tuna, and the inevitable parabolic sailfish and marlin. Here was the decor of a thousand seaside restaurants from Bar Harbor to Key West.

Ernie was immediately swept away to the open bar by a school of sea captains, and so we got comfortable in our booth—Lynne, me, and Chris,

Ernie's son who had come down to visit for a few days. Chris Foster was twenty-three years old, a nice young man with a very serious but engaging demeanor. He was tall and thin and with a shock of brown, curly hair. Otherwise, he had his father's looks, especially the sandy coloration, a mouth crowded with teeth, an easy smile, and an easy way with people. Chris had recently graduated from the University of North Carolina at Chapel Hill. He had a rich baritone voice; by his own admission, he talked too fast, and he sold books and educational materials for a company called Southwest Publishing. A lot of it was door to door, but even in these cynical times, you'd let Chris Foster into your house without thinking twice.

In the lull Lynne and I were left alone in the booth. I had met Lynne, finally, earlier this trip down, when I'd been invited over to dinner in the lovely home they'd built just across the road from the *Albatross* fleet. Ernie was right. Lynne was fascinating, and we had hit it off immediately. She was a stylish woman, but warm and wholly without contrivance or social calculus. She was one of those rare, centered people who smile, look you in the eye, and make you feel interesting and at home next to them, wherever they are. She could wear beautiful fabrics and blue jeans with equal style and was quietly but clearly equal to any situation that arose, social or personal, though she easily hid her gracious mastery. In so many ways she was like Ernie, but for wholly different reasons. Ernie was wonderfully unselfconscious—witness the day back in August when we met and he just began talking to me as if we had known each other all our lives. He was comfortable in his own skin because he knew who he was. It was nothing more complex than that yeoman Popeye philosophy: "I yam what I yam." Lynne was comfortable with whom she was too, but her charming self-forgetfulness grew from her worldly experience. She had tested herself in the high-powered fashion world of New York, and later in London where she worked as an executive marketing manager for Calvin Klein Cosmetics, was married to a tobacco magnate, and moved among the entrepreneurial movers and shakers, the titled and the entitled, with no problem, and from which venue she occasionally sallied forth with husband or friends around the world in search of her collecting passion—fabric. You'd never know any of this, of course, unless you inquired about the mannequin in the corner of their living room draped with a beautiful antique wrap.

She was also like Ernie in his curiosity about all things, in his passion for work, his interest in people, first and foremost, and family, in his oddly left-of-center politics out here on the conservative Banks, and his commitment to community. Ernie had no choice, of course; such commitment had

Lynne Foster (Courtesy of Lynne Foster)

been hard wired in him by his family history. But Lynne had clearly chosen to care civically, again easily and naturally, and had just volunteered to be development director for the struggling Graveyard of the Atlantic Museum at the south end of the village. She had just edited and published an anthology of Outer Banks women's writing so that their voices could be heard. She readily acknowledged that working villages like Hatteras were by nature patriarchies. She wasn't angry. There was no trace of contempt, frustration. As if she were reading my mind, she said, "You know, women don't come down to places like Hatteras Village looking for sensitive New Age guys. They want someone who can frame up a house, fix a toilet. If they fish for a living, so much the better." Lynne Foster, wearing jeans more often than not, her hair ordinarily coiffed, her kitchen cluttered with groceries and fishing gear, was happily, exactly where she wanted to be.

The other thing she shared with Ernie was a demonstrable affection. They were deeply and shyly in love with one another. It was nice to watch. Lynne surely knew the story, but she didn't know Ernie had told it to me a few days earlier when we were out on Diamond Shoals. A cold mist was blowing, and we had zipped the plastic curtains down around us on the bridge. We sat there in big coats drinking coffee.

After a couple of glances back at the lines we were trolling, Ernie just said, "Hope. You can't give up hope."

And then he said, "August 12, 1990."

And I said, "What?"

"The worst and best day of my life."

"What?"

"My wife left me, just walked out and took the kids with her." Even behind his rain-streaked glasses, I could see the tears welling.

"I'm sorry. I guess I haven't gotten over it yet." He went on to balance the equation. "This was up in Manteo. I was going crazy. I had a charter that day down here. I wanted to blow it off, but somehow I knew I should get out on the water, get my mind on fishing. So I drove down." The charter awaiting Ernie was Lynne and her husband. The trip was a happier one than either of their marriages.

"Two weeks later — I'm living in this wretched apartment with no family, I'm miserable, depressed — and I get a thank-you note from Lynne, for the fishing trip." It took Ernie three days to compose a response — "God, was it bland!"

Then Lynne wrote him back. Then there was hope.

Lynne and I watched Chris disappear with his friends toward the open bar. She prefaced the comments she was about to make with a disclaimer to objectivity. Ernie, she said, had been married to Chris and daughter Tiffany's mother for fifteen years. That was the longest marriage for her. Ernie was husband number four out of five total — so far. Ernie and family had lived up in Manteo, north of Hatteras Village, where he worked as a guidance counselor at the local high school, and he commuted an hour and half each way to run his charter fishing business. That's why the kids never grew up in Hatteras Village. Besides, Ernie's wife disliked the provincialism of it all. When they split up, his wife took the kids to Greenville, where she'd begun teaching at East Carolina University. After a pause, Lynne added, "It's too bad, but they never got salt water in their blood, never really took to fishing and the sea. Ernie's really sad that neither of his kids wants to take over the fishing business." Earlier today, when we'd been out on the *Albatross*, Chris had moved about the boat easily, knew the routines, how to net baitfish, how to set outriggers, but he didn't seem nearly as enthusiastic as the rest of us. When I handed him a rod with a king mackerel on it, he seemed surprised and brought it in in a businesslike way. It was hard to tell whether it was his low-keyed demeanor generally or his marginal interest in fishing. Ernie and he kept in quiet touch during the trip through that loving shorthand of small gesture and clipped comment that develops between adoring father and son.

A genial, older man wandered over to our booth and smiled warmly down at Lynne. Lynne beamed back, and I was introduced to Larry Ray Bonney, the owner of the Hatteras Harbor Marina and the man to whom I was paying my motel bills. Lynne and Ernie liked him because he and his wife had come years ago to Hatteras Village, bought the marina, and ended up caring deeply about the town and preserving its unique flavor. We chatted for a while until he wandered back off. Lynne and I surveyed the crowd. I recognized many of the people, but couldn't quite put them on the right boats, behind the right counters, in the right supermarket aisles. Some of the women were wearing sweatshirts and jeans and looked as though they had just come from work. Others wore matronly, Sunday-go-to-meetin' outfits. But most striking were those women dressed to the nines. Some wore elegant, spaghetti-strap cocktail dresses. Some wore slinky, art-opening sheathes. Lynne was checking it out too. She smiled: "This may be the only time in the entire year they have an opportunity to wear 'the outfit.'" A number of the younger women and girls had on sheer black blouses, bare midriffs, hip-hugger slacks with wide, stylishly droopy belts and big buckles. They were happy and self-conscious in their finery. There was a boatload of ass-watching going on as these younger colts wandered through the crowd or went up to claim their raffle prizes ("Two green softhead teasers [trolling baits] go to . . ." Laughter, and then the fishermen put their cigarettes in their mouths and clapped and stomped their feet as a young woman headed up to the podium to get the big blister pack the prize came in).

By now many had made it through the buffet line and were busy eating their seafood and hush puppies and homemade vegetables. Ernie and Chris joined us. Lynne and I took our turn through the dwindling line and came back to the booth. One of the captains was at the podium reviewing the fishing season out of Hatteras Village. "We had a good year," he began. "The numbers are up. We caught 618 billfish. The top boat caught twelve blue marlin, and second was ten." He named the boats. "Now the white marlin. You know they were almost put on the endangered species list. That could have put us out of business. Overall, we caught around two hundred white marlin, about the same number as blue marlin. That means that white marlin numbers are down. We gotta do something about that." And then he went back to the numbers. *Hatteras Fever* was the top sailfish boat. The most billfish released by a boat was eighteen. And the number one boat for billfish this year was . . . *Citation*. Scattered applause. This season two boats, *Gambler* and *Marlin Mania*, scored a grand slam—a sailfish, a white marlin, and a blue marlin caught the same day. More riffling applause, though the feasting and the alcohol-fueled gabbing and laughing were getting in the way. Lynne remarked that in years past, the Captains' Banquet, with its open bar, had often gotten out of hand, with fistfights inside and out in the parking lot. A lot of old grudges were settled. But things, she allowed, seemed to be getting tamer. There were a few weaving drunks here and there, but they seemed jolly and loud and little more.

As we finished eating, a man who appeared to be in his late forties came over to our table. He was handsome and fit and tan, with an expensive, preppy haircut, an Oxford shirt, and chinos. There was an impish, undergraduate quality about him, though the gray at his temples and the few lines in his face were clearly postgraduate. The features of his face were still but seemed eager to do something impulsive. He was Cary Grant with an outdoor job. His good looks were marred only by a deep scar running from the right corner of his mouth to his ear (I learned later it was from a car wreck in his wild youth). His name was Spurgeon Stowe, and besides Ernie and Willy Foster he was the only other remaining second-generation captain in Hatteras Village. He ran the headboats *Miss Hatteras* and *Miss Clam* and the small charter boat *Little Clam* out of Oden's Dock, right next to Foster's Quay. Judging from the barrage of good-natured ribbing directed all evening across the restaurant at his booth, where he and his attractive wife held court, he was a village favorite.

Spurgeon was introduced to our boothful, but his eye remained fixed on his old buddy, Ernie. "Ernie. Damn! You've worn that same sweater for fourteen years. When are you gonna get another one?" He laughed, and his eyebrows danced like Groucho's. Ernie sat in his argyle sweater, smiling, at a loss for words. Lynne chimed in, "Spurgeon, he's got drawers full of sweaters, but he just likes that one."

"Well, get him to open one of them other drawers!" More small talk, more needling. For the first time, not including when I asked Captain Ronnie O'Neal to demonstrate it for me over on Ocracoke, I could hear traces of that famous—and fast-disappearing—Outer Banks brogue: "toyme" for "time," "noyght" for "night." Spurgeon waved and moved on. I'd been wanting to talk with this character from an old village family for some time, even though Ernie had warned me that it would be difficult to get

Spurgeon to hold still long enough to have a real conversation. He was pure nervous energy.

The evening sailed on, the leisurely, bawdy raffle marking its course ("A free man's hair styling and a blow—. . . oh, 'dry'—that's a blow*dry*, goes to . . ."). One of the winners was announced over the din, and a woman in a black evening dress, her hair down almost to her shoulders, stood up and laughed a big gravelly laugh. She'd won a battery charger, and there was no mistaking that Marlboro laugh and those wrestler's arms and the mountain climber legs. It was Dita Young who had mated on my first trip on the *Albatross II* with Tall Bill. She looked fine and happy and still seemed to be with the boyfriend she had waved to on our way out of Hatteras Inlet a year and a half back.

Tall Bill made his way over to say hello and to introduce me to an attractive woman he had taken up with. I didn't catch her name. Tall Bill was shy and mumbling, and beaming. Brian, Bill's just-married son, stopped by just then. Then Ernie and Lynne had to circulate, and I watched the stringy-haired deejay behind the podium getting his speakers wired and cds organized for a postdinner party. But a lot of the older people, many of whom had been out on the water all day, were beginning to leave, and when the winner of the grand raffle prize—an over-and-under shotgun—was announced, more people began to leave to yawns and sleepy good-byes. The deejay was undaunted. A core of young people was staying. The funkapalooza would go on. But we wandered out with the rest. We were beat. On the way, we stopped in front of the oversized framed fishing photos near the front door. Ernie named all the men in the sepia picture. We stood quietly in the wake of his recitation, unsure quite what to do. People came by at last, and we followed them out. At the dreg end of the evening, well past bedtime here in Hatteras Village, the living still paused to remember the long dead.

To understand Hatteras Village, North Carolina, it's useful first of all to know what it's not. As you approach the Outer Banks on Route 158, the billboards and homemade, sequenced signs on sticks—modern Burma Shave fare—conspire to whisper to you, "The Jersey Shore." "Don't Miss Waterfall Park!" "Don't Miss the Waterslide!" "Don't Miss the Super Bungee!" "Woody's Discount Fireworks," "Yogi Bear's Jellystone Park," "Visit The Weeping Radish Brewery." The closer you get to the Wright Memo-

A commercial Hatterasman at the rudder of a fishing skiff, June 1945 (Courtesy of Photographic Archives, Ekstrom Library, University of Louisville)

rial Bridge over the Currituck Sound and onto the Outer Banks at Kitty Hawk, the more shrill and scarlet the ads become—and the more alliterative: "Mako Mike's!" "Bad Barracuda's!" "Dirty Dick's Crab House—'Tell 'em You Got Your Crabs at Dirty Dick's!'" "Try My Nuts!" "Visit Souvenir City—Our Name Says It All." Indeed it does, as do they all. All kitsch, all the time. Come on in. Bring your wallets. The ad frenzy does not disappoint. Dropping down off the Wright Bridge onto the Outer Banks proper, you are delivered a one-two blow from the major retail anchors, Wal-Mart and Home Depot. And then as you swing south, the parade of pastel retail confection continues for fifteen miles, through Kitty Hawk, Kill Devil Hills, Nags Head, and South Nags Head. Of all the cheek-by-jowl tackiness, perhaps the most innovative is the Brew Thru, an electric-green car wash–shaped building that beckons you to drive into its tunnel, pop the trunk, and fill 'er up on the beer and wine, mixer and munchies, arrayed

Dinner from the docks: Hatteras Village, June 1945 (Courtesy of Photographic Archives, Ekstrom Library, University of Louisville)

from floor to ceiling on either side. No need to get out of the car. They'll load you up. You simply pay up, drive forth, and party hearty.

Then just as it seems the schlock will reach some kind of commercial critical mass, that we're headed to Las Vegas and a simulacrum of the Pyramids and Paris and New York, New York, in the middle of the Nevada desert, the neon delirium stops dead in its tracks—to be exact, a hiccup south of South Nags Head, at Whalebone Junction, so named for a nondescript gas station that once had sported an old whalebone on the grass strip out in front of its pumps. This is the end of the glare and blare and very nearly any evidence of the human hand. This is the beginning of the Cape Hatteras National Seashore. This preserve was the first of its kind, proposed in 1933, but not established until twenty years later, and finally dedicated on April 24, 1958. Of all the stretches of beach along the east coast of the United States, only here along the National Seashore can you stand on the beach, look left, and then look right and witness . . . virgin coast. Sky. Sea. Sand dunes, as far as the eye can see. The hand of man has been kept in its pocket. The vista is just the way it was in Columbus's time, just the way it was thousands of years before Columbus. There are a handful of small villages that were grandfathered in when the National Seashore was established: Rodanthe, Waves, Salvo, Avon, Buxton, Frisco, and the end of the line on Hatteras Island, Hatteras Village. But the rest is pristine ecosystem, including a world-class national wildlife sanctuary at Pea Island on the northern tip of Hatteras Island and occasional penned clearings with low lookout towers to spot the famous Outer Banks wild horses, by legend and genetics said to be descended from Spanish horses left here or that swam in from wrecked sailing ships hundreds of years ago.

The changes demarcated by the Whalebone Junction boundary are both dramatic and subtle. The resort development evaporates. The natural vegetation begins like the tracking shot from a gray-green sea epic. But there are other, harder-to-see changes, until you've made the trip much more than once. The "Blow-Out Sale" kitsch at curbside north of Whalebone Junction — bookcases shaped like dinghies on end, windsocks, rowboats full of conch shells, bouquets of windsurfers and surfboards — disappear south of Whalebone to be replaced in those little pockets of human habitation by other roadside objects — peeling boats on long dead trailers, old weed-rimmed Jeep Wagoneers and pickups with rusted-out rocker and quarter panels, stacks of wooden Pepsi crates, or gray, sun-bleached lumber. The roadside down here isn't used as a store so much as for storage.

Likewise, the names of the side streets change. North of Whalebone Junction, they sound as though they came off a developer's drawing board or from some seaside database — Driftwood, East Conch, Dune, Windjammer, Wild Dunes. But as you get closer to Hatteras Village, as you pass through the little towns just north of it, quirky sidestreet names begin to appear: Midgett, Billy Mitchell, Quidley, Fulcher, O'Neal, Jennette, Mirlo, Cemetery Road, and Austin. They are the names of the old families, the famous people (General Billy Mitchell), or the tragic shipwrecks (*Mirlo*), or they just tell you what's down there (Cemetery Road). Just as beachwear gives way to blue-collar shirts and suvs yield to old pickups with a picket fence of surf rods sticking up in front of their grilles, heading south on the Outer Banks, you notice that real history replaces Hallmark sentiments as road names off Highway 12.

'Twas ever thus on the Outer Banks. The first vacation resorts were established on the northern Banks, those at Nags Head predating the Civil War. Back then, to go further south than Nags Head took a major effort. The only earthly reasons for heading down the Banks at all were hunting or fishing or too much George Dickel and a dare involving a large sum of money. Without Highway 12, you had to ride horseback or aboard a wagon along the beach, or, later, drive in automobiles with half-deflated tires near the surfline where the sand was harder. If you made it to Oregon Inlet around fifteen miles south of Nags Head, you had to wave a flag or shirt, or just wait for a primitive ferry—a tipsy raft towed behind a fishing boat—to come across from the tip of Hatteras Island to get you. If you made the treacherous crossing safely, you still had almost forty miles to go to get to Hatteras Village. While history and myth are rife with stories of shipwrecks off the beaches of Hatteras Island, the sea has also claimed its share of cars and old flatbed trucks trying to get down the beaches to Hatteras Village.

The history of modern-day Hatteras Village began on September 7 and 8, 1846. That's when a violent storm with a particularly vicious tidal surge broke through the lower Banks and created two new inlets, one some thirty miles north of Hatteras Village and one right in the middle of the village itself. The inlet to the north, now called Oregon Inlet, after the first ship to sail through it, is still navigable and has a large charter fleet. The second, also still open and passable, is the present-day Hatteras Inlet. Redding R. Quidley, a boat pilot who lived in Hatteras Village, remembered the storm in a letter to a friend some years later: "The day the inlet was cut out, there were several families living where the inlet is now . . . but to their great surprise, in the morning they saw the sea and sound connected together, and the live oaks washing up by the roots and tumbling into the sea." Quidley piloted boats through Ocracoke Inlet to the south and then would walk home to Hatteras Village. No longer. The storm cut up the ancient Indian kingdom of Croatoan, created the present islands of Ocracoke and Hatteras, and forced Quidley henceforth to hitch a boat ride home after work.

Almost immediately, Hatteras Inlet began to change the fortunes of the tiny village on its northern bank. Of the three inlets now on the southern Banks —Oregon, Hatteras, and Ocracoke—it was Hatteras Inlet that proved the most stable and consistently navigable, so much so that by 1862, during the Civil War, Hatteras Inlet would be chosen to accommodate a large Union fleet en route north up the Pamlico Sound to Roanoke Island. And after the Civil War, until the turn of the twentieth century, three separate steamship lines running between New Bern and New York used Hatteras Inlet. Hat-

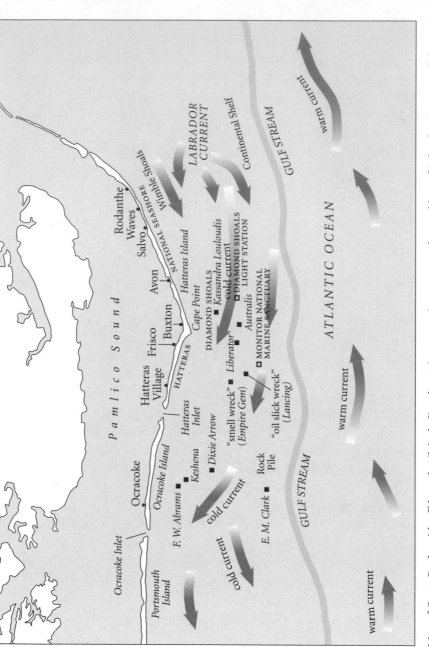

Map of Outer Banks with offshore detail, including the major competing currents, the southbound Labrador Current and the northbound Gulf Stream. The consequent wave action from these opposing currents is pushing the barrier islands southward and westward toward the mainland. Also indicated are the major shoal waters and the favorite fishing areas among charter captains.

teras Inlet almost immediately brought a steady stream of modern commerce sailing daily past the sleepy village doorsteps. It wasn't long before little Hatteras Village became the largest settlement on the Outer Banks.

In addition to a burgeoning commercial trade, there were other indications that Hatteras Village was coming of age. One year after the inlet-opening storm in 1846, Hatteras Village welcomed its first schoolteacher, one John Rollinson from the village of Trent, just north of town. Like just about every other aspect of life on the Outer Banks, John Rollinson's ability to read and write was owed to the sea. Almost exactly ten years before Rollinson became Hatteras Village's first schoolmaster, Joshua Daily, a young Englishman bound from the West Indies, washed up on the shores of Hatteras Island near Hatteras Inlet, his brigantine, *Ralph*, having foundered in a terrible gale. Daily was headed for a teaching job in Virginia, but never made it. He settled in Trent and lived with John Rollinson père, a man of some substance. For the rest of his life, Joshua Daily taught the young of Hatteras Island, and one of his best pupils (except when it came to spelling) was John Rollinson the younger, who ultimately followed his teacher's example in Hatteras Village. Pedagogy was a stern challenge on the lower Banks. There were no books, there was little or no paper, and writing utensils had to be fashioned from goose quills and ink from pokeberry squeezings. Beginning at the age of nineteen, Rollinson taught a four-month term in Hatteras Village. He charged each student $2.50. The rest of the year he fished commercially like everyone else.

Besides the three R's, Hatteras Village also got a fourth one before the Civil War: religion. Back in the eighteenth century, one Reverend John Urmston, a British missionary from the Church of England, threw up his uncalloused hands and declared the inhabitants of the Outer Banks of North Carolina "a nest of the most notorious profligates upon earth." In the throes of the Great Awakening shortly after 1800, the followers of Francis Asbury's Methodism filled their shoes with sand slogging down to Hatteras Village and the other towns on the lower Banks, and were somewhat gentler in their judgment of these hard-working folk; many were indeed "gospel slighters," but there was hope, they felt, for these salty souls. Methodism took firm hold on the Outer Banks and remained that way. Today in Hatteras Village there are two churches: the Hatteras United Methodist Church and the Hatteras Assembly of God.

In the first half of the nineteenth century, social and cultural practices in Hatteras Village, like their religious counterparts, remained relatively uncomplicated. Census figures for Hatteras Island right before the Civil War showed that there were 1,185 people on the island as a whole, among them four "freed Negroes" and eighty-four slaves. Just after the war, the 1870 census listed the island's population at 1,302, with thirty of that number newly emancipated African Americans. Overall, prewar slave numbers were small, and the demographic racial shift after the war (fifty-four African Americans left the island) was negligible. David Stick is undoubtedly correct in his conclusion: all things considered, there was proportionately little slave ownership on the Outer Banks. And after the war it seemed pretty much a live-and-let-live attitude on the Banks. A confounded Confederate soldier stationed on the Outer Banks during the Civil War probably stated the attitude most succinctly: the inhabitants, he said, were "apparently indifferent to this outside sphere, they constitute a world unto themselves." These were—and still are, mightily so—practical, "show me" people for whom hard work and results and minding your own business made up for a boatload of difference, racial or otherwise. For example, in 1878, the negligence of the all-white crew manning the Pea Island Lifesaving Station at the northern end of Hatteras Island led to the deaths of at least four shipwreck victims; as a result the crew was dismissed en masse, which in turn led to the appointment of an all–African American crew, captained from 1880 on by the formidable Richard Etheridge, described as "one of the best surf men on this part of the coast of North Carolina." The all-minority crew distinguished itself through diligence, professionalism, and numerous acts of lifesaving bravery until the station was decommissioned in 1947.

In the wake of the Civil War, Hatteras Village became a bustling, though rough-hewn, trading outpost. A year after Lee's surrender at Appomattox, a member of the numerous Burrus clan opened the first general store in Hatteras Village. It was originally built near the intersection of Fulcher Lane and Highway 12 in the heart of present-day Hatteras Village (where the Lee Robinson General Store is now). The Burrus store was moved in 1900 to the corner of Kohler and Saxon Cut roads and is still there as the Burrus Red-and-White market. By 1884 there were four more general merchandise stores in the village, each owned by a family with a familiar name: the Midgetts, the O'Neals, the Styrons, and the Stowes. All this commerce in a little village whose entire population could not reach 700 if it threw in all the live hogs wandering the sandy lanes.

In the late nineteenth and early twentieth centuries, there was plenty of work for everyone on Hatteras Island, black or white, though much of it was beginning to transcend the family-style and family-sized operations the Bankers had grown used to. Huge commercial interests were moving in and taking over large portions of the fishing industry on the upper and lower Banks, especially on the mainland side of the sounds. The Capehart and Belvidere Fisheries of the Albemarle Sound, the oyster factories at New Bern and Beaufort, and the menhaden factories at Beaufort and Harker's Island made steady wage earners out of hundreds and hundreds of people who had been used to working for themselves in a barter economy. Among these people was Ernie Foster's grandfather, who found work aboard a menhaden boat out of Beaufort.

Large-scale seine netting was the most popular form of commercial hauling, but gill nets and stationary, pole-rigged pound nets also brought in hundreds of tons of fish. Though large commercial fishing operations lured appreciable numbers from the Outer Banks labor force, smaller-scale family operations continued to flourish, as they do today.

After World War I, Hatteras Village's commercial fishing industry would continue to thrive. If you had wanted to go sportfishing in the 1920s and 30s, however, you no doubt would have been greeted by the shaking heads and smirks of locals who found the idea of catching fish for fun an odd one indeed. Yet with a few bucks it was possible now and then to talk local commercial fishermen into taking you out. In those days, Ernie Foster says, there were only about thirty boats in Hatteras. Many had been built right in Hatteras Village in the unique high, flaring bow-and-round-stern design, and all were meant for commercial fishing. "If you wanted to go out fishing with their owners—Vernon Willis, Nelson Stowe, Luther Burrus, whoever —you had to catch them in a good mood and you had to supply your own fishing gear. They would provide wooden fish boxes for you to sit on, but that was pretty much it." Most of the trips were safe, inshore ventures where the water teemed with bluefish and mackerel in the summer months and channel bass in the fall. But, as Ernie pointed out, the Diamond Shoals Lightship was only twenty-one miles from the mouth of Hatteras Inlet, and along the way was Buoy No. 2 and the shipwrecks on Diamond Shoals itself. The lightship and the buoy were sure things for bull dolphin, and the shipwrecks were loaded with huge amberjack, king mackerel, and all manner of bottom fish. But this was the early 1930s, and such "off-shore" trips were rare. The Great Depression was on, and if captains thought they could make more money that day in commercial fishing, they'd simply cancel the odd "angling" offer they had without so much as an apology. Also, most of the boats had six-cylinder car engines in them and could only top out at eight to ten knots (about trolling speed), so the longer trips took time and gas. Add to these obstacles, a healthy respect for the fickle weather at Cape Hatteras and the absence of any electronics on the boats (no loran, no depth recorders, no radio), and it's no wonder offshore fishing was slow aborning on the lower Outer Banks.

While some trips were made in the early 1930s, quite probably the first offshore fishing trip from the Hatteras area was made in the early 1920s by a man named Tom Eaton. Thomas Spurgeon Eaton was the son of a Reynolds Tobacco Company executive. He was also an avid fisherman and a lover of the Outer Banks of North Carolina. These two passions combined to see to it that Tom Eaton played a complex, off-stage role in the development of the lower Banks—Hatteras Village in particular. Regarding the fishing trip, Tom Eaton talked Captain Bill Gaskill of Ocracoke Island into taking him all the way out to the Gulf Stream to fish. A skeptical Bill Gaskill deferred to his son, Thurston, to skipper the boat. They went out Ocracoke Inlet and fished the Gulf Stream, but got lost on the way in and finally came in through Hatteras Inlet, having caught six huge dolphin. This was probably the first real blue-water charter trip off Cape Hatteras. Eaton would later bring writer-friends down, most notably newspaper writers Chet Smith and Johnny Mott, who wrote glowing accounts of Hatteras fishing in the Pittsburgh press.

When Tom Eaton wasn't fishing, he was thinking business. And it occurred to him that the commercial fishermen of Hatteras Village suffered for lack of electricity and refrigeration. Ice had to be shipped to them across the sound, and without refrigeration facilities of their own, they were restricted unnecessarily to relying for their livelihoods on certain types of oily rough fish—like menhaden, spot, and so on—that wouldn't spoil in transit. So Eaton talked local businessman Frazier Peele into running an ice plant, and he did the rest: got electricity run down to the island and to Hatteras Village, built the ice plant, and had the whole thing up and running in 1935. Hatteras Village had entered the Ice Age, and for commercial fishermen that was major progress. Soon Eaton added a sixty-eight-foot freight boat, the *Hadeco* (short for Hatteras Development Company), which held four cars, freight, and passengers. The *Hadeco* for years made daily runs across the sound to Engelhard. Eaton was also instrumental in getting Rollinson Channel deepened and a stone breakwater installed. This opened up huge areas for marinas on the sound side, including Foster's Quay. Eaton often traveled to Washington to talk with Congressman Herbert Bonner about these improvements and the economic possibilities for development on the Outer Banks.

Also during the depression of the 1930s, many of the village men and women who had left looking for work other than fishing returned home as jobs became scarce. Ernal Foster Sr. was one of those prodigal citizens. In an interview conducted not long before he died, he remembered it: "I worked in a sheet metal shop in Long Island. . . . Then in '33, after the election, money people just closed up. And you can't live without work. So I came home. That Depression running me home was the best thing that ever happened to me." But Ernal came back to a family with a father and four boys. It was hard to stretch one boat across all those folks, so Ernal began planning to build his own commercial fisher. Ernal knew something about boat building. The year he returned to Hatteras Village, he had helped a couple of friends, Calvin and Corky Burrus, and Byrum Byrd lay out the bow stem for the *Jackie Fay,* a forty-foot commercial boat made with juniper planking and oak trim and sporting that high bow and rounded stern that was the signature of Hatteras boats. They put it in the water where Oden's Dock is today in October 1934. Ernal's mind was taking copious notes, and when the *Jackie Fay* occasionally took a break from commercial fishing, long hauling, and shrimping, and took out a party of "sports fishermen," Ernal's mind raced forward to an idea. They'd scoff, surely, but he could get his brother, Bill, to do it with him, he knew that much, and then he'd show the rest that it could be done.

Today Hatteras Village remains a working fishing town, one of the few left in North Carolina. Unincorporated, it has 632 permanent residents, seven marinas, and twenty-six cemeteries. Many of the cemeteries are family plots in the front yard of homes or out back by the garage or storage shed. It's hard to drive down a road in the village without seeing a scattering of lichen-covered stones here and there. There are probably more cemeteries, but many of the markers, originally wood, are gone and the little sacred areas forgotten, overgrown, and built over. The handful of mostly mom-and-pop motels in Hatteras Village tend toward the humid and seedy and accommodate mostly fishermen. In the summer, however, the newish line of big, stilted mansions along the Atlantic dune line east of the village fills up with families to swell the town's seasonal population by a large multiplier.

But, for the most part, those tourists whose tastes run to boogie boards, T-shirts, and lattes either stay up at the northern end of the Banks or maybe come on down to Buxton, which has a few emporia catering to such tastes, or take the ferry from Hatteras Village across to Ocracoke Island, whose frou-frou quotient is higher. Hatteras Village is for off-island families too, but mostly for families who like to fish, either from the beaches or aboard the bottom-fishing boats or the blue-water charter boats colorfully dominoed throughout the seven marinas.

But even in the constant thrumming wind, villagers can hear a bell tolling, and they do not have to ask for whom it tolls. It tolls for them and their way of life. Chances are, especially with recent developments, and, ironically, because of their own ingrained, fierce independence, the working fishing village that they and their grandparents and their parents before them knew may become something else. Where I live, in Memphis, it's hard for old-timers to accept that the number one cash crop in the mid-southern United States is no longer cotton but soybeans; it will probably be equally hard for Ernie Foster and his generation to sit around and witness Hatteras Village turn into Nags Head South and high-dollar tourism, not fishing, rule the waves of Hatteras Village and environs.

On one crisp, sunny November day, Captain Ernie Foster and I drove around the town, and he showed me why he and his marine colleagues and friends had this dark vision of the village's future. This morning, Ernie had come in from an aborted blue-water trip because the men headed out for yellowfin drank beer for breakfast, got seasick, and forfeited a chunk of change for the privilege of puking in their own motel rooms. We headed first over to the ocean side along Lighthouse Road. We were looking for the hull of an old shipwreck on the beach. Sometimes it was covered over by sand, sometimes it was exposed, depending on the moods of the sea and the tides. All along the road, huge houses were perched like fat wading birds just behind the dune line, many with their stilts ankle-deep in water from a recent storm. Almost all were rentals. Ernie pointed to a couple of huge new homes under construction. He derisively called them "unsupervised hotels." Like most of the others, they had ten to twelve bedrooms, accommodated a busload of people, and rented for $3,000-$5,000 a week in season.

Here and there on the other side of Lighthouse Road were peeling, single-story bungalows, many with boats on trailers or up on chocks. "These are the real people," Ernie said, nodding to the less-fashionable bungalows. "They live and work here." We drove further along Lighthouse Road. Ernie pulled over. "Look at this." Two signs stuck out of a sodden sod lawn lead-

Mansions along the beach, Hatteras Village. Except for the house in the foreground, all are rental properties. (Courtesy of Lynne Foster)

ing up to a McMansion. One said, "For Sale," and gave the name of the real estate company. The other proclaimed, "For Rent," with the name of a different company. A good number of homes along the street sported the same double signage. "Now you figure that one out," Ernie grumbled. "A developer, backed by deep-pocket investors, builds these places. Supposedly, they're good rental investments"—he added sarcastically. "You come down here in the summer with ten or twenty of your closest friends and fill up one of these monsters. So why," he went on, "if it's such a good investment, are they trying to sell it?" Ernie supplied his own answer. "It's the theory of the bigger fool. With the stock market in the toilet, the fat cats have to put their money somewhere, so they do this"—waving his arm along the gaudy platoon of seaside rental machines. "And right away, they turn around and try to find a bigger fool to buy them."

We got out and walked between the houses and up over the sand dune onto the beach. The shipwreck was covered over today. It was high tide, and the beach wasn't a hundred feet wide in some places. You could see where the waves had been recently lapping at the dune line. We backtracked up Flambeau Lane to Highway 12 and ended up on Kohler Road over on the Pamlico Sound side of the village. It was not very far. We stopped at an

L. N. Stowe House (Courtesy of Lynne Foster)

old house set back from Spanish moss–covered live oaks. It was the L. N. Stowe House built sometime in the wake of World War I. In many ways, it was typical of the structures architectural historians call the "I" home: a two-story, single-pile, side-gable home with a two-story ell. A one-story porch with turned balusters and decorative fretwork ran the length of the facade. The windows were sash-style, two panes over two. You could find the same style dating to the same period throughout the midwestern United States — though not garnished with Spanish moss.

We continued driving in a light rain, talking. On M. V. Australia Road (named for one of the many ships sunk on Diamond Shoals), we stopped again, this time at a beautiful old cottage in a grove of stunted live oaks. It was a quaint little story-and-a-half place covered with sun-bleached green asbestos shingles and plain white trim that gave it a crisp silhouette. A small, latticed porch invited all with aproned warmth and good cheer. This was the Caleb B. Stowe House, moved here in 1888, according to family documents, with "horses and rollers and ropes." Because of storms and hurricanes, a good number of the older houses in the village had been moved over the years, some more than once. I wanted to ask Ernie more about it, but he was looking at another place, a brand-new structure right next door. Its huge shadow easily covered the Stowe House. What Ernie was glaring at was a full-sized, really more-than-full-sized, replica of a turn-of-the-century life-saving station. It was a giant, two-story affair topped by an oversized "crow's nest" room, windowed all around. The second story was vertical wood siding running up the high gables, which were necklaced by open wood tracery. Down below was a shingled first story, with a double-wide concrete ramp leading up to two garage doors six feet off the ground. Such a ramp in the original beach stations was wood and allowed the lifesaving-service men to roll their boats out and toward the pounding surf and ships in trouble. Here the ramp accommodated a brand new Lexus SUV and a matching teal Wagoneer.

Ernie was shaking his head again. "This neighborhood's a goner," he said, more to himself than to me. What did he mean? He pointed to the faux lifesaving station. "Built by Joe Thompson of Land's End Realty. He's on the County Planning Board; he said publicly that he was actively looking for building code loopholes" (the lifesaving station represents a goodly number of them). The more Ernie went on, the angrier he got. "And then Thompson says, 'If I find a loophole, I feel I have an obligation to help others get through it.' Can you imagine? This guy feels an obligation! And this is a man who's supposed to be looking out after the interests and desires of the citizens of Dare County!" If there were ecological "hot spots" where the ocean threatens to cut through and overwash a community or part of the national seashore, there were apparently political "hot spots" as well, with the hottest being the D-word, Development. For the most part, Hatteras Village had avoided the garish seasonal fate of Banks towns like Kitty Hawk, Kill Devil Hills, and Nags Head to the north, and even Buxton only a handful of miles up. They grumbled when the "unsupervised hotels" started going up along Lighthouse Road, and more so when they began lining the beach at the southern end of town down by the Graveyard of the Atlantic Museum. They fumed when a new marina went in right by the ferryboat landing replete with a Holiday Inn Express and a semicircle of flamingo-pink and robin's-egg and putty-gray upscale clothing and beach stores, hissing espresso machines, flapping windsocks, and festoons of tinkling wind chimes.

But things were about to metastasize. Land was already being cleared for two huge developments that threatened to bookend—and dwarf—the tiny fishing village. Just to the north of town was a sandy scar where Slash Creek development was going in. Slash Creek represented the vision of David Hoyle and partners, Gastonia developers. Hoyle just happened to be a state senator and a close ally of Marc Basnight, president pro tem of the state senate, who happened to represent Hatteras. The matching bookend was through the village, also right on Highway 12. It was called Hatteras-by-the-Sea and was the brainchild of another builder, Skip Dixon. Right now, Hatteras-by-the-Sea was demarcated by a sign and a row of ragged, nonindigenous palm trees along the shoulder of the road. Ernie and others derisively called the development "Lonesome Palms." Most of Hatteras Village was outraged about both developments, animated by the quiet seething kind of anger that comes from people who toil from dark to dark and have been used to being respected and left alone here on a spit of land almost forty miles out into the Atlantic Ocean. The stilted, Star Wars monsters Dixon was planning to build on the twenty-seven lots of Hatteras-by-the-Sea would tower over the rest of the village. And at Slash Creek Mother Nature would undergo radical cosmetic surgery, if the laws could be doctored sufficiently by the developers to allow for the procedure. The Slash is a shallow, natural estuary that starts from the Pamlico Sound and meanders inland, under Highway 12 next to the Channel Bass restaurant and almost to Hatteras Village itself. It's a pristine piece of reed-lined water and wetland that is a defining feature of Hatteras Village and its limited surroundings. The developers asked to dredge it out, deepen it, dike it, and make it a canal so that half-million-dollar yachts could tie up in the backyards of million-dollar homes. There's the Wetlands Act, there's the will of the people, and there's politics, and—as is true of people in small towns all over America—the prevailing belief was that politics would trump all else. Senator Basnight was unapologetic. It's progress, he opined, and besides, if the people had been willing to incorporate Hatteras Village and pass their own zoning laws, then Senator Hoyle and his friends couldn't come in and do what they're planning to do. In other words, it's their own damn fault. You want to be fiercely independent? Fine, but there's a price to pay, and that's not having a real say-so in what happens to your unincorporated village. Ernie said that right now citizens were split on incorporation. They knew they could control the zoning, but it was that old fear of being beholden to the "guvment." If you incorporate, you've got to pay for police, and you've got to contract with the county for garbage pickup and all those municipal services. Now it's simple; the county appoints five tax trustees from Hatteras Village (Ernie's one of them), and they figure out how to spend the money allocated to the village.

Talking had pulled us over into the parking lot of the Burrus Red-and-White market. The market was at the intersection of Kohler Road and

The heart of the village: the intersection of Kohler Road and Highway 12 (Courtesy of Lynne Foster)

Highway 12 and just across from the public library, the post office, and the fire station.

It was here, not a hundred paces from where we sat idling, that the citizens of Hatteras Village gathered on November 18, 1861. They were furious that the state government in Raleigh had decided to secede from the Union and join the Confederate States of America. No one had consulted them. Here they accused the state government of North Carolina of treason, drew up a "Statement of Grievances and a Declaration of Independence," and swore their loyalty to the Union. They even formed their own rump government. Fierce independence. Ernie just shook his head. "Yup. Goin' our own way has always been our strength, but these days it just may be what gets this village erased."

––––––––––––

At five the next morning, I could hear Ernie's truck crunching to a stop on the gravel outside my room. We'd agreed to meet and go to Oden's Dock for coffee. He had no charter today (the wind was fifteen knots and climbing). He could have slept in, but I knew he wanted me to witness the scene with Spurgeon and the rest of the fishermen getting their day started around the table at Oden's tackle store.

Men gathered at Austin Store, Hatteras Village, June 1945. The coats and ties suggest it was after church on Sunday. (Courtesy of Photographic Archives, Ekstrom Library, University of Louisville)

Oden's was less than a hundred yards down from the *Albatross* fleet. It was in a large two-story wood structure, the top floor of which was the Breakwater Restaurant. The open deck of the restaurant, looking out over the marina and the Pamlico Sound, provided a patio roof in front of Oden's store, below which mismatched chairs were scattered around. It was too cold today to sit outdoors. The rows of moored commercial and charter boats were bucking like wild horses twenty feet from Oden's front door.

Inside, it was dark and warm and cavernous. Just to our left a small group of men were sitting and standing around a small table whose top was a laminated depth chart from NOAA, the National Oceanic and Atmospheric Administration. It was standard issue on every boat. To our right was the glass counter and cash register and behind it Dan Oden and his helper, Nancy, whom I'd bought coffee from before and whom I'd seen at the banquet last night. Nancy seldom smiled but was friendly enough. Portly Dan

Men gathered at Oden's Dock store, October 2004, with Captain Spurgeon Stowe in the foreground (Courtesy of Lynne Foster)

Oden more than made up for her dour countenance. Beyond the counter stretching into the darkness to the right (the lights were off down there to save money) was the tourist part of the store, with T-shirts, cheap rods and tackle, and souvenir gewgaws. Up in the lighted area by the men was the business end of the store, where supplies — rope, oil, tools, boat hardware, and some charter-fishing equipment, along with breakfast buns and such — were found. And behind that, the two coffee machines were hissing and popping and dutifully dripping.

Sure enough, Spurgeon was there standing, coffee in hand, on the periphery of seated men. He spotted Ernie and me and lit up. We exchanged pleasantries and small teasing, and Spurgeon turned back to the ongoing conversation.

A heavyset older man seated at the small table said, "I finally got the sump working on the boat."

"Oh yeah?"

"Yeah. I pried Kenny out of bed and handed him a bailing can."

Laughter. There was more talk about Kenny's work ethic, and then a great deal more about boat equipment.

Ernie and I were standing behind the ring of men. He turned to me and said in a low tone, "That guy," gesturing discreetly toward the man who finally got Kenny to work, "is a retired electrical engineer. He does repair work on boats now, though he really doesn't have to." Talk turned toward the weather, a vital topic to these men and one that was going to landlock a lot of them today. One of them mentioned the reliability of the daily NOAA weather forecasts. A ruggedly good-looking fellow in waders shook his head: "You listen to NOAA and you starve. You don't listen and you drown." His name was Rob West. He was a commercial fisherman and was active in the North Carolina Commercial Fishing Organization. His wife was too, and she'd published a book on the commercial fishing industry.

"See that guy sitting next to him?" Ernie whispered. A short, bespectacled, plain-looking man in his early forties, maybe. "That's Bill Cowper. He's a commercial fisherman too, but he's also a former Morehead scholar at Chapel Hill. He decided to be a gillnetter." And next to Bill Cowper was "Big Bill" Foster, all six-and-a-half feet and 320 pounds of him. "Big Bill" had come to Hatteras Village in the 1970s to finish his Ph.D. in marine sciences. He stayed, and his degree stayed unfinished. For thirty years he's been active in fisheries issues, local and state.

Another pair of waders joined the group, this time from the rear door, in the shadows back by the coffee machine. "That's Reuben Trent." Reuben Trent was a commercial fisherman too. Some years ago, his father sent him to VMI to get him some military-style discipline and an education. Reuben decided to major in English at VMI, the equivalent apparently of seeking a career in Sumo wrestling at Sarah Lawrence. His GPA ended up being 3.94 out of a perfect 4.0. However, his GPA for attitude—what report cards once called comportment—was not as good. The commanding officer called him in one day. "You're the dumbest guy I know," he told young Reuben Trent. "You will never become a member of the Cadet Corps." Cadet Trent announced to his superior, "Sir, I can accept that, sir."

Reuben Trent looked happy this morning. He looked as though he'd been born in waders. At the table the conversation swirled on, from equipment to commercial netting rules changes to boat repairs to jokes.

Spurgeon announced, in answer to someone, that there were two motivations in life: one got you out of bed and the other kept you in it. Smiling most broadly at Spurgeon's attempt at Poor Richard wisdom was a stunted, middle-aged man whose perfectly round head continually nodded yes, apparently independent of his wishes, his feelings, or the rest of his badly crippled body. His name was Kenny Oden, of the Hatteras Village Odens, of course. Kenny Oden was first cousin to Danny, father of Dan over behind the glass counter. Danny owned the dock. Ernie had grown up with Kenny

Oden. He and his friends would transport Kenny around to their various activities and mischiefs; and when Kenny Oden had one of his many operations that more often than not would leave him in a full body cast, Ernie and his friends would bring their activities and mischief to Kenny Oden. Kenny Oden hadn't been expected to live, but he did. For years he made carved sea birds and such for the tourists, but his motor skills had worsened, and so he had to quit. He owned prime real estate and bought trucks that had a penchant for blowing up or just dying, for which he was teased mightily; he also joined in the opening session of Hatteras Village every morning. Ernie admired Kenny Oden, couldn't fathom how he put up with the pain, plus the operations all those years, and still smiled and bantered with the best of them.

Kenny Oden was descended from Herbert Oden who, according to local lore, was blown up on the beach, a castaway, in March 1856. It had been a harsh winter that year, and the people of the lower Banks were hungry and cold, so much so that a local preacher prayed that if God had a shipwreck in his plans that He make it near Hatteras Village and send some food ashore, preferably pork. Within a week, the *Mary Varney* ran aground and broke up in the Hatteras bight just north of the village. Toward evening, a huge pork barrel came in through the surf and was beached and broken apart. What the barrel contained was not pork but a battered and bruised Herbert Oden. He'd had enough of the sea. He stayed in the village, married, and had a family.

In the cement floor chill of this dark morning at Oden's store, Kenny Oden nodded on, rhythmically. Yes, yes, yes. They—Ernie and Kenny Oden —didn't speak to one another, but every once in a while they made eye contact that held just long enough to acknowledge a half century of familiarity and friendship and history.

To anyone who's lived or lingered in a small town, the scene at Oden's Dock store is familiar community theater. The locals who live and work in the villages on the lower Banks—not the tourists, the seasonal salts, not the megabuck retirees or renters in the huge beachfront/beachview mansions on stilts—but the permanent residents, the people who acknowledge each other when they pass on Highway 12, who talk at the post office and address the postmistress by her first name, who meet for coffee and sweet rolls in the marina tackle stores, who drive up to Norfolk General to visit folks who are sick—these people differ little from people in small towns all over America. In my part of the country, in the small towns across the river in Arkansas or just south of the nearby state line in Mississippi, or east of Memphis in

McNairy County—where Buford Pusser used to be sheriff—the men are farmers, not fisherman, and they meet in general stores or local coffee shops or feed stores instead of tackle shops. But the rhythm and substance and purpose of the meetings are the same: to swap work information, jokes, rumors, to catch up on politics, medical reports, church news, ordinary gossip. Each morning it's an oral edition of an invisible community newspaper. The men don't stay long—often, as in Hatteras Village, they leave as soon as it's light enough to work—but the communal conversation ensures that the center will hold, that the town will remain knit together, that its values will cohere, at least one more day.

Big-game angling has an official birth date
and founding father. On June 1, 1898, Charles
Frederick Holder of Pasadena, California,
landed a 183-pound bluefin tuna on rod and
reel off Catalina Island.
—Fishing historian George Reiger

CHAPTER FOUR

Charter Fishing
Then

Sure enough. There he was, Ernal Sr., moving around the dock by the boats. His gait was spraddled and halting, but, after all, he was eighty-four and just a few years from his death. That lean, wiry body I'd seen in so many of the photos — that body whose clothes always made sense on it and which was so often slouching on one hip or the other beside a hanging marlin with a smile and even a broken arm — I could see was going the way of all flesh, to paunch and jowls now. You could see brother Bill there too, and time seemed to have taken a greater toll on him, but there he was, talking, answering questions the film crew was asking him and his brother. There were long pauses before and after each question. But they would get answered in good time.

"This would have been 1992 or 93," Ernie said of the video we were watching in his small den. "It was a guy named Ackley or something like that and this film crew. They came down from Channel 8 in High Point and wanted to interview my father and Bill about beginning the charter fishing industry in Hatteras."

The production values were worlds better than the home movies we'd looked at together back in August, and it was nice to see Bill and Ernal Sr. as two old salts who'd done what they set out to do, and were now self-proclaimed "wharf rats," doing nothing but talking up the customers, whittling a little, and shaking their heads about how everything's gone "money crazy these days." In fact, at that moment they were summing up lives that had been lived largely within a mile or two of where they now sat on the steps at Foster's Quay. Ernal was saying to no one in particular, "I'm happy. I can't take anything with me; I've done what I wanted to do. What more is there?" The camera lingered on Ernal, waiting for more. But Ernal had risen out of his reserve long enough to speak his epitaph. That was enough. He looked down at his hands, gnarled and knotted and permanently cupped from years of grasping gear in bad weather. The camera slid over to Bill. "I wouldn't change a thing. The world don't owe me nothin'." His voice held traces of pride but also seemed reedy with age and resignation to an imminent fate. If the bodies of these two men were slowly betraying them, their eyes revealed an inviolable youth. Ernal and Bill were used to looking away from people to check the weather, to listen to the boat radio, to search for signs of fish. But they were also by nature men who looked you in the eye, took the measure of you with a gaze, and with that same gaze told you, wordlessly, who it was you were dealing with. Ernal and Bill were not well, yet their eyes were in charge of this moment. Their eyes looked away when they wanted to and they came back when they chose, riveting the camera and cameraman with a wry gleam of a world-weary wisdom, or, in an instant, the playful twinkle of an eighteen-year-old who had recently concluded that the world was an all-you-can-eat buffet laid out just for him.

"I made a deal with those TV guys," Ernie said. "They wanted to talk to my father, of course, but Uncle Bill was about seventy-four and had just been diagnosed with leukemia. They'd told him he had two weeks to live. So we wanted some pictures of Bill. I told those guys if they'd interview Bill too, I'd take them fishing offshore."

Bryan Mattingly, the mate, came in — it was blowing hard out and so boats were tied up for the day. He saw old Bill Foster on the screen, and he lit up. Bryan had loved and respected old Bill. He had even named one of his girls after him — Foster. Bill was just getting to the story of catching the world-record marlin almost exactly forty years ago. It was a wonderful narrative. The fish that would put the Hatteras Village on the map, permanently, remains the stuff of legend these many years later.

For all its color, Bill's account left out a lot of delicious detail, much of which could be filled in by the mate working the *Albatross II* with Bill Foster

Ernal and Bill Foster on the
porch of the dock house, c. 1993
(Courtesy of Ernie Foster)

that day. Ernie Foster was seventeen years old in 1962, but seasoned well
beyond that. They had a party of four fishermen from New Jersey, one of
whom, an elderly gentleman named Sloat, was an experienced fisherman
whose mission in life was to catch a world-record marlin. Fishing the ledges
just beyond the Diamond Shoals Lightship, the *Albatross II* had already
boated one good-sized marlin, over 200 pounds. In doing so, however, the
hook on the old Hawaiian Knucklehead lure had caught on the gunwale
and bent badly. While young Ernie was repairing the Knucklehead (which
had been given to Bill a week earlier by a Richmond fisherman who said
he should try it for marlin), and the other lines were brought in to be reset,
Sloat invited young Gary Stukes, one of the party, to spell him in the chair
while the lines were being put back out. The Knucklehead went back over
the side along with what Ernie describes as the "biggest, whitest, most beautiful squid" he had ever rigged. Within minutes a dark shape was cruising
through the bait spread. It turned up its nose at the fresh squid and went
straight for the repaired Knucklehead. The fish immediately tore off a hundred yards of line, and then tail-walked nearly another hundred off the
spool. Gary Stukes was frozen in the fighting chair, in shock at what he was
connected to. Bill yelled that it was the biggest fish he'd ever seen. Sloat's
reaction can only be guessed at. Bill went into the stern to help the panicked
Stukes, and turned the boat over to young Ernie who knew exactly what to
do in the intricate ballet that always followed getting fast to a big fish.

The fish jumped fifteen times in twenty minutes, but shortly after that
dance tour de force, Bill Foster was up on the fantail with a firm grip on
the cable leader and his heels jammed against the toe rail. For nearly a half
an hour he held that position until a flying gaff (a gaff with a removable

head tied to a rope) could be attached to the fish. Bill Foster was exhausted and needed help. The *Albatross II* lacked a gin pole, a vertical timber bigger and longer than a railroad tie that early boats used to leverage a big fish on board. And transoms that opened to slide fish aboard were still years away. Bill radioed a nearby boat for help and soon enough got it, and soon enough the world-record, all-tackle marlin was aboard ship. The fish was fourteen feet long and sixty-eight inches in girth, and it beat by thirty pounds a fish that had been caught three years earlier off Puerto Rico.

Ernie remembers it as though it were a dream: the fish fighting for its life (it died beside the boat), Uncle Bill holding the fish, waiting for help, the ride home with such a thing aboard, and the crowd at the dock. Besides the village itself, the turnout included all the participants who had come in for the annual Hatteras Marlin Club tournament, which was to start the next day. Though few fishing world records stay in one place very long, it was probably inevitable that the distinction would find its way to Hatteras Village for a while. After all, the waters were perfect for the species, and they were essentially virginal for more than a decade after World War II. Then, of course, there must be the equipment necessary, the know-how, the will and determination of local fishermen familiar with the waters literally from top to bottom, and finally luck and patience. It took almost thirty years (with a world war intervening) for Bill Foster to bring in the world record to Hatteras Village.

Most old-timers agree that the first attempt at fishing for blue marlin out of Hatteras Village took place in 1933. A village fisherman, Lloyd Styron, was there, and in an interview shortly before he died he recalled the occasion. The fisherman was Colonel Hugh Wise from Princeton, New Jersey. He had traveled around the world catching sharks and had in fact written a book about them. But he wanted to try for a marlin. At the time, he was about sixty-five or seventy, Styron recalled— "and he had a bad hip and didn't get around very well. He talked local Captain Nelson Stowe into taking him offshore." Stowe, like all captains in Hatteras Village in those days, had a commercial fishing boat and none of the equipment necessary for a marlin venture. "So Captain Stowe borrowed an office chair from his friend Andrew Austin, and for an outrigger a bamboo pole about ten or twelve feet long that I had found along the beach," and off they went. They didn't catch anything, recalls Stowe, and, worse, poor old Colonel Wise got thrown around so badly both in and out of his office chair that he decided he didn't want to try it again.

Wise's unhappy honeymoon with marlin fishing took place just months after an out-of-work Ernal Foster had returned to Hatteras Village. And according to his son's recollections of his father's account, it was also right around this time a large sailboat, *Alma*, dropped anchor in Hatteras Village harbor. Its captain took a liking to Ernal Foster, and before he sailed off, he gave him the gift of a book: Coleridge's *The Rime of the Ancient Mariner*. "My father had a grade-school education," says Ernie, "but he read that book all the way through, and for some reason that image of that giant albatross, that good-luck bird, stuck with him."

Another abortive attempt to catch a marlin off Hatteras Island was made in 1936 by two brothers, Jack and Paul Townsend, of Ocean City, Maryland. They were aboard their own boat, a forty-foot Elco, and they had better equipment, but their luck was the same as that of the bruised Colonel Wise. Then, in the summer of 1939, a veteran fisherman named Hugo Rutherford came to Hatteras Village. Fishing from his own private boat, he landed the first two marlin ever taken off the shores of the island. One of the fish weighed 590 pounds. Mr. Rutherford also took a fancy to Ernal, this quiet but personable and enterprising young man who had just had a new boat built for himself, and so he donated two red-and-white-banded cane outriggers to the *Albatross*. Outriggers were fast becoming standard gear for serious gamefishing in places a little more advanced than commercial fishing Hatteras Village: Montauk, Ocean City, the Bahamas, Miami (in fact much of the cane for the outriggers came into the port of Miami in bundles on the decks of huge freighters). But Ernal's were the first real outriggers among the boats in the village.

So was Ernal's idea a first in Hatteras Village, or anywhere the length of the Outer Banks: instead of fishing commercially as much as you could and maybe taking out an occasional gamefishing party, why not reverse the polarities? Why not take out gamefishermen exclusively when the weather held—the early spring, the summer months, and into the fall—and then do commercial fishing when the sportfishing season was over? In the Channel 8 documentary, Ernal sat on the wood steps of the *Albatross* office and said, "They laughed at me. Said I was crazy to mess with it, that I ought to get back to commercial fishing. Real work, they said."

But Ernal knew something the commercial fishermen didn't: there was money to be made from tourists and fishing. It was a truth brought home to him as a young boy occasionally helping his father. This was back in the early 1920s. Ernal had been born in Hatteras Village, but his father, Charles, had moved the family to Beaufort further south on the Banks to be near the menhaden fleet running out of there. Every once in a while, when his

Charles Foster, c. 1951
(Courtesy of Ernie Foster)

father wasn't menhaden fishing, he would gather up his son with him on their own boat ("It was very much like the *Jackie Fay*," says Ernal) and take parties fishing near the numerous Core Banks inlets. By 1924, the Fosters were back in Hatteras Village, where they would remain, but Ernal remembered those waters of the Core Sound where he'd grown up. Starting when he was fifteen, Ernal and an older friend would take a borrowed thirty-three-foot boat down sound and spend the summer ferrying bathers from the mainland out to Atlantic Beach. In the afternoons, they'd fetch them back home. The price was fifty cents a head. During the week, Ernal and his friend concentrated on rounding up groups to fish the waters off Cape Lookout. It wasn't hard to find takers.

So by the time Captain Hugo Rutherford had donated that pair of outriggers to the *Albatross*, Ernal had been running it as a charter fishing boat for two summers. Things had been slow at the outset. "That first summer, me and Bill ran four charters at $25 a trip." He chuckled to himself. But the next summer proved much better. Ernal and Bill, who was seventeen now, had developed a reputation. Fishermen who traveled long distances to Hatteras Village could rely on these two young men to keep their word and take them out—and not renege as some of the older captains had for the sake of a good commercial haul. With Ernal and Bill, if the weather held, they'd take you offshore. And there was little doubt that the Foster boys

Hatteras harbor, late 1930s. The *Albatross* is on the right, next to the freight boat. (Courtesy of Ernie Foster)

knew where the fish were. When the trolling action slowed, Bill and Ernal seemed to have an uncanny knack at dead reckoning, of using a barely visible shoreline and who knew what minuscule landmarks to find a handful of old wrecks up on Diamond Shoals or elsewhere. The wrecks teemed with sea bass, amberjack, and big blues.

The only thing occasionally holding back the Fosters, it seemed, was their primitive equipment. Most fishing parties before the war brought their own rods and reels, but Ernal and Bill had their own gear, just in case. It was homemade fare: bamboo rods with twine-wrapped grips and automobile hose clamps for reel seats. The line was braided linen. Twenty-four thread added up to seventy-two-pound test, a workable strength for offshore fishing, but Lord help you if you didn't dry it properly; it would rot quicker than a fall tomato. What reels they had were clunkers with primitive star drags, if they had any drags at all other than your thumb. Tom Eaton, who had brought electricity to Hatteras Island and built the first icehouse, had gone out fishing with the Fosters, and to their operation he donated two beautiful Pflueger Altapac reels. Each cost more than $100, a great deal of money back then (six reels would have paid for the *Albatross*).

All the pieces of a successful business venture were migrating into place, but even here on the Outer Banks in the spring of 1941, you could catch it on any wind—the acrid scent of world war. Hitler had already overrun most of Europe, the Battle of Britain had come and gone, and now the Germans were re-creating Napoleon's disastrous march on Moscow. U-boats were devastating the shipping lanes in the eastern Atlantic, and they were beginning to cast glances westward, toward the American coastline. And in the Pacific, in Honolulu, our fleet lay slumberously at anchor.

———————————

With America's entrance into the war, charter fishing in Hatteras, what little there was of it—Ernal's and four or five other boats—shut down. The men of Hatteras Village were drafted or enlisted. Ernal Foster married Hazel Midgett, of the famous Outer Banks Midgett clan, and then he joined the coast guard. He was assigned to a station in Morehead City, south of Hatteras, down by Cape Lookout. Years earlier, his father had worked out of Beaufort with the menhaden fleet. While Ernal was stationed there, the navy asked if they could requisition his *Albatross* "for the war effort." Ernal agreed and was sent papers to sign. "He threw them in the wood stove," says his son, Ernie. "He didn't trust all the fine print. He just figured he'd get his boat back when the time came." As it turned out, the navy docked the *Albatross* near Beaufort, at Fort Macon. Its chief wartime function was to act as a party boat for officers and their wives and girlfriends. Nothing more military than that. "The trouble was," Ernie recalls, "my father would cruise by on his coast guard cutter and see with his own eyes what was going on aboard his boat." He got angry, a slow, stalled storm front kind of angry. One day he'd had enough and swung the coast guard cutter around and was about to ram his own boat, partyers and all. He had to be physically restrained from doing it.

As the war began to wind down, Ernal went to the local navy brass and told them he'd be wanting his boat back pretty soon. The officer announced to Foster that they had the papers he'd signed when he turned over the boat, and that they'd let him know when they were ready to release the *Albatross.* Ernal shot back, "Like hell you have those papers! Prove it! Show them to me!" A shouting match ensued, and Ernal was thrown out of the naval officer's office. One of Ernal's coast guard friends was waiting outside for his buddy and overheard the whole thing. He was beside himself. "Ernal, are you crazy, arguing with a naval officer like that?" Ernal didn't care. "They'll ship your ass out, Ernal, make you a coxswain on a landing craft somewhere in the South Pacific! That's what they do, you know." His friend's final bit of advice: "You better find someone with some pull, and fast!" Well, it turned out that a few years back Ernal had had a high-ranking naval officer as one of his sportfishing charters. They'd gotten along real well, had kept in touch. Ernal made a phone call. "Let me handle this" was the answer. Ernal got his boat back in a timely fashion. Son Ernie points out that a good deal of items, large and small, requisitioned by the military often never found their way back to their owners. There was a chance that Ernal wouldn't have gotten his boat back even if he had been more polite. That would have been over some dead bodies, of course.

In a way, this anecdote about Ernal Foster in the coast guard sums up the character of the Outer Banks people. They are hardworking and loyal and patriotic and stunningly selfless when such is called for. But, at the same time, these same people are fiercely headstrong, independent, mistrustful of authority, wildly impatient with bureaucracy, and often sleeve-rolling angry with unethical bullshit. What's right is right. Pay a man back what you owe him, in money or labor. Run another man's nets if he's sick and his family needs the money. Give me back my boat when you're through with it. It's just the right thing to do. As Ernal was fond of saying until the day he died, "A man's got to sleep with himself."

Woodrow Wilson said, "The history of America is the history of its small towns writ large." Ernal Foster's values — the same ones shared by his neighbors — are the quintessentially American ones. Commonsense ethics and uncomplicated morality: in a small town like Hatteras Village, it is easier to recognize this sense of decency, honesty, and fair play at work. The beliefs at the bottom of Ernal's dealings with the coast guard ("I bet you boys put your pants on one leg at a time, just like me") are traceable back through the Declaration of Independence, in which we're all declared equal, back to Benjamin Franklin and his Poor Richard, who told us who we were and how to live decently, back even further to the ineradicable Calvinism in all of us (Methodism and Assemblies of God seem most firmly set among the dunes here), back all the way to the Bible and its injunction about righteous living and good works. Of course, the Bible also taught Protestants that life was hard, that "this worlde is but a thorofare of woe." And so hard work, physical and spiritual, was the answer. It made for a sturdy, unfrivolous people, proud of their sacrifices, their families, their labors. Their ministers often quoted Proverbs 22:29. "Seest thou a man diligent in his business? He shall stand before kings."

Look at Grant Wood's famous painting *American Gothic*, the farmer and his spinster daughter before their farmhouse. Take the pitchfork out of the farmer's hand and replace it with a fishing rod; turn his overalls into waders; have his daughter looking up at the sky for storm signs, and there you have it. Except if it had been Ernal Foster in the picture, he would have winked and given a sly grin just as the shutter clicked.

With the war over, Ernal took himself and his boat back to Hatteras Village. Hazel was eager to get on with their lives; little Ernie was toddling; Bill was on his way back from the South Pacific where he'd seen some heavy action; and there was the matter of a business to start back up. Job one was to give the *Albatross* a coat of bright white paint and get rid of that standard-issue navy gray. In short order they were ready. So was the rest of the tiny fledgling charter fleet that had cobbled itself together before the war. The *Albatross* ran charters again in the summer of 1946, and on the threshold of the postwar Eisenhower prosperity, people with disposable income and eager for diversion started coming down once again to isolated Hatteras Island. The same thing had happened after the Civil War. Northerners who had been billeted on the Outer Banks during the war had seen the seas and sounds crowded with gamefish. And so after the war, they came back. Local fishermen, struggling to get by with their small commercial enterprises, would take these Yankees out fishing and welcome the additional income. This post–Civil War phenomenon was truly the beginning of charter fishing on the Outer Banks.

With the war over, the Fosters had more business than they could handle. So in 1948 they launched the *Albatross II*. Now Ernal and Bill each had a boat. The charter fleet at Hatteras Village, nonetheless, remained small. Ernie can tick off the names of the boats and the captains, just as any Brooklynite of a certain vintage can name the Boys of Summer: "Let's see. There was Captain Luther Burrus and the *Jackie Fay*, the *Ursula* with Captain Nelson Stowe, and the *Willis* run by Captain Vernon Willis, and Ronnie Stowe —he ran the *Ronnie* starting in 1951."

And foremost among them were Ernal and Bill Foster. They had started the business in the Great Depression, and now they were running two boats, full time. And if the history of modern-day Hatteras Village began on September 7 and 8, 1846, with the opening of the Hatteras Inlet, you could also argue that the era of Hatteras Village as a modern-day sportfishing Mecca, as the "Billfish Capital of the World," began on June 25, 1951. That day found Ernal out in the Gulf Stream aboard the *Albatross II*. He'd taken more and more to heading out to deeper waters beyond the Diamond Shoals

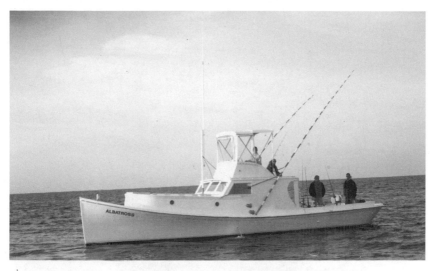

The original *Albatross* today (Courtesy of Ernie Foster)

Lightship. There were big dolphin and wahoo and amberjack out there—species coveted by his customers—but Ernal was also out there on a personal quest. Marlin. A marlin was Ernal's Moby Dick. He wanted one badly, not just for himself but also to show they could be caught consistently in the waters off Hatteras. There were those two big fish Hugo Rutherford had caught several years before the war on his private boat. Now if you could just land these behemoths for paying customers . . . well, then you'd have something, wouldn't you?

There were several impediments facing Ernal. First, many of his customers, especially the older gentlemen, didn't want to fool with those things —too big, too scary. And, besides, the Gulf Stream was teeming with beautiful, manageable gamefish. Why hitch your wagon to a runaway train? The second problem was that marlin were simply too strong for the tackle Ernal had. He had had several encounters with them, and they had ended with busted reels, splintered bamboo rods, and linen line that broke like balloon string. Deep-sea fishing had made great strides, especially in fishing destinations like Miami, Ocean City, Montauk, and the Jersey Shore. Boats from these places would occasionally stop in Hatteras to fish and bring with them advances in the sport, but this was the early 50s, and it would be almost ten years before Hatteras learned about monofilament and cable leaders, swimming mackerel, deboned mullets, squid rigs, strip baits, belly baits, and double lines, flying gaffs, sophisticated fighting chairs, bucket

Ernal Foster aboard the new *Albatross II*, summer 1948 (Courtesy of Ernie Foster)

and kidney harnesses, gin poles, and the like. They would get results, but that was later.

Now it was late June 1951, and Ernal was Captain Ahab. He'd seen a big blue marlin cruising out here the day before, so he'd brought along his new 9/0 Penn Senator reel and twenty-four-thread linen line (seventy-two-pound test) and a three-quarter-pound Spanish mackerel that had been rigged for him by his friend, Lloyd Styron. It was about mid-day and the party was in the cabin having some lunch. Ernal and his younger brother, Gaston, who was working as mate, took the opportunity to put out the Spanish mackerel. There was grumbling from the cabin. But almost as soon as the mackerel was behind the boat a respectable distance, a marlin came up and took it. The fish stayed down. Ernal asked if anyone wanted to catch a big fish. Everyone except Ernal and Gaston thought it was a shark. As Lloyd Styron recalls the story from Ernal, even when the customers aboard saw that it was a marlin, they wanted nothing to do with it. "They didn't want to take the fish, after they saw him. It was just too much fish for them. They were older people." They wanted Ernal to cut the line. Ernal wasn't about to, first because finally he was tight to his obsession, and second, as his son says, "My father hated to cut good line." And so Gaston took over the helm of

BLUE MARLIN CAUGHT AT HATTERAS, N.C. WEIGHT 475½ LBS.
LENGTH 11 FT. 2 INS. GIRTH 56 INS. TAILSPREAD 47 INS.

Ernal Foster and his first blue marlin, June 25, 1951 (Courtesy of Ernie Foster)

the *Albatross,* and Ernal began his fight. With no belt, no harness, and only a primitive wooden fighting chair, Ernal Foster wrestled that marlin for two and a half hours. Near the end of the fight, the marlin died down deep, and so Ernal had to crank up dead weight some thirty-five fathoms by will and main strength. The fish was a beauty—475 pounds. It was Ernal's first marlin, the first caught on an *Albatross* boat, and the first marlin caught off Hatteras since the end of the war.

But the larger importance of the fish to Hatteras Village and the Outer Banks generally was due to a man named Aycock Brown. Brown had recently been hired as publicist for the Dare County Tourist Bureau. As soon as Brown heard about Ernal's fish, he hopped the first ferry across Oregon Inlet and arrived the next morning. He took photos of angler and fish and wrote a story, which made the national media. Brother Bill's world-record marlin some ten years later would add to the mystique and reputation of tiny Hatteras Village and its rich waters, but Ernal's earlier fish put Hatteras on the map. Sportswriters began to refer to it as "Gamefish Junction."

A year later, in 1952, Ernal again made the national news. He had booked long-time husband-wife customers, the Ross Walkers, aboard the *Albatross II*. The Walkers had brought their own reels with them, loaded with new nylon line. Ernal was skeptical, arguing that if they hooked a big fish, the nylon would stretch and expand the spool into the reel frame. It had happened before, he said. It happened again. Not long after they reached the Gulf Stream, Betsy Walker got tight to a good-sized marlin, and, after a long run, the spool began to jam into the sides of the reel frame. Ernal had to do something. He grabbed one of his rods with twenty-four-thread linen line, and took the risk of putting slack in the nylon line holding the marlin. In no time, Ernal had spliced the nylon line to his linen line and cut the line from the original pole so that the transfer of the fish was complete. With a hybrid line and a tenuous splice, they began fighting the fish again. But now more problems: the split-bamboo rod began showing signs of separating. A large fish, a spliced line, a splintering rod: they'd have to go slow. The *Albatross II* was the only boat out that day, so Ernal radioed in that they'd be late. It was well after dark before they reached Foster's Quay. The curious had gathered, and what they saw was a happy couple, a smiling captain, and a fat marlin. Under the direst circumstances, Betsy Walker had become the first woman to catch a marlin in waters north of Florida. Aycock Brown again went to work, and the story and pictures were again picked up by the national media.

In less than a year, the *Albatross III* came off the ways at Marshallberg where the original had been built. It was supposed to have been a carbon copy of the *Albatross II*, but boatbuilders in those days seldom worked from specs, so the *Albatross III* turned out a little longer and broader abeam than its older brother. The other, bigger difference was that the *Albatross III* was put into service exclusively to run charters. No commercial fishing for the *III*. The same was true for the *Twins*, a charter boat that joined the little fleet that same year. It belonged to Captain Edgar Styron who himself would become a local character and legend. A year later "Captain Edgar" added the *Twins II*, the first diesel-powered charter boat, and ran both vessels out of the Blue Marlin Restaurant and Docks, the present site of the Hatteras Marlin Club next to Oden's Dock. "Captain Edgar had a big impact on charter fishing around here," says Ernie. "He was great for the business; he was colorful and outspoken and unorthodox, and, boy, could he catch fish—marlin especially. So could the captains he had working for him—Captain Clam Stowe and Elmer Ballance." But it was Captain Edgar who caught them with flair and derring-do—and quickly. Captain Styron seldom stopped talking, Ernie said. "Oh, he could fill up a room." And he could fill up a boat. "Captain Styron almost always backed up his

Betsy Walker and her blue marlin, summer 1952. Walker, from Richmond, Virginia, was the first woman to catch a marlin on the East Coast. (Courtesy of Ernie Foster)

boasting," Ernie added. "His specialty was catching big fish fast. He'd get a marlin hook-up and get in close on him fast — back his boat down on the fish quickly." His skills and magnetic personality quickly garnered Captain Edgar a national and international clientele. Even with the techniques improving and the charter fleet growing, a big marlin was not an everyday occurrence. A big fish was cause for a village turnout, and it was often left to hang for several days or more (and often towed out of the marina and discarded). Says Ernie, "I can still remember the night in church when it was announced from the pulpit that my father, having battled a marlin for over four hours, would be getting to the dock about the time the service ended. It felt to me like the whole village was there when he docked with the fish."

Then at the end of August 1958, the *Albatross* fleet made the national news yet again. This time it was brother Bill Foster's turn. Bill took out old friends Dr. Jack Cleveland and his wife Elly. The Clevelands were ardent fishermen and committed conservationists. And that day aboard the *Albatross II*, they did the unthinkable. They brought a 400-pound marlin to the boat, cut the

Captain Bill Foster
(Courtesy of Buddy Swain)

leader, and let it go. When they got back to the dock, people were stunned by what they had done. Captains shook their heads. Jim Hurley of the *New York Mirror*, while acknowledging the Clevelands for their "commendable gesture of abnegation in the interest of conservation" also noted that it was like "a starving man refusing a sure-shot at a deer." But what the Clevelands did, as far as anyone knows, was to undertake the first catch-and-release of a marlin on the East Coast. Jack Cleveland not only practiced it; he preached conservation whenever he could. Today, whether by law or conscience, the catch-and-release ethic is standard practice in the sportfishing industry, and fish stocks are the better for it.

In talking about the history of the fleet, Captain Ernie seems prouder of this first catch-and-release than he does of the many hanging billfish his father's boats were responsible for — even the world record brought in by his Uncle Bill four years later. He's quick to add, too, that the *Albatross* boats were also responsible for tagging ten of the first forty marlin along the East Coast.

Not all fishing out of the marinas of Hatteras Village was blue-water trips for billfish. Inside trolling and wreck fishing were still very popular and probably accounted for more revenue than the big-game excursions. Inshore waters teemed with bluefish and Spanish mackerel, and, in the fall, channel bass. Trolling baits, especially artificial ones, remained primitive, with feathered jigs and buck tail (hair from real deer tail) being the overall favorites, while often the preferred rig for Spanish mackerel was the hollow bone of a loon's leg. Ernie will still stake his reputation on the productivity of a feathered jig over the current nylon varieties. Wreck fishing was also popular, especially around Diamond Shoals, which was littered with old wrecks the locals could locate even without loran, depth recorders, or radio direction finders. Then there were the old Diamond Shoals Lightship and the nearby watch buoy, both of which were reliable fish attractors.

But the recent world war had created a bonanza of new wrecks to exploit. Some of these proved easier to find than others. The so-called oil slick wreck was one. This was the oil tanker *Lancing* torpedoed by a U-boat in 1942. The *Lancing* gave off an oil slick four to six miles long. Fishermen simply had to find it and follow it up current until it stopped. More than a half century later the *Lancing* is still sending up its telltale slick. To the west of the *Lancing* lay the *Empire Gem*, a British ship, also sunk in 1942. This became known locally as the "smell wreck" for the pungent gas odor it gave off. Again, captains simply followed the smell upwind to the site. They still do, and if the amberjack or sea bass on the *Empire Gem* have lockjaw that day, the wreck lies conveniently near the edge of the Gulf Stream and its productive lines of floating sargassum weed.

The 1960s brought enormous changes to tiny, isolated Hatteras Village on tiny, isolated Hatteras Island, and with those changes the truth of the old proverb, "Be careful what you wish for . . ." For half a decade, the three *Albatross* boats, captained by brothers Ernal and Bill and their loyal friend Oliver O'Neal dominated blue-water fishing off the Outer Banks. But newer, faster, and better-equipped boats were beginning to show up in the slips to the left and right of tiny Foster's Quay. And other boats from up north and as far down as Miami were choosing to fish all or part of the summer billfish season out of Hatteras. The Hatteras Marlin Club's international marlin tournament in June brought even more boats. The fishing was still good, but elbow room was becoming an issue.

Then, in 1963, the Herbert C. Bonner Bridge was opened over Oregon Inlet at the northern end of Hatteras Island. The bridge connected Hatteras to the upper Outer Banks, and the upper Outer Banks were connected to the mainland. Hatteras Island was no longer an island. In the early 1950s, they'd paved the road from the ferry terminus up at Oregon Inlet all the way down to the village end of Hatteras Island. With the opening of the Bonner Bridge, you could now drive all the way from the state capital, Raleigh, down the highway to the Outer Banks and on to Foster's Quay almost without taking your foot off the gas. Access meant greater prosperity. Few people at the time sensed that the new Highway 12 down the Outer Banks might be a toll road and that the toll exacted might well be a way of life. That epiphany would unfold slowly, over years.

What was more immediately apparent to the village families was that there was a changing of the guard beginning to take place. By the mid-60s, a number of the old commercial watermen who'd taken out occasional sportfishing parties during the depression were quitting the business. Advancing age, staid ways, and an inability or unwillingness to invest in the equipment necessary for a state-of-the-art fishing rig began sidelining many of the first-generation skippers. It wasn't just the different faces, the new names, the disappearing Banks "hoi-toider" accent along the docks now. It was a subtler change, a change in ethos, in the glue that had held a village together for well more than a century. The glue was a body of knowledge that could be acquired only through a lifetime of fishing; and it was knowledge that was shared in the homes, the fish houses, at the cleaning tables, at the tackle shops, while passing tools over busted boat engines, and in the winter chill of the net houses each family owned. Where the fish were, how they'd behaved this year, their curious cycles (not scientific surely, but often more accurate), what waters had shoaled up, which had deepened, the latest commercial techniques, the latest state regulations, the shenanigans of the fish wholesalers, the increasing influx of weekend anglers in fancy clothes. A lifetime of maritime knowledge gained through trial and error and a generation of village gossip and lore and news left to steep in its own rich juices: this was what was just beginning to be lost, the soul of a village, its common pulse of being. As Ernie lamented, "Twenty-five years of experience could be passed on to a mate in three years. Local captains who had learned where and when to go after fish were simply followed by these captains who'd come in from other places." A captain's sixth sense was being replaced by space-age electronics. And it was getting so village neighbors didn't have a chance to visit all summer until the crowds had gone with Labor Day weekend. History, like a shark, must move forward to survive. Progress is impersonal, voracious.

The Foster fleet was struggling to hold its own. Ernal was only in his mid-fifties and Bill almost a decade younger. And it was now that young Ernie, in his early twenties, became a captain, and a few years later Willy signed on as a mate, often sailing with his father, Bill. But it was getting harder and harder. More and more, higher-powered boats could leave the *Albatross* fleet in their wake on the way out Hatteras Inlet. More and more, boats could get to the fishing grounds faster and cover more water. And more and more, boats could offer amenities, creature comforts, what department stores called "the miracles of modern living." Little had changed aboard the Foster boats. Vinyl bench cushions, a tiny head. All they really took with them out to the Gulf Stream every day was their reputation. And that was enough, and the fishing held up. At least for a while.

Things were changing on land too. Development in the 60s was beginning to be a divisive force in the village. The man who owned the marina that included the 100-foot slice called Foster's Quay got sideways with Ernal and Bill about "improvements." The details remain in dispute, but the Foster family had to abandon its wood-frame family home a stone's throw behind the *Albatross* fleet. The house was jacked up and moved, and the Fosters moved across Highway 12 to a one-story brick house. The land just behind Foster's Quay was then sold, to make way for a motel (which I was staying in right now), and only a court order gave the Fosters access to their boats and a few parking spaces for their customers. The little creek that for so many years had served the small fleet of wood-hulled charter boats on the sound side of the village was dredged out now and widened, and it became a full-fledged marina with many more slips for local boats and transients. Hatteras Harbor Marina had arrived, and more and more the *Albatross* boats began to look like quaint throwbacks among the picket fence of sleek fiberglass hulls on either side of it.

In the 70s, time and tide continued to throw a cold shadow across Foster's Quay. In 1971 Ernal came down with a serious lung ailment that required surgery. He recovered, but he would never quite be the same. Two years later Jean Foster, Bill's wife and Willy's mother, died of a cerebral hemorrhage, and a few months later Bill suffered a serious heart attack. That was in late July. Ernal learned about it in the tiny *Albatross* fleet office and was sick with worry. Bill had a party due to go out that day on the *Albatross II*, a fellow named Bill Strahan, who had not caught a marlin in his eight years of fishing with the Fosters. Bill Strahan was willing to call it off. He liked the Fosters too much. But Ernal had made up his mind. When Mark Twain lost his beloved daughter Suzy to meningitis, he said in his autobiography that he turned back to writing for "surcease of sorrow." It was all he had left, all he could think to do to staunch the pain. Ernal Foster turned to the sea for surcease of his sorrow. His son Ernie would do the same thing twenty years later when his wife took their children and moved out, and he was left alone. He still had a boat, a charter booked, and of course that charter turned out to be Lynne, the love of his life.

And so Ernal took the Strahans out on the *II*. They trolled near an area called "The Wrecks," and in no time a marlin struck. Ernal's habit was not to chase a marlin immediately, but to give the angler the thrill of that first big run, when a marlin can reach speeds of over sixty miles an hour, and dance like Little Sheba. This fish did all that, and in the process almost spooled Bill Strahan. There were barely fifty yards of line left on the reel when the marlin slowed. Then, as with most marlin, the heavy work began. But in an hour they had the fish in the boat, and Ernal radioed his son who was out on the *Albatross III* that they had a fish on board that ran more than twelve feet and 600 pounds. They had been fishing in only forty fathoms, and the rest of fleet, listening in, was skeptical that a marlin that size could be found in such shallow water. But Ernal had known better. In 1939 he had caught his first sailfish a mile off the sea buoy, and forever after he was convinced that billfish could be found in closer to shore than most people thought. He'd proved his theory more than once.

The fish weighed in at 625 pounds. It would be the biggest fish of Bill Strahan's life—and the biggest fish ever taken while Ernal was skippering an *Albatross*. Joy and sorrow are seldom out of hailing distance. The picture of the fish shows Bill Strahan smiling and playfully stretching out the hanging fish's dorsal fin. On the belly side of the fish, Ernal's hand is resting head-high on the fish's pectoral fin. He is not smiling, but neither is he frowning. He is simply there, pausing for a moment with this magnificent fish. He had done what he set out to do for someone else and for his own peace of mind—and for his brother. And now he'd go visit Bill in the hospital.

Nature, while it seems to sport with their hopes
and fears, will probably never debar them from
direct communication with the ocean.
—Commander W. I. Muse, U.S.N.,
November 25, 1857, commenting on Hatteras
Inlet, eleven years after it opened

CHAPTER FIVE

Hatteras Inlet

During the summer, the Hatteras Island ferries that run back and forth across Hatteras Inlet from the village to Ocracoke Island are busy around the clock. At high season, there are two or three in service, and they run every twenty minutes or so. Each holds approximately thirty cars, yet still, in June and July and August, the lines of vehicles at the terminus on each side of the inlet are long, though the wait really isn't. On the Ocracoke Island side, people get out of their cars and gather in groups to talk or to picnic on their tailgates. Dogs wag and sprint, children assault the dunes, while couples press "Recline" and stick their bare feet out the windows. The Hatteras side is more orderly. Here, in place of a narrow road flanked by sand hills, is a wide expanse of blacktop with multiple lanes and arrows directing cars this way and that. A little restaurant nearby takes care of the kids and the peckish adults. The bank of kite and clothing and kitsch stores at the Hatteras Landing Marina is reachable on foot. Otherwise, it's sit in the car, roll down the windows, and enjoy the breeze.

The ride across Hatteras Inlet is a four-mile trip and takes around forty minutes. Running down the middle of the ferry is a narrow passenger cabin maybe twenty feet up in the air. It provides a nice view. After leaving the terminus at Hatteras Village, the ferry runs south for a while along a thin spit of land. It has a ragged beach about as wide as the four-wheel drives that you see here and there along its length. The beach is backed by thick scrub vegetation. It's hard to tell how the vehicles and families got through the brown and dark-green tangle to the little strip of isolated beach. Men stand far out in the shallow lime-green water fishing. In front of them is the Pamlico Sound with its patchwork of brown and blue and green waters and low white-sand islands sprinkled occasionally with birds. Behind the waist-deep men, their wives sit under umbrellas on the thin beach and watch the nearby children and dogs. Finally the scrub-spit gives way to the darker waters of Hatteras Inlet itself.

It had been two months since I'd fished with Ronnie O'Neal and Tall Bill Van Druten, and I was back down again. I was standing on the small platform at the top of the ferry's metal stairs just outside the passenger cabin. The view was perfect and the breeze was welcome on this unusually hot day. Next to me was one of the hands on the ferry. He was wearing the distinctive brown-and-cream uniform. He was a slight man, handsome with a thick salt-and-pepper beard and a puffy walrus mustache. If he had been wearing yellow foul-weather gear, he would have looked whittled, lacking only a nameplate below his boots: "Souvenir of . . ."

We got to talking as we crossed the inlet. The fishing and pleasure boats headed out to sea were hugging the dark channel waters on the north side. The south side of the inlet was a murky chop. "When I was a boy," the hand said, "the inlet was back there." I followed his finger back along the spit we had just traversed. "See that TV tower?" It was at least a mile behind us, back toward Hatteras Village. "Right there." I did some quick math. A mile to a mile and a half in thirty-five to forty years. "And this choppy shallow stuff—," pointing in front of us now to the jade turmoil on the southern side of the inlet up against Ocracoke Island, "this used to be solid land." He concluded what I had. "The inlet's moving south, and pretty fast too." Then he added what the geological books had been telling me: "And everything's also moving westward into the sound." Southward and westward.

On the far side, the ocean side of the churning inlet waters closest to Ocracoke, you could see tar-blackened pilings, canted this way and that, like most everything else on the Outer Banks, knee deep in the water: the remains of the Hatteras Inlet Lifesaving Station Number 186, built in 1882 and claimed by the sea in 1955. I remembered seeing old pictures of the imposing two-story structure, shake shingled, high gabled, and vigilant. In front, lined up in their ragtag uniforms, were small, serious, wiry men, much like the one I was talking to right now, except for the high-button leather shoes

The *Albatross III* in Hatteras Inlet (Courtesy of Ernie Foster)

below their dark and too-short pants and mustaches that curled up at the ends instead of down. These were not huge, powerful men, but together, six of them, with a stern oarsman, proved time and again that they could pull through the roughest surf, stay upright, and rescue passengers from sinking ships in howling gales.

But if everything was moving south and west, what about all those million-dollar houses built right behind the dunes facing the ocean in Hatteras, Frisco, Avon, Salvo, Waves, Rodanthe, and especially the cheek-by-jowl monsters further north up the Banks in Nags Head, Kill Devil Hills, Kitty Hawk, Southern Shores, Duck, Corolla? "They don't care," the deckhand said without malice. Malice is a tone of voice you seldom hear from Outer Bankers. "They've got tons of money, and they're all insured up to their gizzards." Hurricane insurance? "There's no such thing," he explains. "Just 'wind and water.' But it amounts to the same thing." It must be expensive. "Not really. It's all federally subsidized. What you do is get your own regular homeowner's insurance—say, State Farm—and then you can add on the federally subsidized insurance, so it's not so bad." But that means we're subsidizing the lifestyles of the rich and famous and their fabulous porch views. "That's right," he said, scratching his beard. It was a lifestyle that was bound to include rebuilding sometime or another. "That's right," he said, again, and once again without malice. He excused himself as we approached the Ocracoke ferry landing.

Hatteras Inlet: it was hard to imagine this sparkling stretch of water filled with pleasure and fishing boats having such a violent birth—over the course of two storm-wracked days in the first week of September 1846, the ocean shouldering and gouging its way through the Outer Banks to the sound, and then, as the storm headed north, the sound waters surging back east and tearing through the same cut made by the ocean a day earlier. This powerful, crosscutting action ripped a deep notch in the Banks, sending Hatteras Villagers fleeing nature's sudden territorial imperative to connect the sound with the ocean. It was equally hard to believe that such a relatively young channel could have such a rich and complex history—much of it as violent as its origins. Only fifteen years after its opening, village schoolmaster John Rollinson would record in his journal, "Troops arrived at Hatteras Inlet to guard it." That was on May 9, 1861, eleven days before North Carolina left the Union. Hatteras Inlet had already become North Carolina's major trade and transshipment route from the sea to New Bern, Elizabeth City, Plymouth, and Washington, N.C. Just as important, ships headed south could cruise down the Albemarle and Pamlico sounds and head out to sea through Hatteras Inlet thereby avoiding Cape Hatteras and its deadly Diamond Shoals. Finally, those looking ahead saw that Hatteras Inlet would provide a major supply artery for the Army of Northern Virginia.

So in May 1861 Confederate troops showed up in Hatteras Village to protect this crucial highway. There were two forts there, Fort Hatteras and Fort Clark. Fort Hatteras was right on the inlet. It was roughly square in shape, 250 feet on each side, made of sand embankments sheathed in wood. The more modest Fort Clark was almost a mile east of the inlet and nearer the ocean. It was located so as to provide crossfire for the inlet channel. According to a contemporary physician, "Mosquitoes held possession of [the forts] by day and night." And there was a "Mosquito Fleet" to protect, as well. This was the name given to a little pocket Confederate navy, a ragtag, ad hoc armada consisting of a larger side-wheel steamer, the *Winslow*, and three propeller-driven smaller boats, designed for river use. Home base for the Mosquito Fleet was a deep slough back of Hatteras Inlet. From here—and using nearby Cape Hatteras Lighthouse as a lookout—they harassed Union shipping in both the ocean and the sounds. They were surprisingly effective. In a few months, the *Winslow* alone had captured sixteen ships. Northern insurance companies howled at their losses, claiming this was not privateering but out-and-out piracy (the distinction remained usefully vague to locals).

Eight weeks after troops showed up to protect the inlet—and the fleet —the Union cutter *Harriet Lane* sailed through Hatteras Inlet and fired a handful of shells at the forts. They were just calling cards, but these few salvos represented the first hostile shots fired by the U.S. Navy at southern-held territory. In August, some six weeks later, the *Harriet Lane* was back, newly outfitted with a fifteen-inch cannon and accompanied by six other ships. Altogether Commodore Silas Stringham's flotilla brought 149 guns to bear on the two forts at Hatteras. In answer, the forts had seventeen guns between them.

The Union plan at Hatteras Inlet was for Stringham's ships to neutralize the forts, after which Union general Benjamin Franklin Butler would land troops on the beaches just north of the village, effectively cutting off the Confederate garrison. The plan worked perfectly.

When Commodore Stringham came ashore on August 29 to take possession of Forts Hatteras and Clark from Colonel William F. Martin, however, he found that his fierce bombardment had not resulted in a single casualty. The furious yet relatively benign little battle was trumpeted in the northern press as a major victory, in large measure to offset the humiliation Union troops had experienced at Bull Run a few weeks earlier. The skirmish at Hatteras Village did, however, succeed in cutting off a major supply route for the Confederate army.

The war wasn't through with Hatteras Village, nor was Hatteras Inlet through with the war makers. A little over a year after the battle for Forts Hatteras and Clark, Union general A. E. Burnside was given orders to engage the rebels on Roanoke Island, just inside the northern Outer Banks in the Albemarle Sound. Storms plagued the fleet from the start, and when they finally reached Hatteras Inlet on January 13, many of the 20,000 troops, including Burnside himself, were violently seasick. The storms had also scattered the lighter sailing vessels in the Burnside flotilla, and passage through the inlet was a disaster. The first ship through, "the splendid and commodious steamer *City of New York*," ran up onto the inlet beach, and in less than an hour was torn to pieces by the surf. In all, seventeen vessels were swallowed by the little inlet.

The storms lasted almost two full weeks, during which time many of the ships' crews staggered ashore at Hatteras Village. Food and water for 10,000 to 15,000 shore-side men was in less than short supply. Typhoid, pneumonia, dysentery, "graybacks," or body lice, and boredom were not. More troops died of sickness on the sandy banks than of drowning in the freezing waters of the inlet. As one officer wrote, "Of all forlorn stations to which the folly and wickedness of the Rebellion condemned our officers, Hatteras was the most forlorn."

The Burnside expedition, or what remained of it, finally got through Hatteras Inlet in early February and headed up to Roanoke Island (where they would eventually prevail). It had been a miserable passage, costly in human life and equipment. And good will: during their brief and desperate stay, the Union troops stripped the village and the villagers of nearly everything edible and then cooked much of it on fires made from the wood of their torn-down homes. The Hatteras Villagers were surely furious. But if truth be known, they had probably been just as mad when Confederate troops decamped in their village a year or so earlier to "guard" the inlet from Union attack. Scavenging, theft, and appropriation are the same regardless of the uniform color, and the majority of Hatteras Villagers just wanted to be left alone.

Cotton Mather, the great Puritan divine, was once delivering a guest sermon in a small fishing village on the coast of Massachusetts. In order to remind the congregation of the religious foundations for their actions, he asked them a rhetorical question: Why, after all, had they made their perilous pilgrimage to the New World? It's recorded that one parishioner somewhere in the back rows yelled out, "To catch fish!" Certainly when it came to the state of North Carolina, and surely more so than in most parts of the fractured Union, the fiercely independent people of the Outer Banks just wanted some laissez-faire. They just wanted to catch fish.

Even slavery wasn't much of an issue with them. Some people owned them, but most didn't, and didn't need them. Demands of loyalty to a larger cause, a bigger government, made them nervous, suspicious. As evidence, when North Carolina seceded from the Union, Bankers held a Hatteras Convention, drafted a statement of grievances, and declared their own independence. They even elected their own representative to the United States Congress. It wasn't that they were traitorous. They were just libertarian by nature and downright contrary when pushed. Ernal Foster would allow his *Albatross* to be appropriated for the war effort; but when it was painted gray, used exclusively for officers' parties, and then not returned in a timely manner . . . well, by God, it was time to take matters into your reasonable hands. Death, taxes, and righteous independence: such have been constants for a long time on the Outer Banks.

Not all Hatteras Inlet traffic makes the treacherous passage with held breath. Spot, menhaden, croaker, summer flounder, and southern flounder make up the great majority of the commercial catch in the Albemarle and Pamlico sounds. The continued existence of these species and many others is dependent on the smooth, swift, alternating currents of Hatteras Inlet and the six others cutting through the Outer Banks. In the late fall these fish migrate offshore to spawn, riding the inlet tides and the prevailing west and southwest winds out to deeper water. From November through early spring, northeast storms drive the currents back westward against the Outer Banks, carrying larvae shoreward and eventually through the inlets and into the sounds. Hatteras Inlet taketh away, but it also giveth.

And what it giveth, what it nurtures and sometimes relinquishes to humans are not always the modest-sized estuarine varieties. In January 1972 the fabled thirty-pound bluefish barrier was broken with a world-record thirty-two-pound twelve-ounce trophy caught by a fisherman trolling in the inlet.

The Foster family also made some history in Hatteras Inlet over the years. Just before World War II shut down fishing off the Banks, Ernal boated the first tarpon caught on rod and reel in the area. He and his brother Hallas were actually fishing for red drum in the inlet. They had taken a party out aboard the *Albatross*. They were casting from the boat, and, as custom and habit had it, each man had staked out a part of the boat — the bow, cabin top, even the wheelhouse canopy. The fish were fat and frequent. As the story goes, a Mr. Creech, who had brought three of his friends with him, was fishing from the cockpit with his bait off the stern. One of Creech's friends, the one fishing from the canopy overhead, hooked a nice drum and sat on the edge of the canopy to fight the fish. Ernal warned the man to be more careful. The *Albatross* was pitching and rolling in the inlet chop. As a young Ernie would find out a handful of years later, his father issued one warning. That should be enough. But it wasn't, and the man fell into the water. Just as he did, Mr. Creech's reel began to screech, and not far from the boat a beautiful tarpon spiraled into the air. Furious multitasking was in order. Hallas used a gaff handle to try to retrieve the fisherman while Ernal maneuvered the *Albatross* toward Creech's tarpon. Eventually both were got aboard, the fisherman and a fifty-three-pound tarpon. There is a picture of Creech, his tarpon, and Ernal.

More than thirty years later, Ernal was in the inlet again, this time with a hunch that the heavy chop on the Ocracoke side of the inlet held something more than drum, and that what had been caught commercially for years could be made high sport with a rod and reel. He was right. Edging the *Albatross* in among the smaller breakers, which came over the stern at regular intervals, he told his customers to pay out line into the murk. Soon there was a heavy strike, and a fat striper surfaced near the boat. Then it was on board. Each time the *Albatross* circled into the waves, there were more hook-ups. These were the first stripers caught on rod and reel off Hatteras Island. Since then, of course, striper fishing has become the staple diet of many Outer Banks sportsmen.

Ernie's cousin Willy Foster had a different experience with stripers in Hatteras Inlet. He was thirteen and out in the inlet with his father netting stripers. It was December and very cold, and they were working the same fussy water on the south side of the inlet that had yielded Ernal's fish many years ago.

"Man, my father and I got into them good, probably too good," said Willy, smiling. "We were standing up pulling in that loaded net and you could feel the boat swamp right under you, just fill up with water. And that water was freezing!" They stood there for a moment, waist deep, feeling the boat settle deeper into the water and begin bumping along the sandbar as the current carried it soundward. Bill quickly got his knife out and cut his own waders off. Then for Willy, it became indelible. "I have this mental image, it'll never go away, of my father, sitting astride the engine block—the wood engine cover had floated off somewhere—madly cutting my waders off." Then they jumped out just before the wallowing boat sank even deeper into the water. They made their way to Ocracoke Island, just barely able to touch bottom, and reached shore, just barely. Right on the margin.

Bill Foster had borrowed that boat from a fellow fisherman, and Willy recalled how upset his father was at having to drive over and tell the man he'd lost it. "We went over to the man's house the next day. He lived over on the sound side of Hatteras, and before we could tell him, he says to us, 'My boat's gone, isn't it?' 'Who told you?' my father asked. 'No one told me. I dreamed it,' the owner said.

"It was the damndest thing, and what made it even spookier," Willy added, "is that a short time later, some of the numbers from the side of the boat drifted into the sound and then up the sound north and right into the slip the owner used to keep the boat."

Willy's story shares a shape and formula found in many tales of the Outer

Banks: the unexpected water-born disaster, the death or near-death experience followed by the drifting back of parts or people to the starting point, to home. It's the formula out here for much apocryphal lore, and you'll hear it often if you listen long enough. It's the myth of the sea village, and it's as fixed and predictable and comforting as the sermon structure: the biblical text, the elucidation of that text, and, finally, its application to our daily lives.

Willy's inlet homily has been preceded by so many of similar shape. One is still sworn to by the faithful at the Ocracoke Methodist Church. It involves the sinking of the *Caribsea* on March 11, 1942, torpedoed by a U-boat off Hatteras Island. By custom, most merchant ships like the *Caribsea* displayed the licenses of its officers in a glass case aboard ship. One of the licenses in the case belonged to James Baugham Gaskill, whose birthplace was listed as Ocracoke, North Carolina. Gaskill was killed in the U-boat attack, but island residents will insist to this day that the glass case with Gaskill's license drifted ashore near Ocracoke Village. And members of the Ocracoke Methodist Church in the village will show you a special wooden cross behind the altar that, they will claim, was made from the *Caribsea* nameplate, which floated through Ocracoke Inlet and was found near Officer Gaskill's birthplace on the sound-side shore. Bringing back a lost sheep to the fold.

Let the lower lights be burning,
Send a gleam across the wave!
Some poor fainting struggling seaman,
You may rescue, you may save.
—"Let the Lower Lights Be Burning"
(Protestant hymn)

CHAPTER SIX

Blowday at Cape Point
Summer

AUGUST AGAIN. This trip down, I'd booked a charter with Willy Foster. Willy's *Ol' Salt* was over at Teach's Lair Marina. When I showed up at the boat in the dark, I still hadn't even talked to Willy. I'd made the charter from Memphis, having called Willy's house and left a message. Willy's answering machine started with the sound of fishing line being stripped off a reel. He talked over it, saying excitedly "As soon as I get this one in, I'll call you back!" The reel continued to scream. "Whoa! There he goes," said Willy, and then there was the beep. That's where I left my charter request. It was 5:30, and the *Ol' Salt* cabin was lit up. A young man came out from behind the boat's varnished cabin doors and introduced himself as John Willis. He'd be the mate today, he said, adding that Willy was probably on his way. The air was anxious and heavy, and lightning was flashing all around us, over the Pamlico Sound, south beyond Ocracoke Island, and behind us out toward the Gulf Stream.

"I don't know about this," said John, continuing to set up the rods. "The weather reports are predicting thunderstorms." We talked in the flickering light. John was a local boy, choir-boy handsome and Boy Scout shy, with a brand-new leaping marlin on the meat of his right shoulder. John's mother was a photographer for real estate agents and for beach weddings. His father was in the heating and air-conditioning business, and John helped him out a lot. That and mating were getting him through college.

Only two other boats in the lineup on our side of the marina were stirring. The rest were dark, vacant. None of the boat flags could seem to make up their minds about what to do, flapping tentatively this way, then that, then going limp. Something was coming through. At 6:00 John excused himself, saying he'd better call to see if Willy overslept. It turned out he had, but he arrived in ten minutes, very apologetic, very embarrassed. He explained he was up late, having gone up to Norfolk General to see a woman who works at the marina. Brain tumor. A bad one. A couple of other captains and hands wandered over as we talked, along with the store owner at the end of dock, to hear how she was doing. Evidently they knew Willy had gone up to see her. "She looked much better, said she felt much better. She was even talking about coming back to her job here. I guess that tells you something." Nods all around. Willy's trip up there, 150 miles each way, wasn't a gesture. The sense of community, of communal concern, was genuine, genuinely touching. Everyone knew everyone. The woman worked here, but was also Fin Gaddy's girlfriend. Fin ran *The Qualifier* out of Oden's Dock, just a few slips down from the *Albatross* fleet. The three of us were alone now at the stern of the *Ol' Salt*. Willy looked up at the light show, slapped at a no-see-um, and shook his head.

"Man, these fronts. They come galloping over here and then half the time they stall out right above us."

Willy Foster was a tall, fit, and handsome man in his mid-forties. If you looked at pictures of Willy's father you could see where he got his good looks from. Bill Foster was central-casting perfect to play the role of rugged boat captain, which, of course, he did for many years. Willy's short, graying hair aside, he looked like a tight end, or like the PE teacher he was for a number of years before his recent promotion to assistant principal of the Hatteras Middle School. While we were waiting to see what the weather had up its sleeve, I asked Willy about his new job. He was really pleased with it, except for one thing. The new superintendent switched him from a ten-month contract to a twelve-month one. Without telling him. For years, he and one other teacher had worked out ten-month contracts because they had "other businesses." Boats.

"The old superintendent was a nice guy, a friend of mine," Willy explained. "He simply wrote a note: 'To Whom It May Concern: Willy has my

Willy Foster and the *Ol' Salt* (Courtesy of Lynne Foster)

permission to go fishing whenever he wants to—as long as I can go with him.'" Willy chuckled. It really used to be almost that simple. But he was not mad at the change. If you lived here long enough, you learned to ride the wind and the tidal changes "I've got someone to run my boat during the week, and I'll do it myself on the weekends." Like most Bankers Willy saved his venom for government bureaucracy. It's the captain's licensing business all over again—trying to get his renewed.

"I took the drug test they required. They screened for seven different things. I passed and sent the results to them [the agency no longer had local offices—just regional ones—in Charleston, South Carolina, and in Baltimore]. They rejected it, said we were only supposed to screen for five things. So I called them and said, 'Let me get this straight; it's kind of like you loaning me $500 and I pay you back $700, and you won't take it because it's not $500. Is that right?'" After a while, Willy said, they agreed to make an exception in his case.

We decided to walk over to the marina store to get some coffee and look at the local weather channel. A few other skippers were standing around looking at the TV. There was a large splotch of bright color back west on the mainland, and thanks to computer fast-forwarding you could see where it was headed. Here. Seas were running four feet and twenty- to twenty-five-mile-an-hour winds were predicted.

"It'll be uncomfortable out there trolling," Willy said. John, his mate, turned to me and said, "Yeah, it's real hard on the equipment, everything banging around. And in these conditions the spread (the various baits being trolled) want to come together and tangle up." But it was the lightning that seemed to bother everyone the most. Sitting ducks—or ducts—out there. And the electronics on these boats ran to thousands of dollars; blow those out with a jolt of lightning, and you're in a serious hole. We took our coffee outside and sat at a picnic table between the store and the boats. The biggest of the boats, *Marlin Mania*, had been idling in its slip. As we sat there, the mate cast off lines, and they slowly headed out.

"I don't know why he's going out," Willy said. "His family—the captain's—has plenty of money." He added, "Most captains who go out in this stuff do it because they need the money. They have to make it while they can. This guy doesn't. And anyway, he'll probably be back soon."

No one else at Teach's was going out this morning. We sat around in the glow of the store and the fluorescent light illuminating a glassed-in blue marlin. Finally dawn began to break, fitfully and piecemeal, through the low-hanging clouds. The no-see-ums were working harder than ever at the end of their shift, but we stayed outside anyway. The exit of *Marlin Mania* offered the opportunity to ask Willy about the state-of-the-art charter boats, the ones with high six-figure sticker prices. I had been wandering around the different marinas the last couple of days, and the upscale boat that caught my eye was the *Big Easy* docked at Hatteras Landing Marina, the newest of the marinas in Hatteras Village and right behind the new Holiday Inn Express with its ice cream boutiques, resort clothing shops, and themed restaurants. This tourist complex seemed more like it belonged up in Kitty Hawk, Nags Head, Kill Devil Hills. A corporate theme park with marina. And in its midst with other new boats was this fifty-seven-foot Briggs Sportsfisherman. Captain Cliff Parker of the *Big Easy* advertised air conditioning, heat, TV/VCR, stereo, microwave, refrigerator, and full-size head and shower, everything "planned exclusively with the fisherman in mind." The armchair fisherman. The boat looked like it had been born in a wind tunnel. I asked Willy about the *Big Easy*. He knew Cliff Parker.

"That boat cost $650,000 to build," said Willy, "and the builder claims he didn't make any money on it." He went on, with malice toward none. "There's no way you're going to spend that much for a boat and expect to pay it off through fishing. Cliff Parker was a heart surgeon for a long time." The clear implication was that making a living at charter fishing for an increasing number of captains was not the point at all. They were doing it because they wanted to and because they had the money. And, according to Willy, they had the clout to push through the paperwork for their licenses. Other boats like the *Big Easy* in the marinas were corporate-born and staffed by salaried captains. As Tall Bill said later when we were trolling for wahoo offshore and listening to the captains jabbering back and forth over the radio, "These guys in the go-fast boats can hear over the radio that there's fish twenty-five miles north, and they can just barrel up there. They can run as much diesel though their engines as they want. They're not the ones paying for it." It was the same thing Ronnie O'Neal had said about the big boats in front of the Anchorage Inn on Ocracoke. Ernie added that they also could get there a lot faster than the *Albatross* fleet, whose trio could top out at around twenty-two knots. The *Big Easy* had twin 660 horsepower CAT diesels. They delivered a cruising speed of twenty-three to twenty-five knots and would run at thirty knots at the top end. That was a lot of diesel. Willy certainly hadn't practiced heart surgery coming up, and while he had his own boat with twin 440s, he had to keep doing the competitive math because he was in chartering to make a living, at least a supplemental living to his assistant principal's salary. He had a wife and a stepson. Chartering made it a seven-day work week for a good part of the year. For Willy Foster, it was no hobby. He had ridden out with his father, Bill, on the *Albatross* fleet when he was nine and ten, started learning the business when he was thirteen, and, when he was still in his teens in the 1970s, had become one of the best mates on Hatteras Island. By the time he was in his early twenties, he had graduated from East Carolina University and had received his captain's license. He even got married aboard the *Albatross II*. Willy's heart was his own business, but Captain Bill Foster taught his son how to use his head. Inshore or out in the blue water beyond, the margin between success and failure, even between life and death, could be measured in inches or less — weather maps slightly miscalculated, a trolling line just a little bit off, a bait weed-fouled for hours, fuel calculations not quite right. Experience, the right kind of experience, was the only thing that widened those margins.

Willy recalled the time his father was headed out with a marlin charter on the *Albatross II*. Another captain who didn't have a charter that day offered him already-prepared trolling rigs. The wire leaders on the rigs were shorter than Bill liked, but he was running late and decided to take them along and use them.

"Dad always felt the leaders should be longer so that if the marlin flipped over, back end to, his tail wouldn't cut the line." Sure enough, on that trip they hooked a huge marlin, and, of course, it pinwheeled ass-end first and cut the line. "My father was madder than hell," says Willy who was mating that day. "He hollered from bridge to change out every damn rig, using longer wire. Well, of course, we did. And sure enough we brought a marlin to the boat." A lesson in margins.

It was clear we weren't going out today, so I took a quick tour of the *Ol' Salt* before we quit. Mate John Willis kept the *Ol' Salt* army-barracks clean. The enclosed cabin was carpeted, with a table and flanking benches. The rods were stowed neatly overhead. There were no TV sets or Barcaloungers or wet bars, but it was as cozy as it needed to be. We made plans to hook up again, and I headed to the car. I was going to walk to Cape Point, unless the lightning had other ideas.

———————

The simplest way to get to Cape Point is to drive onto Ramp 45 off Highway 12 just north of the Cape Point Campground, put it in four-wheel, follow the sand pass through the vegetation-covered dunes, and head for the tiny huddle of other vehicles at Cape Point. But the best way to understand, to sense the drama and to feel the beauty and the complex history of this compact segment of the eastern seaboard, is to begin by walking in at Ramp 45 a mile or so north of Cape Point marked by the black and white spiral of Cape Hatteras Lighthouse. At 208 feet, Cape Hatteras Lighthouse is, of course, the tallest thing around. In fact it's the tallest brick lighthouse in America. And unequivocally the most famous. Since its completion in 1870, it has borne silent witness to more lost ships and lives than any other similar structure.

The first thing you notice about the lighthouse is that it's gone. It isn't where it used to be only a few short years ago. But then, few things are in this land of restless, migrating sand. In this case, however, the change in venue was done by man, not nature. In the summer of 1999, the 4,800-ton structure was lifted hydraulically onto a set of railroad tracks, and, over the course of twenty-two days, it was moved inland 1,600 feet. Ironically that is exactly the same distance it was from the sea when it was constructed in the nineteenth century. But the Outer Banks are on the move too, southward and westward, always have been, and, by the standards of geological time, at a full sprint. By the 1920s, less than fifty years after the lighthouse was built, the Outer Banks had luffed westward and the sea had advanced 1,300 feet toward its quoin-cornered, brick-and-granite base. Jetties, groins, rocks, giant plastic sandbags, artificial dunes, sand fences: nothing could stop the sea from claiming the last 100 yards and its magnificent trophy. Geologists say the new location of the old lighthouse at the eastern verge of Buxton Woods is good for another 100 years.

When I first saw the lighthouse in 1985, it was a different structure. Poised on the very edge of the sea, breakers lapping nearly to its base, it seemed less concerned with lighting ships away from Diamond Shoals than with its own precarious existence. Today, railroaded more than five football fields back into a sandy clearing in Buxton Woods, vigilant Hatteras Lighthouse seemed a study in benign retirement and repose—more Disney than real. It had recently closed to the public, since part of its iron-spiral stairway had given way. The Park Service hoped to reopen it someday, but for now a pleasant park ranger under a sunshade would offer you a narrative in place of a climb.

Along with the lighthouse itself came two white clapboard outbuildings, the lightkeepers' houses. They were creaky-floored museums and gift shops now, one holding a section of the once revolutionary French Fresnel lens made up of a series of thick glass panels, which bent and concentrated a beam of 800,000-candlepower light and threw it more than twenty miles out to sea. Back to the east at the site of the original foundation, and just behind a wire grass and sea oats–covered line of sand dunes flanking the ocean, was a curious circle of jagged granite blocks. The forty large blocks, each the size of a couple of large fish coolers, were not attached and formed a ring approximately forty feet in diameter. The outside edges of the stones had been smoothed and polished, and carved in them were names and dates, two and three to a stone face. They were odd, antique names, forming the circumference of an odd, druidic memorial: Hezekiah Barnett 1849, Pharoah M. Farrow 1821. There were Malachai Swains, O'Neals, more Farrows, Fulchers, Austins, and, of course, Midgetts, the most ubiquitous first-family name of the lower Outer Banks (today the Outer Banks phone-book lists 291 Midgetts). Here in this circle of stone, the names formed an inventory of Cape Hatteras Lighthouse keepers from the first to the last. There were other lighthouses up and down the Banks: the orange brick Currituck Beach Light up north, the black-and-white-banded Bodie Island Lighthouse just the other side of the Oregon Inlet bridge, and the oldest, the squat, white-washed Ocracoke Lighthouse, built in 1825 at the southern tip of Ocracoke Island near the inlet. Each was painted in a different pattern so that mariners could tell them apart as they plied the coastline.

Right here too, just north of Cape Point, was the old Cape Hatteras Lifesaving Station. There was another, Creed's Hill, just south of Cape Point near the present-day town of Frisco, and a third, Durant's Station, had been absorbed into an oceanfront development near Hatteras Village. These were just three—but three of the busiest—lifesaving stations built up and down the Outer Banks in the nineteenth and early twentieth centuries.

The rain picked up to a steady patter. The stones glistened. They had settled unevenly into the coarse sand, but the circle remained unbroken. And surely, if they could, the names at the circumference would laugh at calling today's weather "bad." I headed a short ways south to Ramp 45 and parked. Mine was the only car in the lot. The other vehicles I saw, and there weren't many of those, were all four-wheel drives on the move up the winding, gray-sand road leading through the dunes to the beach. Most had the requisite aluminum shelf jutting out from the front bumper holding a cooler and a fidgety platoon of surf rods sticking up across the front. The vehicles pitched and yawed up the deep-rutted sand to the beach.

It was hard-going with bare feet. The sand was soft and uneven, but it felt good. It was raining even harder now. A break in the intermittent four-wheel traffic, and the silence for a moment was complete. Then the ambient symphony began. The rain whispered on the sand. Here on the low ground between two lines of dunes, the rain made a sharper, uneven rhythm on the wax myrtle, the stunted red cedars, and the meadow hay, the yaupon holly, the bluestem, and the sea elder. And beyond the two lines of dunes further up the winding sand road, I could just pick up the major percussion section crashing left and right. I joined in, my rain gear creaking this way and that as I turned to hear. A gray-and-white rabbit crossed the road ten feet ahead of me. It stopped and stood on its hind legs and looked at me for a long time. It then lowered itself and continued across the road into the bushes, leaving no sound in its wake. There was nothing here, nothing man-made. No houses left or right—only glistening vegetation as far as the eye could see, the taller among them leaning west as angry northeasters and hurricanes had forced them to do, in the process the burning, salt-laden air stripping them of most of their windward leaves and turning them into westward whipping flags. Here, in the puddled swale between the two sets of dunes leading to the beach, there was, for the moment, just me. I couldn't even see the Hatteras Lighthouse. I moved off the road and stood still in the vegetation. The eye swept the horizon, the landscape, looking for something, some object to light on. There was none. The natural, glistening beauty was seamless, of a piece. And a peace, because the eye, gently encouraged to move on by the serene and satisfied face of nature, turned inward in its search for a place to rest. It happened many times to Thoreau at Walden Pond, most memorably, for me at least when I read *Walden* for the first time at fourteen, when he cut a hole in the pond ice and lay down and peered to the bottom—into "the quiet parlor of the fishes," he called it. His eye could not rest there. He knew he was really looking inward, peering into the depths of himself. For a brief moment, he was frozen—in both senses. He came away from this experience with two insights: that nature asks no questions and answers very few that we ask; and, second, that nature quietly invites us inward where the meanings are. Thoreau went where nature pointed him and concluded that "Heaven is under our feet as well as over our heads." Standing here in the strangely windless rain, with a rabbit instead of pond pickerel nearby for company, I felt the same way. A letting go of sorts, something inside me exhaling deeply. I hadn't realized I'd been knotted inside so tightly: by Mo, her illness, and a sampler of other related suburban worries. They'd been slowly bivouacking, I guessed, awaiting orders, and now from this strange, green place, torn and strong and listing, this interdune swale, the troops had been decommissioned. It wasn't the last time this place, low and alone, would have such an effect on me. Eventually I would seek it out.

Thoreau's reverie was interrupted by some winter fishermen and a crew of ice cutters from town, mine by two old Chevy Suburbans bouncing along the ruts past me, headed for Cape Point. I got back into a rut and headed there myself. Up over the last dune was a beach about fifty yards wide. While the ruts turned sharply right and ran along the base of the dunes down to Cape Point in the distance, I walked straight ahead down to the surf line and made my right turn there. The August rain and the August seas were both warm. The gray-green surf was still stirred up from the storm that blew through last night, but as nature's moods go out here, this one was just a minor annoyance. Groups of tiny, needle-billed sanderlings skittled up and back with the wave wash, feasting mostly on fat mole crabs in the wave's retreat, and mincing up the beach for safety at its return. They kept moving down the beach in front of my persistent march. Then, finally annoyed, they took off in unison, flashing that distinctive white stripe under their wings. They made a long, sweeping bank and landed behind me at the water's edge and began to feed again. Larger sandpipers with longer strides did the same. It was raining hard now, a spattering rain, wanting attention. It felt good. I looked up at the skies for signs of lightning, but there was only gray wool. A mile up ahead, a few tiny brushstrokes of color marked Cape Point and its cluster of four-wheelers. As I stood abstracted for a moment, I looked down, and there, just above the waterline, half buried and up on edge was what turned out to be an old Indian-head nickel. It was as orange as a lifesaver. I put it in my pocket.

I got to Cape Point in thirty minutes. The four-wheelers were parked without pattern, some less than ten yards from the sea. Some back hatches were up and had rain tarps stretched out from them, held up with aluminum poles. Women sat under some, reading, knitting, watching their husbands or boyfriends, or just staring out to sea. Others were in the cabs of vehicles.

Cape Point. It really is a point and a dramatic one at that. For a hundred-odd miles the dunes and beach have made a gentle sweeping curve southeastward out into the Atlantic until they reach Cape Point. From there, almost forty miles out to sea, the thin strip of sand suddenly veers almost due west, then seems to change its mind and continues its gradual southwesterly direction the seventy or so miles to Cape Lookout. The result of such fickle behavior is a dramatic arrowhead of sand, literally a narrow point or spit running outward into the sea at Cape Hatteras.

And the sea it runs into: having lived for more than twenty years on the Atlantic, and having been drawn to it inexorably so many times since becoming an inlander, I can say I have never seen anything like the sea at Cape Point, Hatteras Island, North Carolina. Standing on the skinny spit with the barefoot surf fishermen and looking due east and southeast, you see a sea that is in a permanent state of boil and churn. It's a hydrologist's dream. Here at Cape Point you can see every kind of wave in every possible combination—plunging breakers, spilling breakers, collapsing breakers. Perhaps the most dramatic interaction of the waves here at Cape Point is called "claptois," where two wave crests moving in opposite directions slam into one another, causing water to shoot violently upward, sometimes close to a hundred feet into the air. All this as far as the eye can see, even on this calm, windless, rainy day in August. It's not just that these seas are choppy. It's that they are choppy in a mean, random, and berserk way—unless for variety they simply get meaner and more unpredictable. It's not hard to sense some kind of warning in such vast, abiding anger. Out there within sight is where the warm waters of the Gulf Stream coming up from the south at a steady four to six miles per hour run almost headlong into the cold, rugged Labrador Current shouldering its way in the other direction. The result is a natural collision of massive proportions, creating an unremitting turbulence unlike anything else on the eastern seaboard. This warm-cold conflagration is such that each current, as though to prepare for the fight, drops the massive freight of sand it has been carrying along. Hydrologists estimate that water moving laterally along the Outer Banks annually carries between 500,000 and 1 million cubic yards of sand a year. This lateral scouring along the beaches above Cape Hatteras causes them to move westward at an amazing five feet per year.

But when the sand-laden water reaches the triangular protrusion of Cape Hatteras, some of the southbound water slips around the point to the west into the quieter water of the bight, or the south-facing beach of Cape Point. Here much of the sand settles out, extending the Cape Hatteras landmass to the south. Another major part of the southbound water is drawn in the other direction, eastward, away from Cape Point and right onto Diamond Shoals and into the path of the Gulf Stream heading north. This continuing deposit of tons of sand is what makes Cape Hatteras the widest part of the Outer Banks. But more ominously, the same transported sand that settles to the bottom in the waters off Cape Point to the east here, at the eastern tip of Cape Hatteras, is what makes up Diamond Shoals, arguably the most treacherous shoal water in the United States. There's shoal water from Maine to Florida, of course, and even some candidates for most dangerous within hours of here along the same Outer Banks: Wimble Shoals, just north of here off Rodanthe and Waves and Salvo; south of here, Lookout Shoals guarding Cape Lookout; and, further south, Frying Pan Shoals off Cape Fear. But right out there, for fourteen miles south and west of Cape Point, beneath the incessant gray-green boil, is the ne plus ultra, the ain't-nothin'-like-it as people around here will tell you, and these are people who are victimized annually by climatic hyperbole and so have come to respect overstatement and to use it sparingly.

Diamond Shoals runs out from Cape Hatteras just far enough that it almost meets up with the warm, northward-flowing Gulf Stream. The proximity of dangerous shoal water and the Gulf Stream is unique to the Outer Banks. And for southbound ships, especially, it has threatened for more than 300 years to become a trap, a grave. Of the close to a thousand shipwrecks recorded along the Outer Banks from the sinking of the *Tiger* in the Ocracoke Inlet in 1585 to the present, Diamond Shoals has claimed far more than its share. Ships headed down the eastern seaboard from Portsmouth, Boston, or New York, or those coming out of the busy Chesapeake Bay and making the turn south from Cape Henry near the northern beginnings of the Outer Banks, could have a relatively easy time of it, provided the weather held. But steadily swinging east with the bulging Outer Banks, all ships—sail, steam, or motor—when they reached Cape Hatteras had to make a critical decision. They could choose to push on ahead against the combined forces of the Gulf Stream currents and the prevailing southwesterly winds, risking stalemate, or worse. Or they could choose a safer route and swing far out into the Atlantic, a hundred miles or so, and then come back in below Cape Hatteras. But what was the safest was also the most time-consuming. And what was most dangerous could save you days—or number them in single digits—and that was trying to thread your way south down the narrow corridor between the tip of Diamond Shoals and the Gulf Stream currents. Even with a lightship, or now a permanent light station located at the outer end of Diamond Shoals since 1824, this inside passage proved deadly to many an impatient captain and his crew. This is what happened, most disastrously, to the USS *Huron* in November 1877. Confident of his navigational skills, and against the advice of a number of his officers, Commander George P. Ryan decided on the inside route along the Outer Banks. His 542-ton gunboat didn't even make it to the inside passage at Cape Hatteras. Failing to factor in the Outer Banks' easterly curve, Commander Ryan ran the *Huron* aground at Nags Head, some sixty miles north of Hatteras. The *Huron* was only a couple of miles from the Nags Head Lifesaving Station, but the station didn't open for business until December 1. Ninety-eight sailors lost their lives. The resulting furor in the newspapers up and down the East Coast resulted in increased appropriations for lifesaving operations along the Outer Banks.

For those ships that reached Cape Hatteras, there was actually a fourth alternative, which many captains chose, and that was to wait in the waters just north of the cape, hoping for a change in the southwesterly winds. There are a few Outer Bankers still alive today who can remember seventy to eighty sails in a holding pattern, sometimes for weeks on end, north of Cape Hatteras. Back in 1903 a surf man with one of the nearby lifesaving stations reported having counted 105 vessels held just north of the Cape for twenty-six days. Such patience seemed prudent. The trouble was that the other prevailing wind pattern on the Outer Banks is from the northeast, and more often than not, when the captains got the wind shift they had been awaiting, it proved more than they bargained for. Northeasters out here are synonymous with storms, and a wind shift to northeast often reached gale-force proportions before a ship could round the cape. Such a wind, of course, would drive a ship, especially those under sail, right up onto Diamond Shoals.

Ships attempting to traverse the apex of the Outer Banks often seemed damned if they went and damned if they waited. Nature on the Outer Banks has shown that it has not a sense of humor so much as a finely tuned sense of irony. Irony happens when one thing suddenly becomes its opposite, when one outcome is unexpectedly and dramatically turned inside out like a sock. If you stay out here long enough, you can clearly sense in the character of the Outer Bankers—the long-term residents, the old-time families —a grim acknowledgment of the force of this irony and the often fatalistic humor that accompanies it. It's understandable: anyone whose source of livelihood can, in a heartbeat, become the watery instrument of his destruction, surely must have a healthy understanding of irony. The tragedy—and irony—of the *Huron* sinking in 1877—running aground a handful of days before the nearby lifesaving station opened for the four months of the storm season—resulted in expanding and professionalizing the service. In less than ten years, twenty-five lifesaving stations were commissioned from the Virginia line south to Cape Lookout. On average the stations stood seven miles apart along the beaches and were manned by a keeper and a trained crew of six oarsmen. In addition to being able to get a small boat through a huge surf, the crew had to know how to use a Lyle gun, a small cannon that fired a lifeline out to a stranded vessel. They also needed to know how to set up a breeches buoy or a life-car, devices that brought the imperiled in along the lifeline.

Crew members were also expected to continuously patrol the beaches during the storm season (December through March). They were usually afoot, sometimes on horseback. They'd arrange to meet patrollers from the adjacent station halfway between. There they'd exchange tokens (to show they had done their duty), turn around, and head back. As one might expect, the three stations that bracketed Cape Hatteras—Cape Hatteras Station north near the lighthouse and Creed's Hill Station and Durant's Station south between the towns of Frisco and Hatteras Village—were among the busiest stations, and gradually among the most legendary.

On a freezing April 14, 1881, the seven-man crew of the Creed's Hill Station sat down together and quickly drew up their wills. Those who could write helped those who couldn't. The reason for this was that there was a ship aground in the middle of Diamond Shoals with humans clinging to the twisted rigging, and the lifesavers were about to go out after them in seas even veteran fishermen swore they'd never seen the likes of. The leader of the crew, Benjamin B. Daily, brought his men and boat up the beach to Cape Point. They pulled on their heavy gear and cork belts as wet snow whipped at them from the northwest. Daily decided to launch their small flat-bottomed boat off the south-facing beach of Cape Point, where the surf was less angry. This is right where I was standing now, watching a retired orthodontist fish for blues and spot with his grandson. Today's August weather was a far cry from what Daily and his men faced, but you could see that the surf, even today, was indeed calmer on the south side of the cape.

When the lifesaving boat turned east as it had to and rounded Cape Point itself, the full force of the wind and sea hit them like a fist. Just making it out to the *A. B. Goodman* was nigh unto a miracle, but the crew was unable to get in close enough to pull the four remaining souls out of the rigging. Daily anchored a short way off and waited for a wind change. Without that everyone might end up dead. Daily's boat was constantly shipping freezing water. Hours passed. Then, just as the *A. B. Goodman* began to break up under the relentless pounding of the sea, the wind swung around to the east. Daily and his crew quickly snugged up to the leeward of the *Goodman* and, amid the dangerous tangle of spars and ropes, retrieved the four desperate men. With eleven men now in the lifeboat, and a pounding surf to negotiate, the odds were still against them. But Daily skillfully maneuvered the boat through the breakers and got everyone onto the beach. The survivors were taken up to Hatteras Lighthouse for warmth and food and clothing. Daily and his crew headed back to Creed's Hill Station and their wills.

Probably the most famous Cape Hatteras rescue came three days before Christmas of 1884. The 491-ton barkentine *Ephraim Williams* was on its way to Providence, Rhode Island, when it foundered in a vicious storm just north of Cape Hatteras. Benjamin B. Daily, this time leading the crew at Cape Hatteras Station, kept abreast of the vessel along the beach with his boat and crew until the *Williams* raised her distress flag. With Daily in the stern at the steering oar he directed six oarsmen into a huge surf. Observers on the beach said at time the boat was often nearly vertical as it went up the face of waves, the men's feet and the coiled rope and other gear clearly visible in the bottom of the boat. Somehow Daily steered his men through the first line of breakers and then the second larger line further out at the drop-off. Even out at the *Ephraim Williams*, the huge swells were breaking like surf. The *Williams*'s crew had abandoned ship already and were picked up one by one from debris-filled water and the makeshift rafts they clung to, and somehow brought safely ashore.

The U.S. government–run lifesaving service—which would become the U.S. Coast Guard in 1915—gave out twelve gold medals for heroism in its thirty years of operation along the North Carolina coast. Seven of those medals went to Benjamin B. Daily and his crew for their heroism during the *Ephraim Williams* rescue. The surnames of the recipients, again, remain familiar: Etheridge, Gray, Midgett, Fulcher, and Jennet (there were two Jennets). According to Outer Banks historian David Stick, if you go to the quiet little town cemetery in Buxton, you can see the likeness of the medal on Benjamin Daily's tombstone, along with crossed oars, and the inscription "A Testimony of Heroic Deeds in Saving Life from the Perils of the Sea." Daily died in 1914. Had Daily's family been in a more colloquial mood, they might have included the motto for the North Carolina Lifesaving Service that is posted in the restored Chicamacomico Lifesaving Station north of Hatteras in Rodanthe: to an oarsman's complaint about going out on a rescue mission, "Sir, we'll all be kilt!," the crew captain replies, "Boys, the book says we gotta go out. . . . Book don't say nothin' 'bout comin' back."

Even if luck prevailed in the early days and you somehow made it ashore, your travails, at least according to some, were not over. In December 1812 an unidentified ship ran aground just north of Cape Hatteras. Among those rescued by Hatteras Islanders was one Sarah Kollock Harris, wife of Hillsboro judge Edward Harris. She wrote a wonderfully detailed and graphic account of the sinking and rescue. While grateful for the heroic efforts of the local citizenry in saving her life, her Victorian sensibilities apparently took over once her spirits improved. She told her sister that after the rescue, she was "carried like a corpse by two men, one holding my head, the other my feet." She ended up at "a miserable little hut about a mile from shore," where she was forced to sleep in front of the same fire with "four sailors and two negroes." Her rescuers, she concluded, were "wretches" and "a disgrace to humanity. I could not have believed that so much depravity was in human beings," she continued. "Exulting in the calamity which has thrown us among them, though pretending to sympathize in our distress, they would steal the wet clothes which we took from our backs and hung out to dry, and everything belonging to us which they could lay their hand on. They were really a set of harpies watching for their prey, and would actually take it from before our eyes and destitute as we were. Ere we left the island they stripped us of everything they could."

Salvage has a long history on the Outer Banks, some of it legal and some otherwise. Without such largesse from the sea, many families would have starved and been forced to move elsewhere. So great was the sea's tragic bounty that the Outer Banks were divided into salvage districts, each with its own vendue master, or wrecks commissioner, who would conduct legal public auctions of washed-up goods. Sometimes the auctions took place in the small villages, but, more often than not, the goods were piled in stacks right on the beach and auctioned off in lots. The locals were free to keep the odds and ends that came ashore. Some locals recorded that when a ship carrying shoes sank off Ocracoke, it wasn't unusual to see islanders wearing two different shoes or even two right ones or two left ones. Now whether salvage operations included stripping the clothes from the backs of rescued women, as Judge Harris's wife claimed, remains open to question.

On the Outer Banks a fine mist often obscures things, both material and moral.

Meditation and water are wedded forever.
—Herman Melville, *Moby-Dick*

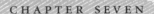

CHAPTER SEVEN

Hatteras in Winter
Cape Point Revisited

JANUARY. I flew to Hatteras again, this time to see the village and landscape in the dead of winter. I came also to ride out with the *Albatross* fleet for bluefin tuna. These fish ran anywhere from a hundred pounds on up, and fishing for them in winter from Hatteras was a relatively new enterprise—only six or seven seasons so far. As usual Ernie and Tall Bill were among the first captains to do it.

Fishing for winter bluefin on the Outer Banks was an iffy business at best. Their migratory routes remained a mystery, and so whether they'd show up at all remained an open question. And then there was the famous Outer Banks weather. In winter, managing to get outside Oregon or Hatteras or Ocracoke Inlet one out of three days was normally considered a stretch of good luck. The prevailing southwest winds bulked up during the winter, and the seas paid the price. Some clients flew in for a week and never got out once. But the rewards were as outsized as the quarry; a hook-up to one of these creatures could be an experience somewhere between the mystical and the chiropractic. And if you got them schooling behind the boat by chunking fatback over the transom, the experience could be life transforming. Arguments still abound in slick fishing magazines and in buck-a-longneck bars from the East Coast to Ketchikan, Alaska, as to which is the hardest-fighting big gamefish pound-for-pound. The final two contestants are usually the bluefin and the king salmon. Blood has flowed like gravy over the differences of opinion.

I flew into Norfolk on the tail end of a freak snowstorm that had swung up through the southern states and blindsided the Carolinas. Dirty snow flanked the runways when we landed. I knew there'd be little snow on the Outer Banks because of the ameliorating effects of the sea temperatures. But it was cold, and as soon as I got outside I could see the wind was predictably southwest.

I figured the wind and my luck were due for a change. Mo's MS-related seizures had been increasing in number and severity over the last few months, and even with nursing help at home, I was worn out by it all. The seizures baffled even her veteran neurologists. The episodes weren't so much physical in nature as they were cognitive. For days she would hallucinate, would be in some strange movie no one else could see, all the while aware of what was happening to her but unable to stop it, and all the while trying desperately to get back to the channel the rest of us were watching. It was heartbreaking to see a brilliant woman trying to pretend she knew where she was or why someone was feeding her. She had had a seizure the morning I left for the Outer Banks. Of course, a nurse was in attendance and would be around the clock while I was gone. I left for the airport more melancholy than exhilarated. But I had to go to Hatteras or go crazy. I looked forward to seeing Ernie and Lynne Foster and Tall Bill Van Druten. I also looked forward to the new cast of characters (in all senses) I no doubt would meet. And if I met a bluefin up close and personal — well that, I hoped, would be the flaming dessert to a weeklong feast.

But as I crossed the Currituck Sound Bridge and made my way onto the Outer Banks at Kitty Hawk, I found myself thinking of the other task I had set for myself this trip, and that was to walk back down the beach to Cape Point as I had done on that rainy day last August. But this time it wasn't to observe the angling practices, nor was it to soak up the rich and layered history of this little spit of land that pointed like a finger out to the thirty square miles of Diamond Shoals, the Graveyard of the Atlantic. No, this time my errand was more personal. I was going to Cape Point to pay my respects to those old New Jersey fishermen who so many years ago taught me how to fish, how to know the sea, and how to understand that fishing could actually provide you with a way of looking at the world. If you connect the dots back far enough, those old-timers were really the ones who caused me to write this book, to be here at all.

I had grown up on the ocean in New Jersey, sixty miles south of New York City and sixty miles north of Atlantic City and almost 400 miles north of Cape Hatteras. Manasquan was a small, mile-long beach resort whose summer population tripled the town's body count. In the summer, my parents ran a hot dog stand right on the beach, a stand-up-at-the-counter affair catering between Memorial Day and Labor Day to bathers and fishermen mostly down from north Jersey or New York City and to the seasonal rental families in the beachfront houses and, behind them, the Jazz Age bungalows stretching back to Third Avenue and Glimmer Glass Lake. For those three hectic months, many of the locals made themselves scarce, preferring the relaxed pace of the spring and fall, when the crowds were gone. Others, like us, catered to the crowds and were, like us, so busy they too remained unseen. Oh, they'd come down sometimes at night for a little gossip, a cup of coffee, and fresh pound cake or German apple crumb cake made by old Mr. Benewicz in his fragrant, powdery bakery in town, but not often. Too many squalling kids, too many drunks from the bars up at Main Beach hollering their grill orders at us, laughing way too loud, too many scantily clad teens in noisy rut. My sister and I worked there alongside our parents, my grandmother, and occasionally aunts and uncles seven days a week, summer after summer, year after year, until we went to college and graduate school, until we married and moved away. I worked there summers from the time I was seven until I was twenty-four. And for those same three summer months, we lived next-door to our little restaurant in one of the oldest houses on Manasquan Beach, a wonderful low-slung, hip-roofed affair that we sometimes rented out and so moved into the two rooms up over the hot dog stand.

Someone once showed us old yellowed pictures of our house sitting all alone among the sand dunes and said our house had been built in the 1890s from salvaged ships' timbers. When I was nine, I crawled under our house (it had a basement of sorts), then wriggled further under with a flashlight, and dug and dug in the chilly sand until I came to the huge support beams running laterally under the floor joists. The massive beams were still raggedly sheathed here and there with copper, and where there was no copper, there were green-headed nails. Myth became history! It was true! The bottom of our house had been the bottom of a ship. In the late fall, when a northeaster was prying at the battened windows on our porch and the needle-sharp sand was taking the paint from the north side of our house, or when a stronger hurricane, especially Hurricane Carol in 1954, was re-moving our front porch (we had not heeded the National Guard's midnight bull-horned warning to evacuate), and waves from the Manasquan River were rocking our car and our '51 Chevy pick-up that said "Carlson's Corner" on each door with a big hot dog logo in the middle between the two arcing words, I would lie in bed feeling the house shudder and shift, groan and crack, knowing water from the ocean was running right beneath us and all around us, but thinking too of those huge, copper-sheathed timbers, and I would pretend that I was on a great and seaworthy sailing ship and that we'd ride this storm out, just as we had all the others.

Between Labor Day, when the tourists went home, and the beginning of November, when we closed for the good and the storm season started, was my favorite time of year. The locals reappeared, including my friends from school, many of whom had been working in the boardwalk restau-rants or mating on the charter and head boats out of Manasquan and Point Pleasant and Brielle marinas up the Manasquan River from the ocean. On Wednesday nights the volunteer fire department came down aboard their vintage hook and ladder, ringing their bells and blowing their horns. In their big suspenders and rolled down boots, they'd order burgers and fries and coffee while kids swarmed the fire engine, ringing the bell and chasing each other in the long-billed firemen's hats. The shop owners from Main Street, a mile inland, whom we hadn't seen for three months, came too: me-ticulous Mr. Wilkins from Wilkins' Men's Shop; Mr. and Mrs. Tassini from the News Stand; Joel Lemansky, the cobbler, with his uncontrollable kids; sweet, giggly Rose Meyers and her silent husband, Lou; Kenny Hartranft from Ralph's Meat Market; florid Johnny Flynn from Squan Tavern; and so many others from the three-block-long business district, anchored at one end by the butterscotch Masonic Temple across from the Esso station and at the other by Quenzer's Drugs. To all of them, my parents were Fred and Mildred, and I was Tommy, and my sister was Nancy, and together we, all of us, ran our fingers over the neat, tight warp and woof of a community we were just now reweaving, at least until Memorial Day of next year.

Of all those who participated in this fall ritual of reestablishing the com-munity, the local fishermen were the ones I most looked forward to seeing again. There were eight or nine of them, older, wind worn, and as regular as migratory birds, fishermen and their fishing wives who came to the stand almost every day and lingered, sometimes all day, especially in the spring and the fall when the crowds were thinner. One of the most vivid snapshots I carry in memory is this group, taking up both of our end-to-end, green-

Carlson's Corner, Manasquan Beach, New Jersey, c. 1955 (Courtesy of Tom Carlson)

slatted benches in front of the stand, drinking coffee, eating pound cake and donuts, talking endlessly, laughing, arguing. I can remember the order in which they always sat as surely as I knew my Boy Scout oath. I know what they were wearing, just how they sat, what they were talking about. From the left, it was Flo Rose and her husband Al, both retired and both round and both with intricate spiderwebs of tiny red veins mapping their cheeks. They never missed the cocktail hour at the Marlin Tuna Camp on Brielle Road, and discreetly took flasks with them out on the jetties flanking the mouth of the Manasquan River. To their left sat Jake Sanwald, a retired detective, hawkish, reticent, sardonic, and a ready audience for the swirl of jokes, practical, off color, or shaggy. Then came old grouchy Doc Meeker, with his white brushy mustache and his thick canvas and gum-soled shoes, sometimes on the wrong feet. Next to Doc was Rocky Luciano, whose olive-skinned daughters I lusted after (in vain); then Stan Osborne and his brother Bart, bachelors both; then George Minier, the plumber; and finally Ed Frazee, the janitor at our high school.

They were customers all, of course, but gradually they became much more than that for me. My parents, working eighteen hours a day, had no time to look after me, to feed me, when I wasn't working. Slowly and without negotiation, the members of this fishing crew became my surrogate parents. Each looked after me in his or her own way. Each helped me to grow up. Flo and Al Rose often took me home and fed me to bursting; they had no children, and Flo didn't know quite how to behave around them. She'd hover behind my dinner chair and exhort me, "Be sure to eat your beansie-weansies, Tommy." I was fourteen years old. Others, usually Jake Sanwald, drove me to Boy Scout meetings and jamborees and dances at St. Uriel's or the Lighthouse in Sea Girt or the firehouse up on Broad Street. When he'd pick me up afterward, I'd sit in the front seat of his '38 Plymouth because he'd let me shift the huge floor shift. In return, I'd have to endure his jokes about all the girls I must have succeeded with. Thanks to Doc Meeker I learned the true meaning of "curmudgeon," learned how grouchiness could rise to the level of a high rhetorical art, especially when the rest of the bench crew short armed him and he got stuck paying for everyone's coffee ("You keep fumbling in your pocket like that, Rocky, and you'll get arrested for playing with yourself!").

But mostly they taught me about fishing, about the sea, how to read the weather and the water, when to expect the blues, the weakfish, the stripers, how to spot the bait school and the birds working it, how to tie a sea clam on a surf rig so it would float off the bottom and away from the hungry crabs, how to drift a live eel at night on an outgoing tide from a concrete stanchion on the Jersey Central Railroad bridge spanning the Manasquan River. Ed Frazee, the high school janitor, showed me how to drift squid strips for fluke and flounder just the right way on the Manasquan River flats, but he also taught me it was possible to live life with grace and dignity and one ear and just the hint of another and a congenitally deformed face that made him look more like Popeye than Popeye.

What they were really teaching me, I know in hindsight, was about life and ways of seeing it, of learning to be patient, to wait for just the right moment, of acknowledging its amazing bounty, its unpredictability, its long silences, its myriad, often cruel, disappointments and ironies as well as its magical generosities.

Jake Sanwald taught me how to fish in the dark at the end of a 900-foot jetty in front of my house, to work a jointed Creek Chub Pikie down along the rocks and catch fat weakfish. He also showed me something more magical. One October, he led me down the beach to one of the wooden bulk-heads that started at the boardwalk and ran low and fat and tarred out into the surf.

Right where the wood entered the sea, a thick incline of water-smooth sea pebbles had drifted up against it. Small waves, four or five inches of wash, moved the pebbles back and forth with their ebb and flow. We took off our

Old-timers on bench, Carlson's Corner, c. 1958. From left to right: Flo Rose, Al Rose (asleep), Jake Sanwald, and Doc Meeker. (Courtesy of Tom Carlson)

shoes and squatted like two Thai laundry women next to the pebble drift. Jake's bare feet shocked me. He was never, ever out of uniform — matching khaki shirt and pants, worn high up on his hips, see-through socks and thick crepe-soled shoes with canvas tops. Above his thin, hawkish features and his white, pencil-thin mustache, he wore a khaki hat with a long green plastic bill and an embroidered life preserver with two anchors running through it. Jake was a detective by trade, and whenever I listened to *Boston Blackie* on the radio, I pictured him. "Be patient and watch carefully," he said over my shoulder, as our bare feet sank slowly in the cold, gray sand. I watched the pebbles moving back and forth, the hiss-and-rattle choreography, the hesitation, then the hiss-and-rattle again as the pebbles danced back toward us and the bulkhead. Over and over, sometimes with brilliant bits of blue and green sea glass and violet shells flashing here, then there, like footlights. I watched the dance, listened to the song, but I didn't see. Until Jake reached over my shoulder and plucked a dime from the receding water and clattering expanse of retreating pebbles. Then a quarter. Then a penny so thin he folded it in half between his thumb and forefinger. "When the water goes out," he said, "the pebbles and shells roll. The coins tumble end over end. Watch again." I did. Sure enough. A nickel. A quarter. And so I could do it myself.

But when Jake died a few months later, and his ashes were scattered in the undertow a short surf cast down the beach from where we now squatted together, it wasn't for the money any longer. Nor is it today, when I go home.

It's for the music—the sea's and old Jake's. Jake Sanwald taught me there was value, real and spiritual, in the most subtle ebb and flow of the sea.

Stan Osborne taught me something else, something I have tried to bequeath to my children. In August 1958, on a weekend, I was out at the end of the jetty, hoping the bluefish would show up. I had a brand new fiberglass rod and a Ru-Mer half-bail spinning reel, and could now cast a plug or a Hopkins metal into the next zip code. It was very crowded at the jetty's end. The blues never showed, but the striped bass did, a large school of fat-bellied sows. There was a fresh incoming tide between the Manasquan and Point Pleasant Beach jetties and a strong southwest wind holding it back. These opposing forces must have created a perfect standoff because a half-acre school of mullet hung right in the mouth of the inlet, and the stripers were cutting them to ribbons. The water slapped and boiled, and the sea gulls above squalled and dove for the leftovers.

A good cast could reach the fracas, but the fish wouldn't hit a thing offered by the many fishermen lining the dark jetty rocks down below at the water's edge. Except for a Yellow Atom plug one of the fishermen tried. The Yellow Atom is a large, plastic yellow plug, translucent and shallow diving. The man pulled in twenty-five-, thirty-, thirty-five-pound stripers. And then a huge striper snapped his line.

"Come on," Stan said, and we headed in off the jetty to Bill and Em's Bait Shop behind our hot dog stand. They didn't have a Yellow Atom. Stan said, "Come on"—he was a gentle man, of few words—and we crossed Riverside Drive to his old boxy Nash. It was a thirty-minute drive in the holiday beach traffic across the Manasquan River to the Ship Chandlers store in Point Pleasant. I was bouncing in my seat I was so impatient. I put the towel rag I had tucked in my belt on the hot metal door frame so I could put my arm out the window. Stan was his usual quiet, steely calm. He stared straight ahead, his wrist on the wheel. His thick pompadoured hair lifted and fell in one piece as the breeze came and went. I could smell the Wildroot Cream Oil and the salt air and the hot fabric of the seat. Ship Chandlers had one Yellow Atom. Stan bought it for me. I think it cost three dollars.

When we got back to the end of the jetty, the feeding frenzy was still on, but it was more crowded than ever with fishermen drawn to the action. No one could get tight to a fish. No one had a Yellow Atom. The man who lost his to the bull earlier had left. It was elbow to elbow on the rocks below us. Many of the fishermen had no idea what they were doing. It was far too dangerous to go down there to try to find a spot and avoid the flying treble hooks. Stan tried to comfort me, but I was beyond consoling. We just sat on the concrete light-tower platform and watched. A man came up from a prime spot down below. His brother was still down there, holding his place on the rock for him. The climber's tackle box was near us. He was frantically going through it trying to find something, anything that might entice. I heard him talking to himself, in German, probably cursing his luck. He was around forty, dark haired, and handsome. I looked at Stan. He looked at me, smiled, and danced his eyebrows up and down. I took the Yellow Atom, still in its cardboard box with the see-through cellophane top, over to the man. "Here. Use this," I said. "You'll catch one." He looked up at me, studied me for a moment, and then took the box and studied it. "Vott is dis?" he asked. "It's a Yellow Atom plug. It's the only thing they'll hit. You'll get one." I don't know if he understood me, but he did say *Danke* and took the little box with him back down to his brother.

On his first cast, he hooked a giant. I saw his rod bow over, and for a long time, he just stood there with braced legs as the fish stripped line from his reel. Then gradually the man began reeling him in, pumping the rod and then cranking, then stopping to allow another line-peeling dash, then more slow pumping and cranking. Everyone else had stopped to watch. It took half an hour, but finally a huge silver-green fish with black stripes was on its side in the wash four or five feet below the brothers' rock. It went at least forty pounds. Without asking if anyone had a gaff, the brother without the pole simply jumped in the water, grabbed the fish, and lifted it like a fat barbell up over his head and onto the rock. I could see the brothers jumping up and down and hugging each other. They petted the fish as though it were a Labrador retriever. Then the other brother took the pole. On his first cast, he caught a twenty-five-pounder. This time the dry brother jumped in after it. Two casts. Two fish. Two wet, happy men.

Then, just like that, the school of stripers vanished. But that was enough, anyway. The German brothers worked their way up toward the light tower where we still sat. Soon two huge fish were at our feet, flopping languidly in a crowded semicircle. And I was being hugged repeatedly by two wildly grinning, waterlogged Germans. They jabbered away. All I could understand was *Danke schön*. One brother made a flat palm with one hand and a writing motion with the other and pointed to me. Stan gave me a pencil and a scrap of paper. "They want your name and address," he explained. I wrote it down and handed it to them. More jabber. More hugs and handshakes, and then off they went. We had to laugh. Instead of taking the big fish by the gills and walking them in vertically, the brothers carried them sideways in the crooks of their arms, like new brides across the threshold.

For the next five years or so, I received beautiful Christmas cards from each brother from Germany. There were long messages inside each, which I managed to get translated by Mr. Gruenwald, the German teacher in the high school. I always saved the cards to show to Stan when we opened the hot dog stand in the spring. It was these fishermen, these teachers and surrogate parents, who would gather in the cool September air with our hot coffee and tell fishing stories, lavish, byzantine, dramatic, hilarious fishing stories, mostly about stripers and bluefish, but sometimes about absent members of the unofficial club—"Heart Attack Jim," "Four Roses" Fred, Lazy Harold Dunphy, Old Man Tice, and the rest.

But what I remember most was their elaborate plans to do their fall fishing at some place called Cape Hatteras and Ocracoke, where it wasn't so cold and where, they claimed, the surf fishing was world class. It was my first introduction to these names—Cape Hatteras (by which they meant Cape Point and Hatteras Inlet) and Ocracoke Island. These places became mythical to me as year by year the fish caught there grew in size and reel-screaming strength. I didn't get to go there until I was forty-one years old, with children of my own. And I didn't make it to Cape Point until fifteen years after that. And now I was going to Cape Point again, six months after my first visit, to think of them—these characters more vivid and important to me than they ever knew, all gone now, all crossed over the bar—to pay tribute to them, to thank them for helping me to see what really mattered, and for creating in my life a passion that has not abated after half a century.

I reached Hatteras well after dark. The office of the Village Marina Motel had closed at 5:00 (winter saw little business), but my name was taped to the window of my room, the door was unlocked, and the key was on the little kitchenette table. Such are the arrangements in a village where the crime rate is near zero. (I once asked Ernie if there was anything like theft in Hatteras, and he said, "Not really. If someone steals something of yours and starts using it, everyone in the village is going to see it and know it's yours. Theft doesn't make sense here.") I unpacked and went out for some pub grub at one of the few places open in the village.

In talking with Ernie before coming down, I had mentioned how much it would mean to me to go out with him on the original *Albatross*, the one his father had built for $805 in 1937, the one that started the whole charter fishing industry on the Outer Banks. I knew Ernie didn't take the original

Albatross blue-water fishing—it was pretty narrow abeam and had only one Cummins 250 diesel in it—so I suggested striper fishing inshore, either in Hatteras Inlet or on Diamond Shoals. He'd agreed—Lynne told me later that Ernie loved to take the *Albatross* for stripers and drum with friends—and tomorrow was the day settled on. I called home and found that Mo was doing much better, and so my attention turned to my pulse, which was more noticeable as I turned in.

At 5:30 the next morning, even in the half dark I could see that the fountain grass out by my car and the line of wind socks across the gravel lot at the marina store were being whipped by wind out of the southwest, not the north-northwest as marine forecasters had called for. A north wind coming over the land would flatten out the winter sea; a southwest wind would stir the offshore pot, maybe dangerously. My motel room was only a hundred feet from the *Albatross* fleet, so I gathered up my small duffel and my thermos and walked down the arcade porch toward the boats. I could hear the voices before I saw their owners. Ernie and three other men were standing on the dock by the stern of the *Albatross.* It was cold, and the wind was making it colder. I got introduced around. Tony Lamm was a cheerful, semi-retiree with a beach home down here; he had helped Ernie through his messy divorce some years back even as he was going through his own. They'd been fast friends ever since. There was Bryan Mattingly, a Brad Pitt–handsome thirty-year-old local who had that easy, unself-conscious Hatteras manner and who'd worked as a mate and captain for the *Albatross* fleet on and off for years. He'd opened a restaurant further up the island, had a boy and a girl from a previous marriage, and mated part time—just couldn't get it out of his blood, he said with a smile that would have caused a director to terminate the casting call.

And then there was Mike Scott whom I'd met last November at that dinner party with Ernie and Lynne and Spurgeon Stowe and his wife. Mike was forty-something and a dead ringer for Lyle Lovett. For some reason Mike chose to wear one of those furry, flappy aviator hats that nerdy kids in the 1930s sported during the winter. Mike was an incredibly smart man, though it took awhile to cut through his soft-spoken modesty to find that out. An autodidact with a vengeance, Mike had opened a boat yard, had taught himself the business, had built forty-odd boats (we'd pass a couple of his artworks a few days later), and had just sold the whole business to a California couple and was in the process of doing what he loved best—flying around the world for surfing adventures. Did he remember Bruce Brown and *The Endless Summer*? Oh yes. Had he found the perfect wave? No, he smiled, but he was working on it. It turned out his favorite place to surf was Peru. Wherever he surfed, he read widely on the culture before he flew there. Once there he'd check the navy's satellite read-outs and if they were showing that the surf was not going to be up, Mike would grab his backpack and take a local bus or whatever inland and soak up the local culture on the local level. He was clearly a man who was curious about everything and knowledgeable about almost as much. If encouraged sufficiently — he was quiet by nature — he could hold forth on Machu Picchu with the best anthropologists, sort out global politics, and assess the nuances of native cuisine with self-effacing ease and alacrity. As Ernie had told me earlier, "Mike is not your average surfer dude." Indeed.

As we stood there talking, the *Tuna Duck* went by the bows of the three *Albatross* boats, headed out. At fifty feet and broad abeam, the *Tuna Duck* was a much bigger — and newer — boat than the *Albatross*. We turned our attention to the business at hand. Would the old *Albatross* be able to go out? We piled into Ernie's cab-and-a-half truck and drove to a narrow spot north of the village, climbed over a small dune, and took a look. Not good. The seas were running three to four feet and the forecast was for worse to come. We drove back to the dock, just in time to see the *Tuna Duck* coming back in, right by us. You could feel the disappointment of the party, a family, standing back by the fighting chairs. At least I could, because I was feeling the same thing, maybe more so. No one else seemed to. I was anxious to ride aboard the original *Albatross*, the boat that started it all down here, to feel its signature through the water, to see Ernie standing where his father had for so many years, so many years ago. And, running a close second in my desperation was to catch a rockfish — a striper in New Jersey parlance — because, as I admitted to Ernie and the rest as we stood around the dock stamping our feet against the cold, I had never caught one. Even though I had fished for them since the Eisenhower administration, I had never caught one. I told them I had even tried for the freshwater variety on the Cumberland River in Tennessee with no results. They were amazed. I felt vaguely embarrassed by the admission, as though I were a frat boy admitting to his brothers around a keg of beer that I had never been with a woman. In fact, the metaphor that developed to correct my condition was just that. "Well, we'll help you lose your virginity," Tony said, and everyone laughed. I didn't tell them that it wasn't some kind of biological urge or a long-delayed ego gratification. Because it was too complicated for the cold moment we now shared, I didn't tell them about Stan Osborne and the Yellow Atom plug and the two German brothers there at the end of the

Manasquan jetty in 1958, and how happy I had made them, and myself, and therefore how much catching a striper would mean to me, and, hokey as it might seem, how it would somehow complete a circle in my life.

Ernie was anxious to show Mike his handiwork aboard the *Albatross*, so we all went aboard and down into the cramped forward hold. Ernie had rebuilt the curved underside of the boat's forward deck. Above and in front of us was raw wood, neatly arced, and glued and blocked. After quizzing Ernie about his techniques ("Did you . . . ," "Did you remember to . . . ?"), Mike gave his stamp of approval. We then adjourned to the tiny *Albatross* fleet office thirty feet away. It was unheated and cluttered with fishing equipment and engine parts. We seemed between moments, trying to decide what to do with the day. The office still held the magnificent wall of photos under Plexiglas—the whole history of the Foster family and most of the village they lived in. We all edged around the clutter on the floor to look at the pictures through our breath. Maybe because Ernie was headed to Morehead City at the end of the week to join a group fighting for North Carolina fishing rights to the bluefin, we began looking at pictures of those great balloonish bass fiddles standing on their heads, some taller than the baggy-pantsed fishermen who'd caught them. Ernie knew many of the complicated laws governing the harvest of this species, laws international, national, and state. He sorted them out, compared them, pointed out the inequities in their application. There were no limits on bluefin in the Mediterranean or in Japan. But here apparently there was a complex of laws governing and limiting catches more tangled than the worst monofilament backlash. There were special fine-print laws governing commercial and recreational fishing for bluefin. Just how many you could take was the bottom line, and that had recently been made more complicated by the discovery that eastern and western Atlantic stocks apparently mixed more freely than anyone had previously suspected.

Such lobbying and bluefin lawmaking was more than bureaucratic masturbation: big bucks hung in the balance. Japanese buyers came into Hatteras Village a few years back and paid more than $20,000 for a single bluefin. For North Carolina fishermen, at least for this year, two things were certain: one, because northern catch quotas had not been met, North Carolina charter fishermen were allowed to keep one fish per trip (the fish had to measure at least seventy-three inches from tail fork to the lower jaw); and two, North Carolina fishermen were getting screwed again. What fish there were this year, and they hadn't turned up in big numbers yet, were uncommonly close to shore. Apparently they were feeding on the massive schools of menhaden not far off the beach. Normally you had to go out twenty miles or so to the Gulf Stream and fish the temperature changes around its edges to have a shot at them. Rumor had it that someone recently caught one off the pier in Avon. My striper funk lifted a little because I had also planned this trip down to ride out with Tall Bill and Bryan for bluefin. Maybe we wouldn't have to go so far out in search of them.

Inevitably the conversation turned to the numerous pictures of monster marlin on the wall. They were Ernie's favorite fish, and he never tired of talking about them. He once told me, "The most beautiful and powerful thing I've ever seen in nature is a marlin." He was talking now about their eyesight. "I've seen marlin trailing our baits at fifty yards in choppy seas trying to decide whether or not to feed." Bryan added, "And it's not just marlin. King mackerel have keen sight too, and, man, are they smart. When you lean over the boat to bring them in, they'll take off, likely as not. And if they see the gaff, they fly!" Ernie was back on marlin. "Did you know, if you club one, they light up all over with electric stripes?" He told of the time they boated a 439-pound marlin. It reached all the way from the stern into the open cabin of the *Albatross*. They clubbed it and thought they had it subdued. But it revived, and—with Ernie straddling it—it went crazy. "That dang thing flipped the fighting chair up into the air like a tennis ball," Ernie recalled, "and almost got me. I broke my club on it, and it was still going crazy. I had to go down below and get a stilson wrench—and beat it to death with that." Something he wasn't proud of, he said. But what are you going to do with something that powerful in close quarters?

Bryan brought up the story of the marlin caught out of Morehead City five or six years ago. Everyone nodded solemnly, except me. They knew the story. A film crew was aboard the charter boat when they brought a good-sized marlin alongside. The mate was experienced and had the leader wrapped and the marlin in position. The filmmakers wanted a better shot, so they told the mate to hold on a moment longer while they set up the shot. Just then, the marlin did a full back flip toward the stern of the boat and then took off. The mate's hand got tangled in the leader, and he was pulled overboard, attached to the fish. The other mate grabbed the fifty-pound test line and jumped in to help his friend. But the line snapped and the leader, which of course was stronger, didn't. They retrieved the second mate, but they never saw the first mate or the fish ever again. "It's all on videotape," says Bryan, "but no one wants to watch it."

By now few of us in the little office could feel our feet, so Plan B was proposed: to go over to Ernie's to see videos of his recent trip with Lynne to Venice. As we went out onto the back porch of the office, all Ernie could talk about regarding Venice was its boats. "Those gondolas are the strangest damned things. They're all the same, except the ceremonial gondolas. And by decree," he added, "they all have to be the same color — black. The decree was issued in the twelfth century! You think we've got history around here."

I begged off the viewing, citing my work back at the room. Ernie said fine, that they'd be back if the wind died down a little or if it swung around to the north. Chances of that were slim. I knew Ernie had set up this striper expedition for me, and he realized how anxious I was to ride aboard the *Albatross*, out of the dramatic inlet, across mythical Diamond Shoals. He had added his other friends because he enjoyed their company and knew I would too. Yet neither Ernie nor any of the others showed any disappointment at all when it got called off. This fascinated me. If you live here long enough, in this land of moving sand and petulant winds, Plan B is more often than not simply a way station on the road to Plan C or D or F. Yet I remained disappointed. I had flown half a country over to sail on the *Albatross* today, and this was the day I wanted to be aboard — and lose my virginity. I knew I was being childish probably, but the best I could manage was to try not to let it show.

"Tomorrow's another day," Ernie called from his truck. "Be at the dock at 11:00. I've got a dentist appointment. We'll go out." And off they went to Venice.

I decided to go to Cape Point. Maybe my spirits would improve if I quit thinking about myself. I would make my planned pilgrimage today. I went back to my room and had another cup of coffee; when the feeling returned to my feet, I headed to the car. In August I had parked north of Cape Point and hiked through the dune lines and up to the beach on the sandy road labeled Ramp 45. This time I decided to walk to Cape Point using Ramp 44. It was a little further south — in fact right behind Cape Point, due west of it — and therefore a shorter trek. But that wasn't my reason for choosing it. In August, barefoot and alone in a gentle rain, in a swale between two lines of massive dunes I had had that strange and wonderful peace-that-passeth-understanding experience in the ambient silence shared only by a staring rabbit. Somehow I felt it would be a violation to go back to that place. Besides, there was something near Ramp 44 that I wanted to visit again after more than seventeen years. Just a couple of hundred yards north of the ramp was a huge seawater pond between the first and second line of sand dunes. In 1985 I had taken my children there to see the wreck of the

Altoona, which had run aground at Cape Point in the fall of 1878. Although its seven-man crew was saved, the huge wooden two-master was taken by the sea and the sand. Then in 1962 it popped to the surface again, its ragged stern like a tombstone, its ribs curved like a giant dinosaur's. My children, Winnie and Dan, had played on it as though it were a jungle gym.

I walked up the sand road for 200 yards or so and then turned off into the wire grass and low scrub toward the huge seawater ponds I had remembered. The sun played off the riffles, its shards lazing, then racing in the late morning wind. It was still coming from the southwest. I scanned the lake for any prominence above the stunted yaupon and cedars, but saw nothing. The *Altoona* had been on the ramp side of the lake, I was quite sure. My kids wouldn't have had the patience to hike all the way down to the far end of the water. I looked up toward the first line of dunes between me and the beach at Cape Point. There was a cut through the dunes as wide as a four-lane road. It was a dry riverbed now, but you could tell it wouldn't take much of a storm to send the ocean through the dune line and back to where I was standing by the lake. No doubt the *Altoona* was gone. For almost thirty years she had dried her wide and bony wings in the sun like some giant cormorant, and then, like everything else eventually out here on the Outer Banks, she moved on—gathered the wind and the water under her, enough so to migrate, maybe piece by splintered piece, but migrate nonetheless south and westward into the inevitability of the Pamlico Sound.

I followed the edge of the lake toward the beach. The sea gulls floated in quiet, Quakerly groups nearby, unconcerned by my intrusion. These were the big gulls, the ones I had grown up with on the Jersey Shore, the ones that, at first light during the fall, would drop huge sea clams on the roof of our beach house to claim the rich yellow meat inside. It was hard to forgive them on school days. I also saw possum and raccoon tracks along the edge of the water and other, larger tracks I couldn't identify. Ernie later told me they were probably made by a species of small deer still extant on the island, which had probably wandered over from Buxton Woods to the west.

Every so often I came upon the splayed and desiccated remains of a sea gull. In its balletic contortions, the posthumous flutter of its parts, the delicate rictus it displayed, each was oddly beautiful. These were the birds not of Audubon but of Morris Graves, a lonely, brilliant artist who spent much of the first half of this century painting birds, mostly dead, some blind, many of them sea gulls. In them Graves found a glimpse of the Zen satori, that sudden moment of intuitive enlightenment or illumination. In their lifeless bodies he saw life—ours—in all its delicate beauty and loneliness. These sunken birds lay amid clumps of wire grass. The fickle wind had made each clump of grass draw a perfect circle around itself in the sand. Out here, where it's risky business to expect the land to be where it was last week, out here, for some reason, you find yourself looking for signs — not meanings, that's too much to expect, but sidelong signs — sudden swellings rising from the depths of the sea into the air, an eye's blink, the smooth glidings, the choreographed banking in on a frozen sheet of air to splashless landings, the wind's work, constant and deadpan, moving the sand like a chess piece down the board, leaving you to wonder at the larger calculus involved. Meanwhile 400 miles inland cars wound down the spine of the Blue Ridge Mountains, their owners absorbed with their own serpentine motion, indifferent to the ancient, unmoving mountains beneath them. The mountains abide; not so the Outer Banks. They're too restless. Maybe that's the difference. Out here on the Outer Banks, maybe it's the very mobility and temporariness of all things, the sudden appearance, the shocking flash and disappearance that reminds us of our own mortality and makes us yearn for a sign of something, anything, larger at work in the world.

I turned left and followed the dry riverbed to the primary dune line. I could see the now-familiar collage of colorful four-wheelers up ahead of me at Cape Point and the jade petulance of Diamond Shoals beyond that. When I got to the Point, the fishermen were clustered where they had been in August — on the thin finger of sand that ran, half under water, right out into Diamond Shoals. The fishermen out at the end of the sand finger were having a tough time keeping their balance in the turbulence. I counted thirteen fishermen. High season at Cape Point ran from about October to December. That's when the big drum and stripers were most plentiful. Ernie said it wasn't unusual to see 200 people fishing in this small area. And, he added, when someone got a big drum on and it made long lateral runs, there was an etiquette of helping the hook-up go over or under your rod, or even bringing in your line to get out of his way. "Of course," he said, "there were always two or three guys — not locals very often — who would refuse to move." Then arguments started, even fistfights. "I know a lot of people who just won't go down there anymore," shaking his head as if they'd closed the Sistine Chapel to the faithful.

Thirteen wasn't a crowd, and there seemed to be room for everyone. You could tell the locals from the off-islanders or big-beach-house immigrants. The locals favored vintage four-wheel-drive pickups or old Wagoneers with ragged quarter and rocker panels. The nonlocals came down the beach in Range Rovers and Lexus SUVs, or an occasional Yukon, all fitted with shiny

Surf fishing, Cape Point, Hatteras Island, fall 2004 (Courtesy of Lynne Foster)

chrome rod holders up front (not the homemade PVC setups made by the locals). In the surf, the locals wore baggy olive waders, old plaid shirts, and duck-hunting hats. The upscale species fished in tight-fitting, chocolate neoprene Cabela waders and L.L. Bean shirts with epaulets; they sported expensive haircuts with aviator sunglasses and no hats.

Today at least everyone seemed to be getting along. Those who had been fishing there the longest often turned their backs to the sea and shouldered their big rods like rifles, to rest their arms and backs. As I sat on a convenient shelf of sand created by a previous tide, I watched the rod of one of the locals out at the end of the finger double over. He set the hook and just stood there as the fish made its long, initial run. After a while, the man started gaining line back. Then he'd wait again. Each run was shorter, and the fish was moving left toward the beach. The man went with him, and the etiquette this day worked perfectly. Everyone made room. Soon he was a few feet from where I was sitting with a twenty-pounder by the gills. He posed proudly as I took his picture and congratulated him. He walked the fish up to his truck and put it in a big cooler in the back. Back out on the Point, one of the neoprene boys was kneeling, trying to get a writhing sand shark off his hook.

Surf fishing, Cape Point, 1930s (Courtesy of Buddy Swain)

Things quieted down as the afternoon moved along, and so I had time to think about why I'd come today to Cape Point. I looked out at the cluster of fishermen and tried to imagine Rocky Luciano and Stan Osborne and Jake Sanwald out there in their waders. I tried to picture Al and Flo Rose, sitting in their canvas beach chairs, watching their rods in the sand spikes, chatting and drinking coffee out of their big ribbed thermos, adding a little to each cup from their flask. I thought of old Doc Meeker grumbling about something or other, but making everyone laugh that night in the little fish-net-draped restaurant in Hatteras Village. It wasn't hard to do.

Then I remembered that this wasn't the exact spot they had stood on, because on the Outer Banks nothing stands still, most especially the Outer Banks themselves. In my backpack I had a book about the ecosystem of the Outer Banks. In it was a chart showing Cape Point and where the point probably was at different times in history. Like everything else Cape Point was migrating south and west. The broken line on the chart for around forty years ago, when my old mentors would have been here, showed that Cape Point was actually about 1,000 yards north, up the beach. So I paced it off and stood there. Of course in the 1950s Cape Point was also further east—and that meant out beyond the breakers. I couldn't manage perfect historical accuracy, but I had brought with me that orange nickel I had found in August during my first walk down to Cape Point. I took it out of my pocket and walked down to the wave line. I recited all of their names in the order they had sat on the benches outside Carlson's Corner from left to right, and then I said, "This is for all of you. Thank you." And I threw the nickel as far as I could into the sea. I hoped it landed somewhere near where they had stood those many quick years ago.

I walked back down to Cape Point. A chill was sitting up in the late afternoon air. I sat there a long time watching Diamond Shoals buck and charge and spin back on itself like a pen full of wild mustangs. I watched the surf fishermen, knowing so well their sweet sense of expectation — it couldn't be eager because you knew it would have to last maybe all day, maybe all week, maybe days beyond that, and so you had to ration it, but the rationing was delicious because at its end was that feeling like nothing else in the world when your rod gracefully doubles over and a mysterious, hidden energy moves up your rod arm, to your shoulder, to your neck, and you wait just a beat and set the hook; then that feeling, again like nothing else, that split second at the quick end of which you discover if you're tight to the fish you always imagined at the telescope end of your carefully portioned-out expectation. And then the delicate, brutish ballet begins between two creatures tethered by what seems the thinnest spiderweb of line. The reel-peeling runs so far out, then later the thrum-thrum-thrum of the fish in the surf now, tired, shaking its head from side to side trying to throw the hook, rolling in between the waves, a vast white belly, a tail appearing just for an instant like a glistening opera fan. Then the wading out with the gaff, or better still, just you, thrusting your hand up in behind the gill cover and lifting it out of its world, and it looks at you and you return the stare, a moment as primitive as fire in a cave, and then you bring it to the beach.

This beautiful sleek thing, this creature so often seen, but maybe capably captured in paint by only one artist in a generation (why is it easier to paint a beautiful woman, to display her loveliness and even her soul, than it is to succeed similarly with a striper or bull red, a dolphin, a marlin, a king mackerel?) — this thing now in our world, where the fate of beautiful creatures is decided by such things as size and slots and numbers allowed per fisherman. And finally by the fisherman's mood, his inclination. These days, mercifully, more often than not, fishermen take the fish into the shallow wash, right them, rock them forward and back to get water moving through their gills, until they slowly tail outward away from their gentle grip and back beneath the surf. When I was growing up, the inclination was otherwise. Keep everything. Bring it off the jetty, off the beach, parade it by everyone and finally get it weighed in at Bill and Em's Bait Shop around the corner from our hot dog stand. Maybe a photo too. To this day, when I sand a piece of wood or sweep a gritty patio floor, I flash on my adolescence, on the shh-ah-shh-ah-shh sound of a huge striper tail being dragged by a fisherman along the sandy sidewalk by our restaurant. In Ernie Foster's little office next to the *Albatross* fleet, there are dozens of photos, most faded or yellowed with age, depicting men and women standing or kneeling beside hanging fish — great marlin, a brace of sailfish, bluefin tuna, many with the weight painted in white across the belly. Kill-and-hang bragfests. I asked Ernie what happened to the fish after the pictures were taken. "Well, they often hung there until they started to smell," he said; "then we'd cut them down and take them outside the marina and dump them." He paused and then added, "I'm glad we don't do that anymore."

I headed back to the car through the same dry wash cut through the dunes I'd found this morning. My morning's striper funk seemed like ancient history. Ernie was right. We'd get out tomorrow.

Only connect!
—E. M. Forster, *Howards End*

CHAPTER EIGHT

Portly Stripers and Eager Virgins

The next morning before first light, I walked out onto my little motel porch in my skivvies and checked the fountain grass and wind socks across the way. Yes! The wind had switched around to north. It was a lot colder, of course, but if the wind held, we'd be going out fishing. Aristotle believed that babies were healthier if they were conceived when the wind was coming from the north. He didn't say anything about fishing. But today the fishing promised to be healthy. My virginity was imperiled, and right now I was freezing my joyful ass off. I went back inside and made some coffee and ate a light breakfast in my room. I watched the Weather Channel and all systems seemed go—except we're talking weather, and this, of course, was Cape Hatteras. I kept my fingers crossed.

Then, into a second cup of coffee, I turned to CNN to see if the rest of the world was still in place. The way I was feeling right now, if they announced that it wasn't, that some errant asteroid had sheared planet earth into a ragged, half-eaten apple that contained only the east coast of the United States and parts of Newfoundland, I'm not sure I would have cared. All I wanted was for the wind to hold north northwest for one day, January 8, in a twenty-square-mile patch of salt water on what remained of Mother Earth. January 8! It struck me the way detectives got cold cocked in Philip Marlowe novels. Today was Elvis's birthday! Moments later, CNN confirmed it: "Today, Elvis Presley would have been . . ." Who cared? For me Elvis would always be twenty years old and cool and on the Ed Sullivan "Toast of the Town" show with the bottom half of the screen blacked out so we couldn't see what he was doing down there. CNN, of course, showed Elvis in Vegas, the bloated rhinestone wind sock. I'd been writing about Elvis for years, and so I wasn't surprised. Anyway, where there were rhinestones I was seeing stripes. Elvis not as rock star, but as rockfish! Here was an omen!

Ernie had said to meet at the *Albatross* at 11:00, so I got down to the business of writing for a couple of hours. At 11:00, from the open door of my room I could hear the single diesel of the *Albatross* burbling down and around the far corner of the motel. Tony and Mike and Bryan were standing on the dock talking. The north wind was a knife on this side of the building. It felt wonderful. Bryan was warming up the engine as we waited for Ernie to exit a dentist's chair somewhere in the village. He was here in short order. We loaded our gear aboard, slipped the lines, and in no time were out of the narrow marina entrance and heading south toward Hatteras Inlet and the open sea. We stood around the fighting chair talking, joking, and drinking coffee. I decided to head up the wooden ladder through the open square in the bridge floor to join Ernie. It was even colder up here, but heavy plastic curtains zippered around three sides of the bridge helped some.

Up here the view of Hatteras Village was lovely. The tallest structure was the water tower. Everything else was trimmed low and tight to avoid the wind. The long, unpopulated finger of sand and scrub that ran south of the village to the inlet was suddenly brindled by the sun that was joining us by increments. Right below us was the sound water turned mocha by yesterday's blow and, closer in, the rich aquamarine paint of the foredeck. Ernie explained that his father had chosen that color to cut the glare. That was back in the days when sunglasses didn't always do the trick.

Ernie was clearly pleased to be taking friends out fishing. There were none of the pressures or protocols that come with charter parties—no need for forced politeness, no need to answer dumb questions or caution against stupid behavior. No need, as a last resort, to tell the occasional angry or drunken customer, "The ride out is free; what you're paying for is the ride back in." For Ernie, this was just the best kind of busman's holiday. My obvious enthusiasm for the history I was riding in got Ernie talking about the boat. The original *Albatross* was his favorite of the three, certainly for sentimental reasons, but also, he pointed out, because of the boat's magical physics. By this time we had turned into the light chop of the inlet pass, the *Albatross*'s Cummins purring like an old cat in the sun.

After a long communal silence, Ernie explained the physics part: "Narrow boats may have their drawbacks, but if you want to tune into the water, if you want to feel connected to the sea, well, ride this boat." Another long silence as we negotiated the heavier chop where the inlet opened out into the sea. Connectedness to the sea was obviously important to Ernie. Just as obviously it was something he'd done a good deal of thinking about. No doubt he'd had the opportunity to ride the new fiberglass models, "plastic" boats they're called derisively by the old-timers—boats almost as wide as the *Albatross* was long—even the line of boats named after his hometown. He'd take his fleet, anytime. Ernie Foster was no mindless sentimentalist. His father had developed some of that curmudgeonly resistance to change. That was understandable. But he hadn't passed it along to his son. Ernie knew that the future lay in the big plastic boats with their warp speed, NASA electronics, and Malibu beach house amenities, that these waterborne space ships with wall to wall carpeting, TV, Nintendo, fridges, card tables, Serta Perfect bunks for naps, and electronics able to identify fish species, size, number, and probably gender at forty fathoms would eventually put him out of business. He also knew that in the process something important would be lost. Connectedness. It was probably a better word than most. Connectedness: it made me think of that little poem by Walt Whitman.

A noiseless patient spider,
I mark'd where on a little promontory it stood isolated,
Mark'd how to explore the vacant vast surrounding,
It launch'd forth filament, filament, filament, out of itself,
Ever unreeling them, ever tirelessly speeding them.

And you O my soul where you stand,
Surrounded, detached in measureless oceans of space,
Ceaselessly musing, venturing, throwing, seeking the spheres to
    connect them,
Till the bridge you will need be form'd, till the ductile anchor hold,
Till the gossamer thread you fling catch somewhere, O my soul.

Here, Whitman spoke of the soul's attempt, like the spider's, to connect to something larger than itself. And Whitman instinctively turned to a nautical metaphor: "oceans of space," "till the ductile anchor hold." For many of my students, Walt Whitman was a little too loud, even a blow-hard bard—"I Walt Whitman of the Cosmos" ("Yeah, right."). But Walt Whitman was a quiet man, introspective, and he lived on Long Island and knew the sea—and fishing—intimately. If one of his soul's "filaments" had managed to attach itself somehow to Hatteras Village, Whitman would have felt right at home.

I had time for all these thoughts because in the short time I had known Ernie—and Tall Bill too—we had become friends, not writer-and-subject-friends, but friends in the real sense of being able to sit together for long periods without feeling the obligation to say anything at all. In fishing, unlike almost any other sport, it is the silences, the rich, resonant, comfortable library silences that most deeply characterize its activity.

By now we'd cleared the inlet and swung north, maybe a half mile off the beach. "Look!" Ernie tapped me on the arm and pointed off the stern on the port side. Just as I did, a set of huge flukes rose slowly into the air, hesitated for a split second, and then slipped beneath the sparkling surface in the same smooth parabola. Then a spout, and then another, two flags of spume frayed in the wind. Bryan and Mike had seen it too and were yelling up to us. "A humpback," Ernie said. "A humpy. They're not uncommon around here this time of year." It was headed south across the mouth of Hatteras Inlet. I had never seen one before. I watched it until it disappeared beneath the water and the cold, flat light, and continued watching, hoping it would come up for an encore.

Ernie called down to Bryan to put two rods out. Up ahead gannets were diving on what looked like a huge school of menhaden, or fatbacks, as they were often called on the Banks. Menhaden were the blue plate special for a huge number of predators. We were hoping there were stripers underneath them. Up ahead too lay Diamond Shoals. I was hoping we'd fish it. The Graveyard of the Atlantic. Just yesterday I sat at Cape Point, looking out on Diamond Shoals, transfixed by its random moods, its varied angers, its showy playfulness. To catch a striper, my first one, to lose my virginity in these hallowed waters, and aboard the original Hatteras charter boat that was christened the same year as the Hindenburg disaster, the same year Frank Lloyd Wright created his architectural masterpiece, the house called Fallingwater, . . . well!

We trolled onto the shoals. The birds we'd been watching had moved further offshore, but there were more, lots more, dead ahead of us. I could see the surf fishermen at Cape Point and their bright four-wheelers huddled askew, scattered like LEGOS behind them. We took an inside line across the shoals (the *Albatross* drew only two and an half feet of water). Bryan kept checking the Magnum Stretch 30 plugs we were trolling, a chartreuse one close in and a bright blue one further back, and both were coming in every time fouled with weed. There were still more birds working up ahead of us near Avon Pier, so we headed up there to get away from the grassy water on Diamond Shoals.

I went back up on the bridge and sat with Ernie. He was on the radio. "Yeah, yeah. I see them. But there's more ahead of us!" He hung up and laughed. "We're being followed," he said with a grin. "What do you mean?" "See that truck on the beach?" I looked, and there was one paralleling us north along the surf line. "That's Spurgeon Stowe, trying to tell me I'm missing the birds and stripers. He's looking at the birds behind us." Ernie left the wheel and told Tony and Bryan and Mike down below about Spurgeon over on the beach. Spurgeon stories sprouted everywhere. "Man, some of the things he does on his boats," Bryan said; "he'll just yell back to some woman bottom fishing, 'Hey Fatso, move over so some other people can fish!'" Bryan continued: "One time I saw him go up to a woman in a tank top fishing with her husband. He hooked his finger into her top and pulled it out and looked down, and said 'Lady, you better cover those things up. They're getting red!' Man, if anyone else had done something like that, they would've gotten punched out by her husband. But somehow crazy Spurgeon always gets away with it."

We fished up to Avon Pier. The schools of menhaden were so thick in places you could see the rod tips dancing as they blundered into our plugs. We turned around and headed back south toward Diamond Shoals. The sun had come out with its hands up. We each peeled a layer or two. It had turned into what they called out here a bluebird day, a beautifully anomalous day of clear sky and flat seas in the midst of a season of gray storms and moody water. About a mile north of Diamond Shoals, the port rod bowed over. "Hop to it, man!" Tony said, looking at me. I grabbed the rod, and in a few minutes a nice striper lay in on the floor of the boat. "There goes your virginity," Bryan announced. Indeed. My first one (*O Hymen, hang thy bloodied wedding sheets from yon bedchamber window!*). They took my picture holding it. They took my picture kissing it. I said I was going to mount it. Tony said he wouldn't take a picture of that.

We had time before we reached Diamond Shoals, so I went and sat in the open cabin. The others were waiting their turn at the rods. I thought of all the old striper fishermen again, as I had yesterday. I thought particularly of Stan Osborne who had worked so hard to help me catch a striper almost a half century ago. I got a shiny penny from my pocket and tossed it past the red and white outrigger behind me. "Stan, I did it," I said to myself; "I finally did it." Then I took another penny and threw it too. "And Elvis, thanks too."

I must have caught a loner because we had no more action until we got back to Diamond Shoals. This time Ernie headed the *Albatross* a little further offshore. I was watching the depth finder with Ernie when we suddenly shallowed up on a small dome, maybe ten feet below the surface. Two rods went off together. In short order we had two twenty-pounders in the boat. Ernie swung the *Albatross* around for another run over the dome. Again both rods doubled over in unison, I grabbed the starboard one and hung on. This one was peeling some serious line. I looked up and saw Ernie cast out a bucktail he had on a rod up on the bridge. He got tight to a fish almost immediately. A triple-header. Mine was the last one in the boat. It was the sow-of-the-day, a thirty-two-pounder on the scale back at the dock. This time, posing for pictures, I found myself thinking of those two German brothers I'd given the Yellow Atom plug to at the end of Manasquan jetty in 1958. This was the size fish each of them had caught. So that is what it felt like. I hoped they were alive and still remembered. I was seized with the desire to hold the fish in my arms, crosswise, as they had done when they walked happily in off the jetty, but the explanation I'd have to give Tony and Bryan would be longer than the fish. So I just turned around and whispered *Danke schön* to the fish as I put her into the fish box in the stern.

We had eight fat fish in the box, more than enough for everyone, and certainly enough for the dinner Ernie and Lynne were going to have over at their house tonight. It was getting late and the temperature was beginning to drop noticeably, so we stowed the rods and headed south off the shoals and toward Hatteras Inlet. I went up on the bridge and joined Ernie on the slat bench. We sat in silence, enjoying the sunset over Hatteras Village and the sound behind it. Then I told him, all kidding aside, all issues of virginity shelved for the moment, how much this day had meant to me—his company and his friends, the old *Albatross*, Diamond Shoals, the stripers. Without going into all the details, I tried to explain to Ernie how this day connected importantly to a day in my life in 1958, how I felt a circle completing itself. I knew such talk of feelings, of sentiment, of anything bordering on the intimate anecdote did not make Ernie uncomfortable. Ernie was a man's man, certainly, but I knew he allowed, even welcomed, such moments of self-reflection. I was still surprised by the tender, vocal side of these people—that even among the commercial fishermen, as rough and calloused as their hands, room could be made for a moment of tenderness, a gravelly whisper from the heart. The only rule governing such moments seemed to be that they be kept short, tight as a knot in their telling. A cup of soup—not a bowl.

Just a few days earlier we'd been sitting in Ernie's cluttered little den watching old video footage of the *Albatross*, some made by him, some of it sent over the years by various customers. We came to that footage of his father, Ernal, being interviewed by a local television station about having started the charter fishing industry on the Outer Banks. Ernal was eighty-four and two years from his death. Ernie hit the pause button on the remote. "You know," he said, looking at the TV, "my father wanted only two things out of life. He wanted a successful fishing business so he could support his family, and he wanted to send his only son to college. He said to me, 'Son, if you get an education . . . ,'" and Ernie stopped. I looked over, and he had tears in his eyes. He waved his hand, asking me to wait, but he couldn't go on. He got up and came back with a Kleenex and unabashedly wiped his eyes and blew his nose. He was determined to finish the sentence. He did so, but his voice cracked several times. "He told me, 'Son, if you get an education they can't ever take it away from you.'" I put my hand on his forearm, and told him, "Ernie, my father had an eighth-grade education, and he told me the same thing." It was true. Ernie didn't say anything. After a while he started the video again.

So I knew sitting up on the bridge in the gathering cold, I hadn't embarrassed Ernie by the connections I had felt today. He remained quiet as we swung into Hatteras Inlet. I knew he was thinking about something. He pulled his thick insulated coat collar up around his ears. Finally he spoke from behind the newly erected fence. "When my father was older—well, you saw it on those videos—he used to sit at the dock office and whittle and wait for us to come in. He was always whittling—a stick of juniper was his favorite wood, same wood these boats are made out of. Well, if he came to a knot in the wood, he wouldn't try to get rid of it by main strength. He'd whittle around it, a little on this side, then some on that, until it stood up like a post. The point was to get to the end of the wood beyond the knot, and my father always got to where he wanted to go, even if he had to go left and go right to get there." Patience, single-mindedness of purpose, even stubbornness. Ernal had wanted his fishing boat built a certain way, his way, and he went left and right, carrying his own lumber with him, until—it was the fourth boat works he'd gone to, the Willis Works in Marshallberg on Core Sound—he found someone willing to shape the juniper the way he wanted it. The result was the beautiful, functional physics we were riding in right now.

But I sensed there was something else embedded in Ernies's parable about his father. He waited awhile to supply it. Another cup of soup, never a large bowl. "My father learned to treat the elements the same way, to skipper his boats the same way," Ernie said as we approached the narrow mouth of the marina. We were close enough that the pelicans were heaving themselves up from behind the marina breakwater, like old men out of stuffed chairs, to see what we might have to offer. "And he taught me the same thing too. Don't fight the elements—the wind, the currents, the weather. Learn to use them to your purposes, to go with them or around them if you have to, like that knot in the wood, without fighting them. Let the world work with you," he concluded as he swung the boat up to Oden's Dock to refuel. Connectedness. To accede to the energy in the world; to become one with what one does. There was something Eastern about all this, something Zen-like in these people straddling a spit of sand that bowed toward the east.

The refueling didn't take long. The *Albatross* had hardly used any diesel. We swung down the way to our slip. It was almost dark now, and the temperature had dropped another ten degrees. Bryan heaved the stripers up on the dock, and Ernie and he and Mike filleted them by droplight and flashlight while Tony and I hosed down and mopped the boat and fish box. I got up out of the boat and weighed my Diamond Shoals baby on the hanging dock scale before they cleaned it. Thirty-two pounds. When Bryan cut it open, he carefully slit the stomach and out shot a two-pound menhaden. Bryan threw it in the basket already filled with fatbacks from Tall Bill's commercial fishing that day. Recycling. Mike saved the head and tails and innards in a plastic garbage can to plow into his garden. More recycling. We were cold and tired and happy. But dinner was in an hour, and the entree was still sitting freshly hosed down on the cleaning table, so we headed off to clean up and reconvene.

The shower stung my cold hands and feet the way it used to years ago after skiing. Though Ernie let on out in the boat that Lynne would be working all day on the dinner, he also said she loved every minute of it. I suspected that the dinner would be elegant and understated, like Lynne. I knew too that this was Hatteras, and all else would be informal. A clean shirt and jeans, an odor manufactured by something other than a fish, and no scales on your shoe tops. That would do it. I grabbed a bottle of wine I'd gotten at the marina store yesterday and walked from my motel room across the narrow highway, two houses in to Ernie and Lynne's. I stood in the middle of their sandy little

side street and took in the house they had built a few years ago. It was a taste-
ful two-story affair with a screened-in porch on the east side. Perfect. The
stars above the house were achingly apparent, and the house glowed warmly
under them by candlelight. When I walked across the narrow porch, I passed
the bank of kitchen windows. Lynne looked up and smiled. The smell of
garlic joined the cool salt air. I stopped in my tracks. Ambrosia. If heaven
has a fragrance, I thought to myself, I hope it's this. Fresh-cooked garlic and
salt ocean air.

When I got inside, Tall Bill and Ernie and Mike were sitting at the dinner table talking. Lynne was just a few feet away working her magic on a
small cooking island. Greetings all around, and then Lynne asked if I was
alright. I guessed she'd seen me turn to stone outside the kitchen windows.
"It was the garlic," I explained. She began to apologize profusely. If she had
known I didn't like garlic . . . Things were soon clarified. Ernie got me a
beer. "House brand," he said smiling. I looked: Foster's. I joined them at the
table. The kitchen and living room were one big, uncluttered space with a
huge cathedral ceiling. I had worked up a theory, endorsed by my wife, that
you could gauge the relationship of a couple by the connection or absence
thereof between their kitchen and the living room. According to my theory,
Ernie and Lynne's marriage was a true partnership. It surely enjoyed the
connectedness and sweet, seamless physics of the *Albatross*.

Dinner was served. The garlic with other spices Lynne recited for us was
served over fresh, steaming shrimp. Eventually the striper made its way to
us, square and silver-black and substantial, and atop it a geometry of green
and red and yellow strips of pepper. It looked like a Mondrian painting. It
didn't taste like one. The variety of foods Lynne had encountered in her
world travels, first as a flight attendant, then as the wife of a wealthy tobacco
magnate and herself as an executive for Calvin Klein Cosmetics in London,
had obviously not been lost on her. The conversation was as delicious and
as varied as the dinner, as broad as Hatteras Island was narrow. After re-
hearsing our day for Lynne (no mention of virginity or its loss was included,
mercifully), Ernie averred that the values of a culture are always found in
the monuments it has erected to itself. "And for years," he said, "the only
monument in this village was the world-record marlin in the glass case on
the wall of the little village library. Fish worship; we're a primitive people,"
Ernie concluded.

I said there was now a second public monument: the *Jackie Fay*, an old
Hatteras-style commercial fishing boat, restored and under an open shed
for the public to view just north of Hatteras Village. Ernie started laughing.

He knew the captain of the *Jackie Fay* when it was still a working boat. He described how the captain pulled into Oden's Dock with a boatload of fish right where we had fueled up earlier this afternoon and went into the store for a minute. Tall Bill started laughing. He knew the story. "Well, when the captain"— Ernie mentioned his name—"came back out, his boat was jammed with pelicans, eating the fish. In fact it was so jammed with pelicans that none of them could spread their wings wide enough to fly away when he got to the boat. Man, he was mad! He just climbed on board, got in among those birds and started heaving them out one by one, cursing and heaving, until there was enough room for the rest of them to fly off." We were all laughing now. "And this is an endangered species!" said Ernie.

Talk turned to commercial fishing regulations, to fears that anal-retentive OSHA would begin managing the charter fishing industry (a fear ironically realized the very next day when Lynne presented Ernie with a fresh e-mail from OSHA addressed to all licensed charter captains announcing that the agency planned to do just that). Finally talk tacked back toward geopolitics and culture, first in Central and South America and then to the Far East. Ernie wanted Lynne to tell about her adventure with the wali of Swat. Lynne laughed nervously. Clearly the story was a family favorite, but to be asked to launch into it on demand . . . I told her we weren't leaving until we heard it, and so she began a fascinating narrative that predated her marriage to Ernie. It involved Lynne and a woman friend, both collectors of antique fabric, heading by themselves, and against much advice to the contrary into the remote valley of Swat, then a tribal territory in what is now northern Pakistan. Because of its rugged beauty, the Swat valley today is known as the "Switzerland of the East," and remains famous for its unique fabrics, especially embroidery. Lynne and her friend managed to get to the valley and were soon intercepted and ushered to the palace of the wali, or supreme tribal ruler of the valley, who treated them like royalty. Lynne told the story with humor and rich detail. I got the feeling that her adventure with the wali of Swat was just one chapter in a longer book she had in her head. I had noticed on entering their house mannequins of sorts here and there displaying beautiful old fabric, blouses, skirts, and wall hangings. Things fell into place.

The conversation moved gracefully ahead, but not for long. In the lower part of the Outer Banks, most people start their jobs in the dark, and so our pleasant dinner party ended early.

Nature is what we know—
Yet have no art to say—
—Emily Dickinson

CHAPTER NINE

Smoker Kings and Bluefins
Now and Zen

THANKSGIVING WEEK. "If you watch the way a big king mackerel hits a live bait near your boat, it'll probably change the way you look at life," Ernie said with a wry smile as we made the short drive though the predawn darkness to the *Albatross* fleet. Ernie was hardly given to such dramatic or mysterious pronouncements, so I heaved myself up out of my coffee-less stupor. "What do you mean?" I'd never caught a king, so I was genuinely curious. "Well, you'll see. It's beautiful and savage at the same time. They don't give a damn about anything but that fatback in front of them. Not anything. It's that single-mindedness and the power, I guess," he said. "It sure makes you realize your place in the food chain, and that it's a couple of notches lower than you thought." I wasn't sure what he meant, but I guessed I'd find out. King mackerel fishing had always been a part, though a minor one, of the sportfishing scene out of Hatteras Village. Mostly it was a commercial venture. We'd see a lot of commercial boats out where we would be today. Ernie himself often fished kings commercially aboard the *Albatross*, trolling with planers, heavy tackle, and electric reels. At around a dollar a pound at either of the two fish houses in the village, you could pick up some nice fall and winter pocket money.

But the sport or charter side of fishing for kings had grown steadily over the years, bringing hearty souls down Highway 12 willing to wait out three days of bad weather to go out one good day. Also, the trend in recent years had been to lighter and lighter tackle for kings, the larger of whom were called "Smokers," not because of how you prepared them, but what they often did to your reel when they grabbed your live fatback. Today we'd use light rods and small Shimano TLD 15s and thirty-pound-test line with the necessary wire leader. Sometimes Ernie would go down to twenty-pound test, but, as he said, "that allows a really small margin for error — if the line touches the side of the boat or it hits other lines or the gaff or the fish, whatever, it's usually all over."

When we got to the *Albatross II*, Karen, the mate, was already busy setting up the rods and getting the sinking gill nets we'd use to catch some live fatback just off the beach before we headed out to the Gulf Stream. Karen Crawley was a very pretty young woman and clearly very athletic. She had just graduated from Virginia Tech on a soccer scholarship, and it showed in the way she moved. I got pieces of her story on the way out. She had come down to Hatteras with her family and booked a charter aboard the *Albatross*. The mate that day was Justin Buxton, the young man who'd mated for us a summer back. Justin had done a stint in the coast guard at Hatteras, and when he'd finished up, like so many, he'd fallen in love with the place and stayed. To finance this love, he began to work as a mate for Ernie. Justin was young and fit and *GQ* good-looking, and according to Ernie probably the best mate he'd ever had. He said, "You know, there's a bit of Ahab in all of us captains — yelling for crew to do this and this and this all at the same time, getting mad when we lose a fish, hollering — always at the mate — because of this or that . . . But," he added, "I have to say I never saw Justin get frustrated with me or even close to angry; in fact he usually did things before they occurred to me to holler down for him to hurry up and do them."

Well, the inevitable happened: Justin and Karen fell for each other instantly and totally, and now were inseparable. She stayed on in Hatteras Village when her family's vacation ended and, never once having mated, signed on with Ernie and Tall Bill. She instantly picked up the nuances of a difficult, demanding job, one that takes a complex body of knowledge, finesse, strength, patience, intuition, and social skills. Her only shortcoming was a chronic and violent affinity for seasickness, which she kept under control now with a small scopolamine patch behind her ear. I noticed that as Ernie talked with

Karen, there was an extra fatherly sweetness in his tone, a gentle jokiness. He was actually quite sad as I found out. The *Albatross* had done it again. Ernie had met Lynne aboard the boat and married her; Willy had literally married aboard the boat; and now another liaison had been forged in the same spot. But this time it was carrying the lovers away. Justin was from a restaurant-owning Louisiana family. He'd grown up in a kitchen foggy with spices and roux, and now he and Karen were headed in two days to St. Augustine, where Justin was going to enroll in a culinary institute. Ernie had effectively lost a son and daughter to a failed first marriage, and now I could sense that he was having those melancholy feelings all over again with these, his surrogate children. He and Lynne had planned a farewell breakfast for them the day of their leaving, and all that was left was two more trips out.

Justin showed up shortly, and he and Karen embraced sweetly in the dark shadows of the *Albatross* office. Justin was going to take the original *Albatross* out with some friends—a kind of farewell cruise—and troll around with us for kings. It would be a fine day, with friends, and two *Albatross*es side by side. I would be able to watch the original boat move through the water off Hatteras Island for its eighth decade.

As we headed out of the marina and down the Pamlico Sound toward the inlet, there was hardly a wisp of wind. The ferry from Ocracoke passed us. It held a single milk truck. In its wake, we could see Tall Bill headed out west aboard *Net Results* to harvest his gill nets. As we turned east into the inlet, Ernie was commenting on how the inlet channel had shifted south and west so recently and so quickly. He'd never seen the likes of it except, of course, after a storm. He wondered what was making it shoal up so suddenly. The coast guard was going to have to sprinkle some new buoys through here. Ernie liked the coast guard, but they could also be a pain in the ass and dumb as stumps about the sea, especially by old-timer standards, and so it was fashionable to complain about them. Hatteras fishermen couldn't tell Polack jokes because there were no Polacks down here. The coast guard was a handy stand-in. "I swear," Ernie said, "The coast guard takes the dumb ones and says, 'You're on buoy detail.'" He then proceeded to give a logical layout for the new buoys in a tone that suggested that any third grader could get it right and that the coast guard surely wouldn't.

As he talked, I watched the sun come up a brilliant orange and red and fuchsia directly in line with our bow. High up to the south of the growing light, an electric-orange vapor trail pointed down the coast. Behind us the pale disc of a full moon lingered long after the last stars had gone home. Ernie finished his lecture and looked over his shoulder toward the sound.

He smiled: "Lynne and I got married between the sun and the moon, like this." That was almost ten years ago. I remembered Lynne telling me about it. They'd gotten married up in Manteo, she said, and had liked it so much they got married again a year later in 1993. That was in the town of Waves north of Hatteras Village. And then, she said, the sun was setting over the sound and the full moon was rising over the ocean. Bracketed by heavenly bodies, the two *Albatross*es headed out with their cargo of warm memories and young love and imminent parting. I was up on the bridge with Ernie. A voice on the radio asked for a moment of silence. Then the same voice, that of the captain of another vessel outward bound, said, "Father, thank you for allowing us to do what we do. We pray for those we've lost; we appreciate the calm waters you have given us today and for the great bounty of your seas. Amen." Ernie added his amen. There were high spirits and laughing aboard the *Albatross* behind us.

We turned northeast and headed up the beach toward Cape Point and Diamond Shoals. We needed to get some live fatback for the king mackerel. We cruised along the beach, Ernie eyeing the depth-finder looking for a good mark—a nice bright red cluster that indicated a school of baitfish —where he could signal Karen to toss the nets. Like most charter captains, Ernie used 100- to 150-foot lengths of sinking gill nets to catch bait. These were nets whose bottom weights were heavier than their corked top fringe. They were buoyed on each end and sat on the bottom, a nylon curtain the fatback would blunder into.

Ernie wasn't finding a good mark, but when he saw scattered red, in twenty-five feet of water, he called to Karen to set the nets. Soon there were two buoys behind us, 150 feet apart. Then another set near the first one. Other captains were complaining about the scattered baitfish. Ernie was too. As he swung the *II* around to pick up the nets, he said "I think we're gonna get a water haul" —meaning we'd bring in nothing but the ocean. But as we retrieved the nets, we got a scattering of fatback. And then some more. And a few more. Soon the live well was filled. Justin and his friends nearby in the *Albatross* were also slowly getting what they would need.

Spurgeon Stowe came on the radio, with that unmistakable brogue. "Ernie! Come on out here to this seventy-four-degree water." Spurgeon had the *Miss Hatteras* out in the warm waters of the Gulf Stream. He was near the Diamond Shoals Light Station, about fourteen miles out. He was apparently into some fish. We headed out to join him. The wind had picked up from the southwest, but it was still pleasant, single-sweater fishing weather. When the water temperature gauge rose dutifully at the edge of the Gulf

Stream, Ernie called down to Karen to put the lines out. We were going to troll live fatback, exclusively, using a tandem rig of 4/0 treble hooks, one through the nose and the other behind the dorsal fin, but not so far back that it impaired the swimming motion of the baitfish. We ran out two flat lines, one long shotgun line from up on the bridge, and a longline from each outrigger so that the fatback would be dipping in and out of the water with the pitch of the boat.

Things went slowly. Nothing doing. Up on the bridge, Ernie and I got to talking about his years as a student at North Carolina State in Raleigh. He'd gone there because he'd wanted to be an engineer and N.C. State was the engineering school in the state system. Chapel Hill was education and liberal arts. Ernie went to State from 1963 until his graduation in 1967 but changed his course of study and left with a bachelor's degree in science (he'd later get an M.Ed. in counseling). Prior to his going to State, Ernie had been off the island only a handful of times, to a few 4-H camps and to visit his uncle and aunt in Norfolk, the first reasonable population density you hit when you got off the Outer Banks some 150 miles up from Hatteras Village. He'd had five teachers in his four years at the little high school on Hatteras Island. He'd never seen a football game because there weren't enough boys in his high school to make up a team. He was scared to death when he got to Raleigh, North Carolina. "It took me a year to ride a public bus," he recalls. "I knew how to get on the bus, but I had no idea how to make it stop . . . you know, pull that cord overhead." He laughed. We dieseled on. Then he added, "But all along, I was very aware that I knew a world, a way of life—this one right here—that no one else knew. That knowledge always bolstered me, made me feel good about myself."

Ernie suddenly swung around and yelled to Karen. Something had spooked the two portside fatbacks. The rod tips were twitching as they swam frantically, trying to get away from something. The one hanging from the outrigger clip got so panicked that it pulled the line out of the clip. Karen picked up the outrigger pole and held it a moment feeling for some activity. She then reeled it in. The back half of the fatback was gone, sheared off as if run through a band saw, right behind the rear treble hook. The flat line fatback was abridged too, but more raggedly. It set an odd and frustrating pattern of half baits for the next hour or so. Ernie was clearly frustrated. "Man, these kings are either real smart or real lucky. They're feeding at supersonic speeds and missing the rear treble hook by millimeters."

Then slowly our luck began to change. We were getting hook-ups, fish that made it all the way to the box. Eight-, ten-, twelve-pounders. Feisty and fun, but smallish. At least it was action. Then the shotgun rod went off like a cannon. We had known it was going to because we'd been watching the spread and seen this fish, a huge one, come clear out of the water twice chasing the panicked fatback. The third time was the charm. I reached up and took the rod from Ernie leaning over the bridge and slipped the butt end in the fighting belt around my waist. I braced my knees against the side of the boat and watched the reel scream as though I were free-spooling the bumper of a car. I tightened down the drag just a little, and finally the fish slowed. I began the pump-and-reel to get back my lost line. It came steadily but very grudgingly. I knew what was going to happen because I'd been warned. Fifteen minutes of back-burn to put line back on my reel ended in a heartbeat when the king saw the boat. The reel started screaming again, this time across and almost under the stern of the *Albatross*. I had to race to the transom and hold the rod as far out over the water as possible to keep the line away from the props. The reel screamed on, then slowed to a crackle. I started in again to get back what I'd lost. By this time, my arms had pretty much stopped working, and my knees stung from their bracing and banging against the wood sides of the boat.

Then the fish started acting oddly, veering erratically, playing dead, staying up almost on the surface. And then up on the surface: forty feet out in the light swell, we could see that the big fish had become tail-wrapped—the line tangled around its rear fins so that it faced away from the boat and was in effect hog-tied. It would be easy to break the line like this, so I made my dead arms come to as much life as they could muster. Twenty feet from the boat, the now-placid king started twitching and trying to dart. It seemed odd. Then we saw why. A huge hammerhead shark rose up to the surface behind the king and headed straight for it. "Damn! Look at that!" It was Ernie up on the bridge. "Get that fish in! Quick!" I cranked sloppily. Karen was next to me with the gaff. The king planed compliantly across the surface of the water, exhausted or resigned to the bad ending that waited on either end of it. The shark was gaining. It was a good nine feet long, its stalk-shaped head easily three feet across. Ernie had never seen one that big. I certainly hadn't. I wanted my fish badly, but I was glad I wasn't the one who had to lean over the side and face that shark. Karen would have to do that. She'd have to do what Hemingway said only the honorable bullfighters did—work in the territory of the bull: when the bull came past, the brave bullfighter held his purity of line, exposed the femoral artery in his thigh to the horn of the bull. It was easy to fake it, to pretend you were doing that, when you were really bending over at the waist and staying as far away as you could from this frightening beast who was faster than a polo pony and could throw one straight over his back.

The big king and the shark met at the boat. Then I couldn't see what was happening. Karen was in front of me, wedged in next to the fish box. She had the leader, and then the top half of her went over the side. Then there was a big splash, and I saw her legs straining. Her upper half reappeared. She was holding the white gaff handle down close to the hook as she staggered backward and a huge king came into the boat headfirst, skidding across the top of the fish box and crashing to the deck. I looked back over the side. The hammerhead had turned and was swimming toward a flat line bait. "Bring in the lines!" Ernie was yelling. Karen and I grabbed a pole apiece and began reeling to keep the bait away from the cruising shark. We got them all in. The hammerhead sank smoothly out of sight. Then we turned back to the king. It was big and beautiful—an aqua-dynamic missile with finishing nails for teeth and ancient coins for eyes, dark on top and silver beneath, but really no one color at all so much as a sheen, a desert shimmer of tea greens and pinks, sage, vermilions, peach, lime and bleached blue and parchment. Of the gifted fish illustrators from Hoen to Jardine to Bloch and D'Orbigny, and Sherman F. Denton, only Denton, working at the dawn of the twentieth century, had consistently captured the restless rainbow of color in fish like the king mackerel. I always thought his touches were whimsy, self-indulgent poetry, but they weren't. They were true, brilliantly, subtly true. I kept the fish box open and stared at the king, trying to fix the torpedo-shaped painting in my memory before the world turned him dull and flat. Even with her adrenaline still racing, Karen seemed to understand when I tried to answer her question about what I was doing.

It was getting late and Ernie had a charter fishermen's meeting to go to that night, so we decided to head in. In the growing darkness a mile from the mouth of the inlet, we put out a couple of lines for stripers, but up ahead we spotted the *Albatross* becalmed; so we brought the lines in and went over to see what was up. Justin had noticed the boat running hotter and hotter on the way in, and instead of risking a burned-up diesel, he had shut down and waited for us. As it turned out, the impeller was shot, and the engine probably would have burned up. They threw us a line, and we towed her into Hatteras Harbor Marina. It was dark and getting very cold and Ernie would miss his meeting, but that was fine. We were back safe and sound, Justin and Karen were holding hands near Ernie, and the fishing had been good. A Citation or trophy-sized king mackerel was thirty pounds. Mine weighed in at forty-two pounds. Justin and his friends slid some big fish

The author with a king
mackerel, fall 2003
(Courtesy of Ernie Foster)

up onto the dock planks too. One was a thirty-eight-pounder. They said it
had come clear out of the water, like a missile, five straight times after the
bobbing fatback on the outrigger. Each time, Justin said they all gave it a
woofing cheer as if it were Shaquille thunder-dunking a basketball. Finally
it got the bait, and all hell broke loose—minus a curious hammerhead. We
were all tired and cold and hungry, but Ernie hooked up a drop light at the
cleaning table on the dock and filleted two of the fish. He took a couple of
my fillets, including one of the Citation slabs, and the next day presented
me with more delicious smoked mackerel than I could consume in a year.
My friends in Memphis would be friendlier than ever.

At 5:30 the next morning, I checked the wind using my two usual indi-
cators. Not good. Southwest and gusting. And the Weather Channel was
hedging on afternoon conditions. I got myself ready just in case. At 5:45 I
heard diesels and looked out the door and saw the *Tuna Duck* headed out

The *Albatross* fleet was the first to employ women as mates. A reunion picture of the pioneers. From left to right: Dita Young, JoAnne Coyle, Carol Teague Etheridge, and Karen Crawley. (Courtesy of Ernie Foster)

of the marina. A mixed sign. Then at 6:00 I heard the familiar *Albatross* diesels. Or diesel. When I got around the corner of the motel to the boat, Tall Bill and Bryan were closing the cover of the starboard engine on the *Albatross III*. It wouldn't turn over. When we were under way, they said, it would wake up.

I guessed that meant we were going out, and I eagerly clambered aboard. Bryan was busy with the equipment, and Bill was saying we needed to stop to fuel up at Oden's Dock next door. No one mentioned the weather, so I didn't either. While they were pumping diesel out on the end the dock, I went into Oden's store to get us some coffee. A handful of captains and mates were gathered around a small table covered with a laminated Cape Hatteras depth chart. They were talking darkly about the forecast. They weren't going anywhere today.

I got back to the boat, and we headed for the tiny marina entrance a hundred yards away. Bryan and Tall Bill were still busy getting the *Albatross* ready to go, so I gave them their coffee and climbed up onto the dock. I didn't mention the store conversation. Just then Ernie drove up. He wanted to take the rest of the king mackerel over to the fish house and sell them. They were still in the fish box aboard the *Albatross II.* I heaved them up from the box to Ernie on the dock, where he put their stiff bodies nose down in a plastic garbage can. Their parchment tails leaned up and out of the container, like an old, dried flower arrangement. We set the three garbage cans on the tailgate of Ernie's truck for the short drive over to Jeffrey's fish house. When we got there, we each grabbed a handle on a garbage can and lifted it down. The tails hit me in the face, knocking my glasses onto the gravel parking lot. Ernie was laughing hard. "You know who the real cowboy is?" Ernie asked as we lifted the next can down from the tailgate. This time I leaned away from the tail bouquet. I bit.

"No, Ernie, how can you tell the real cowboy?"

"Well, he's the guy who sits in the middle of the truck seat. That way he doesn't have to drive and he doesn't have to get out and open the gates to drive through." Then he added, "Now, do you know how to tell the real fisherman?"

"OK, how?"

"It's the guy on the side without the tails." Then he laughed again, slapping his leg. As he did, I spun the third can around on the tailgate so that the tails leaned toward him.

Inside the small fish packinghouse, it was cold and concrete and wet. One of the men at the culling table nearby greeted Ernie. Another man appeared from a small room that was the source of a Merle Haggard song, and they scuffed over in their white rubber boots to see what we had. They did not assess the fish like sportsmen. This was business calculus—size and pricing. Nothing was said. The men dragged the garbage containers over to a small room heaped with chipped ice and open cardboard boxes of fish of various sorts. The room was kept cool by heavy plastic strips forming a curtain of sorts. In this room they sorted and tossed our kings onto a hanging scale. We had 105 pounds of large kings and twenty-two pounds of mediums (king mackerel under fifteen pounds). They'd fillet them here, pack them in ice and cardboard boxes here, and take their cut. Then the fish would be sent on to the Fulton Fish Market in New York City, where you had to hope for a good price. Right now, Ernie was told, kings were going for around a dollar a pound.

Before Ernie dropped me back at the *Albatross* boats, I stood up on the tailgate of his truck. The Pamlico Sound was a moving Morse code of whitecaps as far as you could see.

"Is Bill planning to go out today?" Ernie asked.

"Yes."

Ernie didn't say anything. We agreed we'd meet up later, but left it vague. Ernie had his usual busy, odd-jobs day ahead of him.

I joined Tall Bill up on the bridge. He was deep into his morning cigarettes and coffee. If he was concerned about anything, it was his rear end. He'd sat down in the cup-shaped fiberglass captain's chair on the bridge without checking. It held a couple of inches of cold rainwater from a shower last night, and now his pants had inherited it. "Jesus, I'm going to have a wet ass the whole way!" And then he laughed at himself. The closest Bill came to mentioning the ominous weather was his explanation that, with this southwest wind, we'd be heading south out of the inlet today down around Portsmouth Island below Ocracoke, and then fish our way back. I assumed that was so that we would be fishing in a following sea and not be pounding our brains out at the same time we were trying to catch bluefins. Hatteras Inlet was running two-to-three-foot swells, and when we got outside and swung south, it got even bumpier. It was very cold. This wasn't going to be like yesterday. No bluebird day this day. Spray was flying into the boat from the starboard side in a steady rhythm, so I went inside (unlike her older sisters, the *Albatross III* had an enclosed and heated cabin) and put on my foul weather gear.

Going south, we were up against both the wind and the wave action. We were taking a beating, but not a bad one. For some reason, I thought of the gray-muzzled hunting dogs I used to see in the back of pickups in the Arkansas Ozarks where I often fly-fished. The trucks would be parked in a farmer's field near one river or another, and the dogs would be in the truck beds, dreamy eyed yet alert, often in a cold drizzle, just standing there happily, every once in a while shaking themselves in sections, their tags clinking, and then resuming their happy stares. The *Albatross III* seemed to be doing the same thing. Her other engine had long ago kicked in, and she was in her element and happy.

We made our way the length of Ocracoke Island, across the mouth of the inlet at its southern end, and reached the shores of Portsmouth Island. Ocracoke and Portsmouth weren't islands in the traditional biomorphic sense and shape; rather they were part of that thin ribbon of sand called the Outer Banks that started up near the Virginia border. I had never been down the ribbon this far. Portsmouth Island represented the northern end of the Cape Lookout National Seashore, which was a continuation of the Cape Hatteras National Seashore. At one point in the late eighteenth century, the town of Portsmouth, located on the northern tip of Portsmouth Island and the Ocracoke Inlet, was a flourishing port and the largest town in North Carolina. In 1846, however, when a storm opened Hatteras and Oregon Inlets, coastal trade was drawn up the coast. Then during the Civil War the citizens of Portsmouth fled the advancing Union army. Afterward few returned home. Today Portsmouth is a ghost town.

Unlike Hatteras and Ocracoke, Portsmouth Island, from the *Albatross III*, showed no signs of life. The ghost town was apparently tucked behind the massive dunes somewhere. If you looked closely the only human evidence you could make out was a line of barely perceptible telephone poles behind the deserted beaches and the dune line. Surely what I was looking at was much the same that Giovanni da Verrazano, the first European to explore north of Cape Fear, gazed out upon in 1524—a turbulent sea mottled with foam and shards of chromium light reaching a long, steady brushstroke of sand topped with green as far as the eye could see.

Finally Bill swung the *Albatross III* east and headed out for the Gulf Stream. The wind was up to fifteen to twenty knots, and the seas had built to four-to-five-foot swells. We were rocking and rolling to a rhythmic clatter of gear and a pulsing whistle through the outrigger lines. We were going out to fish the temperature breaks along the edges of the Gulf Stream. Here, where the warm water from the Gulf Stream mixed with the inside southerly push of colder water was where bait often got trapped, where nutrients churned up by the eddying currents attracted hungry predators. Bill said the ideal temperature for bluefin this time of year was fifty-seven to sixty-one degrees. Bluefin fishing had been lousy so far this season. Just too warm. Rumors were that the fish were holding north of here. A real muscular cold snap might get them moving south, but that hadn't happened yet. Bluefin were around, just not in numbers, and, oddly, a sizable number had been caught in close in six to ten fathoms—skinny water by bluefin standards.

Up on the bridge, the pitching of the boat was magnified. Bill complained that he'd take the *Albatross II* any day over the *III*. The *III* we were in was wider up front and tended to push or plow, he said. (Before the day was over, we'd get a graphic demonstration of what he meant). Ernie had ordered the *Albatross III* to be a carbon copy of the *Albatross II*, but it wasn't. "They must not have used plans. Just eyeballed it," Bill concluded. The two boats differed in length and width. He went on. "When you dock the *Albatross II*, and you throw one engine in reverse and one forward, she seems to have a perfect pivot point, right in the middle. Not so the *Albatross III*. The same maneuver with the *III* gets the stern swinging, but the bow wants to stay stationary."

Bill called down to Bryan to put the rods out. We'd fish only two rods with those big, gold Penn 130s, eighty-pound-test line, 120-pound-test leader, with ballyhoo for bait. The wind continued to build, but riding with it was more topographical than teeth-rattling, as it had been on the ride south. We trolled for two hours. Nothing doing. Bill was on the radio. Only three boats had gone out of Hatteras today: us, the *Tuna Duck*, and *Contender.* Three other boats had gone out of Morehead City down below Cape Fear. That was it. Six boats had the whole ocean to themselves, and I was willing to bet we were easily the smallest of the six. The *Tuna Duck* was a sleek, fifty-foot, custom-built job; *Contender* wasn't much smaller. The *Albatross III* had to stand on tiptoes to make forty-three feet.

Everyone was taking a beating. It was apparently now acceptable—and probably wise—to talk about the weather conditions. They were clearly deteriorating. The Morehead City boats had lost a fish and boated another. The Hatteras three had been shut out thus far. Bill was working hard to keep the boat crisscrossing the temperature breaks. It wasn't easy holding any kind of line up and down the swells with a strong wind. I got the feeling that Bill had gone out today only because he knew how badly I'd wanted to go. Tomorrow's forecast was worse, and I was leaving the day after that. He must have been reading my mind as we bucked and pitched along. He began talking about his fishing philosophy regarding customers. "I fish for my customers. For a family of five or six in the summer, I don't try to bail sixty dolphin in the hot sun. I try to put them on some good-sized fish so they can sit down and bring them in, so they can have time to sit and visit and enjoy the day. What are they going to do with sixty dolphin anyway?" By way of summary, he added, "I try to cater to the customer, not the catch." On we trolled. Below, hanging onto the fighting chair with Bryan was even more dramatic. The swells were up to seven and eight feet now. You looked up at them down here. Except for the bright sun, this looked like some old film footage from *Victory at Sea.*

Then Bryan yelled, "Here he comes!" And a split second later the portside rod went off like a rocket. I was staring at the spool of the 130. I had never seen line strip off a reel that fast. "We got a good one," Bryan said. "Get in the chair! Quick!" In moments I was strapped and harnessed and trussed up like a Christmas goose. Bryan lifted the rod and brought it over and shoved the butt into the metal gimbal between my legs. The reel was still screaming. "Hang on to it! Be careful!" I heeded him as he attached a clip and a line to each side of the reel. Unlike the bluefin, I wasn't going anywhere, which suited me fine. I'd heard stories of inattentive anglers getting yanked over the transom by these freight liners. The more I resembled Hannibal Lecter in stir, the better. Bryan crouched behind me, keeping the fighting chair and rod pointed at the fish, calmly giving instructions.

My virginity was once again in play. This was my first bluefin, but I knew the drill, had studied it so I could do my part. Let the fish make its initial run (you're not going to stop him anyway), and when he slows, turn him, and reel and pump so he doesn't get a second wind. Conditions couldn't have been much worse to perform these maneuvers, especially with a good-sized fish. The *Albatross III* was rising and falling two stories at a time in these swells. And the wind had picked up. At one point, as the boat rose up, I could see my line telephone-poled in and out of three massive swells, one behind the other. What Tall Bill was doing, how hard he was working up on the bridge I didn't have time to imagine, maneuvering the boat to match the bluefin's moves, angling the *Albatross III* just right, backing it down when the fish took too much line, moving ahead to help pick up the slack in the line. It was almost impossible to keep a tight line in these conditions, but we were working together, doing our best. Several times we thought we'd lost him. But Bill tightened up the line using the boat, and I cranked as fast as my dead arms could. Miraculously the fish was there again. And off he went on another reel-howling run. "Show him who's boss," Bryan said from a crouch behind me. "Show him who's boss." Bryan had no idea of the Pavlovian hold that phrase had on me. I flashed on Key West, a monstrous tarpon . . .

Only after this bluefin drama was over, and I was lying in the cabin exhausted, winded, unable to lift my arms, my fingers still in a curl, did I have time to think about it. "Show him who's boss." It was the early summer of 1997. Mo and I had gone to Key West and rented a beautiful place just off raucous Duval Street. It had an old tin roof and had once been a little cigar factory. We were vacationing, but we were also seeking respite from a depressing situation. Mo's father had died recently. Her family was very close, all seven of them, and it had been hard on everyone — anyone, really, who had known Ed. He had been a doctor at the Mayo Clinic in Minnesota. When I was courting his beautiful daughter in the late 60s, and I met him for the first time, I asked him what his specialty was. He said he was a bronchoscopist. Trying to be clever, I said, "I thought they were extinct." He just looked down at me, not a single part of his six-foot-six-inch frame smiling. He eventually forgave me my idiocy, and for the next twenty-plus years, we—Mo and I and our two children—joined Ed and his wife Winnie and a constantly changing and growing gaggle of brothers and sisters, nieces and nephews, cousins and friends at their lake house outside Hayward, in northern Wisconsin. Ed loved fishing almost as much as I did, and it's safe to say I spent more time in a boat with him than with any other human being on the face of God's aqueous earth. Fishing for muskies. Always muskies. The space between muskies is often as vast as West Texas and so we had ample time to talk about almost everything under the sun, and sometimes the pouring rain. In the process we became fast friends.

Some evenings, after dinner, looking out at the stars over the lake and deep into a second bottle of Chardonnay, Ed and I would swap fishing stories. Among my favorites in his repertoire were his trips as a young boy to Miami and then on by Hemingway-era boat to Key West to fish for tarpon. He would describe how shoals of tarpon, pushing wakes ahead of them and rolling to take a look at you, would shoot past like the tails of a thousand comets, how the fish often proved too much for the linen line and the old bamboo rods, and how they would explode the drags on the old Penn Senator reels.

My mission during our trip to Key West, I had decided, was to catch a tarpon for Ed, and then to march directly up Duval Street to Sloppy Joe's Bar, Hemingway's favorite watering hole, and hoist a frozen margarita to my departed partner. I hooked up with a guide named Jeff Burns, whose speedy center-console boat was docked a stone's throw from Mallory Square at the foot of Duval Street, where crowds gathered every evening to drink, watch the street theater, and of course take home movies of the "Most Beautiful Sunset in America." Jeff had come down to Key West some time ago to train Navy Seals at the facility there. He had fallen in love with the Keys, a woman, and fishing (he didn't indicate the order of events), and was guiding now full time since he'd done his twenty and retired. He talked about what was going to happen this morning. He said we'd be free-spooling live bait just about a mile outside the harbor. When the tarpon hit, he said (not if, but when), he would show me how to lock down on them, how to bend forward when the fish jumped. If he had raised his voice just a notch, had frowned just a little bit more, he would have had me shouting, "Sir! Yes, sir!" But he was patient and kind, at least until he got to the last part of his lecture. Then he was a Navy Seal who had reconned the enemy. "These fish are incredibly smart. If they sense, even for an instant, that they have a chance to escape, they'll fight even harder, and we'll be here all day. Right from the get-go, you've got to show them who's boss!" "Show them who's boss." There it was. I was eager, but I hadn't a clue how to send that assertive message through a screaming spool of eighty-pound-test line to a fish who spoke no English.

Well, the school came, and I got tight to something that rose out of the water like a chrome-slick tailfin. In moments it was apparent who would be calling the shots. The best I could hope for was a promotion, and that seemed less and less likely. My boss, Mr. Silver, was large and in charge. I moved to the bow and watched as the fish made for crowded Key West harbor. I turned him a couple of times, but he spun me as many and dipped me too. This was a tango, and I was wearing the dress. Before long Jeff was maneuvering us around anchored sailboats, vintage Chris-Crafts, and sleek yachts dotting the aquamarine waters between Mallory Square and a nearby island that framed the harbor. After about an hour, the Boss came up to the boat, almost voluntarily it seemed, and lay still. He seemed moody, even contemptuous, impatient to get shut of us. We released him. He swam off with slow dignity. I saluted him. Jeff was smiling behind me. I had done it, thanks to a skillful skipper and as much skill and dignity as I could muster.

It was easier for me to be the boss at Sloppy Joe's where, in its cool, late-morning emptiness, I saluted Ed with not one, but three margaritas. Mo was reading under the bougainvillea when I got back. I told her I thought I'd lie down for a while.

"Show him who's boss." After forty-five minutes with this bluefin, my back and shoulders were aching, and I had to will my arms to pull and crank. Half the time they wouldn't listen. Little by little, nonetheless, we gained on him, cranking, backing the boat down. Thank God the stern of the *Albatross* was round. If it had been conventional—square across—we would have been soaked. The fish was twenty feet from the boat, a huge dark shadow in the heaving, sparkling water. And then he was gone. He had pulled the hook. Bryan stood up behind me and uttered, "Damn!"

I wasn't disappointed. Maybe I was too tired to be, but I'd seen many bluefin before—at various docks, on film, at Ernie's office, and so on. They weren't breathtaking works of art still vital beside the boat, the way, say, marlin and sailfish, or Citation dolphin were. Bluefins were interior line-men, iridescent blue-steel engine blocks with eyes as black as the darkness, eyes that would never look at you, but willfully look right past you to something more significant in the middle distance. It made you feel small. Such a fish will take your spiritual measure, all the while hidden like a priest behind the screen of a confessional. The spiritual news may not be good, like the writing Daniel saw on the wall at Belshazzar's feast. *Mene, mene, tekel, upharsin.* Weighed, weighed, and found wanting. Not the fish. You. What if the line doesn't break? What if the fish is stronger, smarter than you? What do you do then?

All sports test your mettle in one way or another. But this kind of blue-water fishing ups the ante in special ways. Certainly a great part of the attraction of fishing is the chance for victory, of landing the big one. But the other equally powerful attraction, unique to fishing (the attraction beginners don't understand and aficionados of fishing don't often talk about), is the possibility of defeat, not just coming home skunked, but hooking up to something out there that gets the better of you, humbles—even humiliates—you, makes you lose control in the most alien (we are land creatures) and unstable of nature's settings, so that you come home not just empty-handed, but spiritually chastened. No other sport, in its practice, offers such a wide margin for self-definition. For the first time in my life I had been attached to something from another world whose strength and will seemed superior to my own. Determination was not enough. I needed a bucket harness and rod clips, and, even then, this hidden force threatened to make a coward of me. A tarpon is a huge, silver quadriceps, often frightening in its sudden whip and torque, but more often it displays its strength not so much in brutish, roadhouse violence and raw power as in muscular arabesques, pliés, ballonnés, and Gypsy Rose shimmies, which both dazzle and rattle your teeth. Bluefins fight you in the dark.

We talked awhile about the magnificent mystery we'd just glimpsed. Then Bryan set about rerigging the rod. I went into the cabin to think about who was boss. I found myself hoping we didn't get another hook-up. Having to ask Bryan to take over for me would be the probable outcome, and I didn't want that. We trolled for another hour. I finally got my legs back under me and went out into the weather. I went up to the bridge and told Bill I'd had my close encounter and was happy and humbled. He said that the *Tuna Duck* and *Contender* were headed in and that we might want to start thinking about doing the same. Fine. My arms and back and shoulders still held the ghost traces of that fish. It was like an arm you lost but thought was still there. That was enough.

As we headed back to Hatteras Inlet, we saw the *Tuna Duck* a mile of so off to starboard. Our twin 210s were no match for her drive train. She'd easily beat us to the inlet. *Contender* was somewhere behind us. The seas were quartering as they had on our run earlier out to the Gulf Stream, and the pitching and rolling was getting more dramatic. Bryan and I held on down below and talked when we could. Bryan was saying that he learned almost everything he knew about fishing, from rigging mackerel to piloting a boat, from Ernal Sr.'s brother, Bill Foster. Ernal, he said, was a nice man, but got kind of grumpy and resisted change as he grew older. "Bill would never laugh at you for trying something new," Bryan said, but added with a smile, "he sure would laugh if it didn't work." I asked Bryan if he'd ever been scared out here, either as a captain or a mate. He answered quickly. "No. Never. I've never seen anyone afraid out here. If you're afraid, you can get in a lot of trouble in a hurry. People who get afraid out here either don't come out here anymore or they disappear."

We were approaching the mouth of Hatteras Inlet. Bill was calling from the bridge. We looked around. The humpback whales were here again, two of them, very much closer this time. One rolled on its side and you could see the long, distinguishing pectoral fin, blunt and scalloped, dappled white on its leading edge. Finally it righted itself, sent its flukes into the bright air and disappeared. Bryan smiled, pleased to see them. I was transfixed, once again. Lynne had recently told me about her first encounter with hump-backs off Hatteras. It was her first trip out on the *Albatross*, that fateful char-ter that would lead to her union with the captain. "Ernie actually pulled in the lines, and took us over where he'd seen whales before. And there they were! We were so close to them we could hear them breathing, and we actu-ally got splashed by their spouting!" In a place like Hatteras, nature offers a wonderful running conversation in images, not words, but we seldom listen. We're too busy living in it to pay it much mind. But every once in a while, maybe because of our inattention or because we're ready for the conversion experience, nature will raise up a pair of gleaming black flukes into the brilliant, biting air, or send a marlin spiraling into that same air like a muscle-bound parenthesis, just to remind us what we've been missing. It was hard not to believe that there was some kind of divinity glistening in this common miracle I'd just witnessed at the mouth of Hatteras Inlet.

We soon turned our attention to the narrow mouth of the inlet. The *Tuna Duck* had made it through apparently, but the water in the inlet looked bad. I had read that in a good wind, the seas will race through Hatteras Inlet at twenty to twenty-five miles an hour. The *Tuna Duck* could probably outrun such swells, but the *Albatross* sure couldn't. And these weren't just swells. These were fifteen- to twenty-footers and many of them were curling and breaking. The secret, I knew, under such circumstances was to stay on the backside of the wave, to ride the shoulder in. If you saw that it was going to break, then you slowed down. That's what Bill was doing, staying up on its shoulder. We seemed to be doing all right though Bill was working hard to hold a line. Then behind us, Bryan and I saw a huge wave building. The top of it curled and foamed a little, and it looked as though it would roll under us. But then it seemed to slow down and gather itself behind us. We were drawn back with it. It built itself into a perfect curl, and the *Albatross III* was poised at its apex. Instead of letting us settle onto its safe, sloping backside, it caught us and threw us down its cupped face like a surfboard. Bryan and I, facing backward, watched, frozen, as we shot down the wave above us.

When we reached the bottom, the *Albatross III* pushed, just as Bill had complained it had a tendency to do. It nosed deep into the water. We yawed to starboard, almost sideways, and heeled over radically. Everything loose in the boat clanked and clattered to the port side. The outrigger nearly touched the water. For a moment I thought we were going over, but Bill somehow righted us and got us back in line with the channel and the serial swells. After picking myself up and reassembling my parts, I climbed the ladder to the bridge to see if Bill was all right. He turned around and grinned: "How'd you like that ride?" Bryan said he'd had the same thing happen to him, that in bad weather it wasn't all that unusual. But I sensed it wasn't all that usual either, including worse outcomes than the one we'd just had.

I remembered clearly one late afternoon in the late summer of 1958, when I was fourteen years old, watching from the end of the 900-foot jetty in front of our old beach house in New Jersey as huge charter and pleasure boats tried to get in through the twenty-five-foot waves curling and breaking unexpectedly in the mouth of Manasquan Inlet, watching as they surfed down the face of the wave, engines racing to try to beat its curl and crash, only to burrow in at the bottom of the ride, dig in bow first at the base of the nearly vertical green wall and swing beam on to the heavy water and roll over as the wall advanced, turn upside down and disappear completely for a moment as the huge whitecap of the wave fell onto its upturned hull, watching as other boats did the same, broached at the wave's base and the captain flung from the bridge, but then somehow righted themselves and, engines wide open, run themselves driverless up onto the rock jetty where I sat, splitting open their bows on the rocks, so that I could see inside, see the forward berths, the pillows and coats and orange canvas bags, watching as the wave tossed the occupants overboard, to be picked up with the captain by the coast guard idling in two boats just inside the deadly surf (the sea is a giver, but it is also a gatherer, and today, that day those many years ago, it was harvesting).

Tall Bill hadn't been afraid surfing down that wave in the mouth of Hatteras Inlet. Bryan hadn't been afraid when we spun sideways at the bottom and stood on our ear. I had been afraid. But as young Bryan and all the old salts eventually let on, there was a world of difference between fear and respect, and more than a world of difference in the result that can happen at the butt end of each of those disparate emotions.

At the house a few days earlier, Ernie got to talking about his father running the charter business in the early days, when you could count the number of charter boats on the fingers of one hand. "I was just a kid, and I'd ask him if I could do something with my friends and he'd invariably say, 'No, too dangerous.' And I'd say, 'Daddy, you go out into the ocean in a wood boat with an old car engine you found in a junkyard, with no radio, no nothing, and sometimes you're the only boat out there. You tell me that isn't dangerous?' You know what he'd say? 'That's different.' That's different!" Ernie laughed. "You couldn't argue with the man."

Again, the subtext of the story wasn't merely the stubbornness of Outer Bankers. It was wisdom, respect. Ernal wasn't being foolhardy. No doubt he'd done the calculus of going out to sea in a wooden boat with an old flathead six, and, short of an act of God, the equation worked. Go with the grain, steer around the knot, and you'll get to the end of the juniper just fine. Ernal Foster Sr. was reticent, as most Outer Bankers were, but their few words cut to the chase, and sometimes to the quick, or the spare language reached out and gave you an awkward hug. "*Hey mister is this here* Albatross *air conditioned?*" "*Well, sure it is. Just open the cabin windows and you'll get all the air you want.*"

Years ago, Ernal Sr. was sitting in the middle of the kitchen in their old house next door to the net house. He was heating some metal with a blowtorch, making his own gaff. Little Ernie was at that inquisitive age and fascinated by the bright blue flame. "Don't touch that, son." A few minutes later: "Don't touch that, son." Again, "Son, I said you'd better not touch that." Then no more words. Ernie shows me the scar he carries on his hand to this day.

... our net ... product, derived by subtracting
our real losses from our real gains ...
—Wendell Berry, *Home Economics*

CHAPTER TEN

Leavetakings and Homecomings

A few days after our bluefin trip and with only two days of my visit left, Tall
Bill had agreed to take me out with him commercial fishing. It was midmorning, and I was sunning myself on the little porch of the *Albatross* office
when Bill's battered F-150 pickup crunched to a stop. Ernie was over on the
II making some minor repairs. Bill squinted through the biting bright-
ness over to me on the porch. We chatted, but the sound of banging metal
on the *Albatross II* was irresistible, so we walked the twenty feet down the
dock and joined Ernie. Soon Ernie and Bill had arranged themselves into
that universal still life: "Two Men Hunched over Engine." I went up to the
bridge. Even I could see, with the wind blowing and with whitecaps on the
water to the east of us, that Tall Bill would be setting his nets in the sound
and not in the ocean.

Finally Bill helped Ernie put the engine cover back on, and we headed
over to his truck. We unloaded baskets of nylon netting and brought them
over to the stern of his boat, *Net Results*, which was moored behind the *Albatross* office. I helped him splice the netting together and feed it, basket by
basket, onto the huge hydraulic wooden spool that took up the back third

of his boat. We worked in silence. Then Ernie wandered over. Bill stood up to take a breather.

"You know, I learned something new the other day. I thought I knew everything about commercial fishing by this time, but, by God, I learned something new."

"Yeah? What's that?" Ernie asked.

"Well, you know angel sharks, right?" Bill turned to me and explained. "Angel sharks are more like large skates with big mouths like monkfish, and they get caught in the nets sometimes." Bill turned back to Ernie. "Well, the usual 10,000 pelicans were there bothering the hell out of me as I'm bringing in the nets . . ."

Ernie interrupted him. "Any of 'em not make it?"

"Yeah, one," Bill replied with a mixture of sadness and annoyance. He turned to me again. "Pelicans have this little hook on the end of their bills. It wears down on the older birds, but on the young ones it's real sharp, and sometimes when they're stealing fish out of the net as I'm bringing it in, the younger ones get tangled up and some of them drown. What's worse," he added, "is that sometimes the metal band the fish and game people put on the pelicans' legs isn't pinched shut all the way and the band gets caught in the net.

"So, anyway," he continued, "I'm hauling in this net and a good-sized angel shark comes up with it. And you know what? I notice that when the pelicans see this shark they take off. Every damn one of them. So I put two and two together, and I get a piece of rope and tie it around the tail of the shark and let him float just off the stern of the boat. Bingo. No more pelicans!"

This was new to Ernie too. "Maybe you should go into business. Make rubber angel sharks and sell them."

Bill finished securing the huge spool with the 1,500 yards of four-foot-wide gill net, and we were ready to go. The northwest wind had even more shoulder in it now. It was going to be a little hilly out there. Bill was hoping to get a haul of sea mullet or gray trout, both of which were going for around ninety cents a pound at the fish houses just now. Gray trout, called kingfish up north, was the winter money fish on the Outer Banks. Fishermen here accounted for 70 percent of the entire East Coast haul, and most of those fish were processed through the fish houses in Dare County. Less desirable were croaker and menhaden, but Bill would take what he could get. Even though the price these days for menhaden was low, they would go fast because the bait shops wanted them to sell to fishermen for striper and redfish bait and to the charter boats to chunk for tuna. Most of the fish, though, would be iced down and sent up to Wanchese on Roanoke Island and then on to Philadelphia or Boston or the Fulton Fish Market in New York, where prices were set.

We moved up into the small stand-up cabin of *Net Results*. It was littered with screwdrivers, pliers, hammers, rubber boots and gloves, old Winston boxes, and rusted aerosol cans. In a few minutes we were out the marina entrance and into the sound. Bill was on the radio. Gregarious and a talker by nature, he clearly enjoyed the banter and camaraderie of the job. He had been doing this for so long he knew almost everyone. He also knew most of the traditional hot spots where the fish hung out. Trouble was, so did many other fishermen. Etiquette was required when hanging your sets in an area. You didn't want to crowd anyone, cut off anyone headed to the same spot.

A high-bowed shrimper strolled along to the east, its net booms out, birds like confetti swirling behind it.

"Who's down south of the pound nets?" Bill asked a skipper.

"Where are you at right now?"

"I'm not trying to crowd you now . . ."

"That's alright."

When we got to our spot, Bill threw the boat into neutral and went back to the spool. Pelicans and gulls of all sorts had settled in on the water behind us. There'd be more if we were bringing in the nets, but we were just setting them out and the birds seemed to know it. They didn't have their hearts in it. They would tomorrow. Bill grabbed one of the many regular small boat anchors with chains and attached it to the bottom of the gill net. From the roof of the cabin he grabbed a buoy with a stick and faded red flag and attached this to the top of the net on the spool. He tossed that rigged end overboard and, satisfied it had deployed correctly, put the boat in gear and slowly spooled off 250 yards of net, then disengaged the engine and put an anchor and buoy on the other end and tossed that over. We drifted downwind for fifty yards or so and repeated the process. Altogether we put out six sets, each time the net neatly crackling off the big spool and over the transom between two vertical pieces of four-inch PVC pipe set up four feet apart. The depth gauge said sixteen feet.

It was 2:00 P.M. and we headed in. On one of the sets, the net had gotten caught up in the propeller, and the engine wasn't acting right—the flywheel maybe—so we had to take it slow. Bill was fussing with his left hand, looking at his index finger and thumb. Then he held them straight out, palm to palm. These were not Dürer's *Praying Hands*. If they were, they'd been left out in the weather since the Renaissance. "Fish poison," Tall Bill allowed. The words were said less as identifying a medical condition than the title of a little science lecture he was about to give. "It's annoying. It's actually not a poison. It's the mucous of the fish. Blues, trout — if you get stuck by their fins, you can get this irritant under your skin . . ."

A big, high-bowed trawler was headed up the sound to the east of us. Bill turned around and looked at him.

"See those guys? He's headed up to Wanchese. Fifteen, twenty years ago, there were forty or fifty of those boats working offshore. They were all out of Wanchese up on Roanoke Island. They were doing great. In the 70s the Feds had moved the U.S. territorial waters out to 200 miles and kicked out the big Russian and Japanese factory boats — so the Wanchese boys were making serious money. But then the market got flooded, and the prices dropped way down. It wasn't economically feasible for them anymore to work way out for high-dollar fish." Bill lit a Winston. "So they moved in here, started harvesting croaker and such. They can work in any weather, pretty much. I can't compete with 'em." A boat like the one we were looking at off in the distance was around eighty-five feet long. It could fill 700 boxes a day easily. A box was a hundred pounds of fish. If they were croaker and the market price was fifty cents a pound, that was $35,000 right there. Twenty boxes a day was a very good haul for Tall Bill Van Druten — a thousand dollars — but out of that had to come all his expenses: the mortgage on the boat, fuel, license, insurance, etc. And then there was the wear and tear and the unexpected stuff, like the drive-train problem we were having right now because of the net getting tangled in the prop. Tomorrow Bill would have to go to the boatyard up in Frisco, pull out the *Net Results*, and hope he could fix it himself.

The trawlers, his own rising overhead — these weren't the only problems for small operators like Bill. There were the frequent market floods — huge numbers of bluefish from New Jersey, kingfish from Florida. There were the crab fishermen from Stumpy Point, Belhaven, Swan Quarter — when the water cooled down and the crabbing slowed, they were converting to gill netting now. More competition. And then the general changes in lifestyle and eating habits. "You know," Bill said, "not too long ago, a wife would go to a fish market or the fresh fish section of her supermarket and take a whole fish home for the family dinner. Nowadays, women are working, and fish, for them, is processed fish, easy-to-prepare breaded squares — you know —

Gordon's or Mrs. Paul's. Croaker and gray trout—which run a poor second, table-wise, to their more popular cousin, the speckled trout—they don't lend themselves to this kind of processing—their flesh is too soft—so the kind of fish we're netting down here aren't as attractive in the new marketplace."

And, of course, fish stocks were up and down, but most steadily down, and the state's response was to open and close, but mostly shorten, the fishing seasons. This was done arbitrarily, it seemed to Bill and others, by sudden proclamation. The commercial quotas on stripers, for instance, would be announced—100,000 pound for gill netters, 100,000 pounds for dory fishermen (seine netters off the beach), and 100,000 pounds for trawlers, with a 47,000-pound buffer. That's 347,000 pounds statewide. The fishing season would be three days long, ten fish per day. "It's crazy," said Bill. "It's also dangerous," he added. "If the weather's bad those three days, the fishermen have to go out anyway. It's their only chance." For Bill it wasn't worth it, especially with stripers holding at around two dollars a pound. Quotas for other commercial species went up and down capriciously, and the fishing seasons for them blinked open and shut and open and shut. Like most workers at the beginning of the manufacturing or market process, commercial fishermen believe the system is run by pointy-headed intellectuals (in this case marine biologists from Nebraska or Mars) who have a fondness for bureaucracy, a cocked ear for politicians, and no clue what it's like to set nets or pick fish. They love to come up with expensive devices for commercial fishermen to buy, like the TED, or turtle excluder device, and they're in bed with the powerful sportfishing lobby, which sees all nets as weapons of mass destruction.

Assaults on a livelihood from so many quarters, in so many guises. No wonder the seething anger, but mostly weary resignation, of the commercial fishermen on the lower Banks. In this way, they're like Steinbeck's Okies in *The Grapes of Wrath*. "Mister, you can't shoot the system," the farmers are told by the land agent serving them notice. "Then who do we shoot?" they ask. "Brother, I don't know. If I did, I'd tell ya."

The next day I went out fishing with Ernie, but I saw Bill at dockside when we came in. He said our set had produced almost 900 pounds of gray trout and some scattered sea mullet. It was a reasonably profitable run. As it turned out, gray trout were currently at eighty cents a pound—not too bad. In a week, it could be thirty cents. Bill told me that two months earlier, he'd set 600 yards of net on undersize croaker and came up with a tremendous haul. He picked fish out of the net from 2:00 P.M. until 10:00. Then he just shoveled them back overboard. "The market price was too depressed," he explained. "It was a shame, but it just wasn't worth it." That's how it went for commercial fisherman; like farmers, they were pawns in a far larger game.

One thing was sure: the fish houses always got their cut—and the wholesalers and retailers got theirs, without the heavy lifting. There were only two fish houses left in Hatteras Village—three, really, but two of them were owned by the same company, and the one at Hatteras Harbor Marina where Ernie and I had taken our king mackerel was scheduled to close. So Bill Van Druten had two choices, which in fact were no choices at all. There was no real market competition for Tall Bill's product. And it was going to get worse —from no competition to no fish houses, period. Everyone knew it. If there was anything commercial fishermen shared, besides being involved in the most dangerous profession this side of logging, it was an unrelieved fatalism. "We're doomed, we're dinosaurs," Bill said on our way back to the dock. "Once upon a time, not too long ago, oh maybe fifteen or eighteen years ago, there were maybe a hundred drop net boats running out of Hatteras Village. Now it's down to thirty, and it's still dropping. We're going to be gone with the wind, but the fish houses will go before we do. That'll be the kiss of death for a lot of us."

It was the "D" word once again. Development. Waterfront property. Deepwater access. In Hatteras Village, and wherever else they existed, fish houses were smelly, financially precarious eyesores sitting on prime condo property. They could be sold for millions, bulldozed in a half a day, and in no time turned into pastel "Soundside" and "Soundview" communities. And so they would be. Until recently, Michael Peele ran the Hatteras Village fish house Bill took his catch to. Peele said of his operation: "There's been a fish house here as long as I can remember, and as long as I live there will always be a fish house here." But then he acknowledged the truth of the matter: "I'm probably the last one in my family to do this." He had a son, but he actively discouraged him from becoming a fisherman. His son was now a massage therapist in Raleigh. Like Ernie Foster and so many others, Michael Peele had no one to pass his business on to.

Peele ran the business, but it was leased out to Quality Foods over in Elizabeth City. Quality had four or five big rigs that it used to deliver seafood to Philadelphia, New York, and smaller markets along the East Coast. They had agreements with Food Lion and Winn-Dixie. In 2002 there was a mild winter and the trout harvest went way down, so far down that Quality Foods stopped sending trucks to Peele's fish house after twenty-six years. Locals feared the inevitable, and developers sat up. But Michael Peele was

Tall Bill aboard *Net Results* (Courtesy of Lynne Foster)

as good as his word. Rather than take the millions and run, he leased his operation to Jeffrey's, another fish dealer in the village. Tall Bill was probably right, though. Peele's gesture was noble, but it was also only a stay of execution. In ten years there would likely be no fish houses in the fishing community of Hatteras Village. Instead there would be a small off-loading facility, just sufficient to get the catch onto a refrigerated truck but not so big that valuable water frontage was wasted in the operation.

Less than twenty years ago, Bill Van Druten went commercial fishing out of Hatteras Village with a hired hand to help with the setting and hauling. In 1986 he cleared $45,000. Twenty years later and twenty years older, Bill Van Druten is still setting nets. His mobile home is paid for and his truck runs most of the time, but he's barely getting by. Today, his concern is more basic: "Ten years from now, where am I going to keep my boat?"

Tall Bill and I had planned to go back out on *Net Results* on my final day. But when the alarm went off at 5:30, I could hear the wind without even getting out of bed. The spot and croaker and menhaden would live to school another day.

The wind was southwest and gusting, and when the sun came out, it had the makings of a nice land-locked day. I decided if I was grounded today, I'd make it literally a ground day—a cemetery day. Hatteras Village had twenty-six cemeteries, and I wanted to visit at least some of them. I began by driving around randomly in the west-side section of the village behind the Burrus Red-and-White market. It became clear very quickly that Hatteras Village was an oxymoron in the making. Snooty street names—The Thames, Bluebird Way—featuring snooty, designer homes competed with streets like Oden's and Midgett Way—the old names, the original streets lined with their old wooden bungalows flanked by the inevitable wooden boat up on blocks or a rusting trailer or dented house trailer accented by old trucks, their windows down (or gone) and fringed with weeds. The smoothly paved roads in the new developments invited you in, then swept you around and out like a bouncer with the grace of Fred Astaire. The pocked and pitted blue-collar streets simply stopped abruptly, forcing you either to back up or pull into someone's driveway to k-turn it back out the way you came in. And all around, without respect to income or class, old headstones sprouted randomly like mushrooms, two here by the driveway, one there by the rotting hammock, three between two weathered cottages, one in the manicured entrance to a high-tone development. Out here on the Banks, it seemed, the living did not relocate the dead to make way for the future. Out here, a final resting place was just that—final.

The graveyard I'd really been wanting to see was Buxton Cemetery just north of Hatteras Village in Frisco. I particularly wanted to find the grave of Benjamin B. Daily. I'd read his amazing, fragmented narrative—mythic hero among heroes in the lifesaving service on the Outer Banks, the winner with his six-man boat crew of seven gold medals for saving lives aboard a foundering ship. Daily's family had the lifesaving medal put in bas-relief on his tombstone—and I wanted to see that too.

I drove north on Highway 12, and just past Hatteras School on the left was a tiny, overgrown trail called Buxton Cemetery Road. I inched down the steep, sandy incline. I wondered if my little rental car would make it back up to the main road. The ground here pitched and rolled in every direction. These were not the "sweet fields beyond the swelling flood." These were the swells themselves, and floating like buoys upon them were an asymmetry of tombstones. Compared to the mainland variety, this was a small cemetery. Out here, though, it was a good-sized gathering. Pine needled and so overgrown that at times you had to pull back the thick carpet of vines, there lay the expected roll call of Midgetts, Fulchers, Whidbees, O'Neals, and Rollinsons. Some of the stones had fallen, others were listing badly, and still others freshly set out. The oldest were wooden, jagged on top, and so deeply runneled by the elements and the years that they spoke no names. Others were readable. Husbands and wives lay together, some with parents, some with adolescent offspring taken too soon, others with stillborn babies. Masonic symbols and Woodsmen affiliations were announced in silent chorus. But try as I might, moving from swell to trough and back to swell, I could not find the grave of Benjamin B. Daily.

Before I left, I stood still, looking over this narrow shoal of souls. Just south of the sandy road and the dense undergrowth, you could hear the schoolchildren laughing and squealing at recess. On the north side, again unseen, you could hear the angry complaining of chainsaws and hammers rapping. In between these disparate sounds of growth and progress, the uneasy sleep of the original settlers, their children, and their grandchildren.

When I returned to my room, there was a note taped to the door. Ernie and Lynne wanted me to come over for dinner. "Leftovers," it said. This night I was the only guest. I was flattered. It was more informal, but not leftovers. Lynne had worked up some delicate fish cakes and various other dishes that looked like no leftovers I'd ever seen.

I couldn't hide my concern—about Mo. I had just called home from the windy outside pay phone on the Village Marina porch, and Mo was having another seizure. The nurse was there with her. I'd done everything I could medically and care-wise going on almost ten years now, and the doctor finally warned me to take care of myself. Caregiving carried its own dangers, he'd warned. I told Ernie and Lynne that the best therapy for me was right here, right now. They knew what I meant. They knew I was grieving and they may well have known too that these trips, besides being literary, were also a form of letting go, of my practicing being alone. This last part was the hardest of course, especially when MS is involved. With cancer victims there is usually a general timetable; even with other forms of sclerosis—say, amyotrophic lateral sclerosis, or Lou Gehrig's disease—there's a more-or-less predictable trajectory so that the survivor might prepare for it psychologically, even make plans, imagine a future. With MS, there was no timetable, no markers along the way. Each day was a crapshoot. You could wake up paralyzed from the neck down, or blind, or deaf. You could wake up dead. Doctors finally knew no more about the disease than I did. They could see what I could see, sense the decline, and give it long Latin names, but in the end, who knew what was next, and when? It was this uncertainty that was cruel to everyone involved, but to Mo and me first and foremost. My trips to Hatteras Village had become a labor of love as well as a deep respite. And I was falling in love with the place. Having grown up in a small beach and fishing resort in New Jersey, I knew well the rhythms of a place like Hatteras Village: the hectic Memorial Day to Labor Day tourist madness followed by a subtle reknitting of the community in the fall and winter. But what I was being reminded of daily was the quiet kindness, the natural generosity, and native intelligence of the people who made do with what they had and started and often ended their workdays in the dark. I couldn't say all this to Ernie and Lynne. It would go beyond the cup to the bowlful. Too much. I just hoped they sensed it.

We talked during and after dinner about my day's cemetery adventures. I lamented particularly that I hadn't been able to find the tombstone of Benjamin B. Daily, the sculpted medal and so on. Ernie excused himself from the table. He returned a few moments later with a book and a black velvety little box. It looked like the kind old watches came in. He turned up the lights and then slowly opened the hinged case. In it was the coveted Gold Life Saving Medal of Honor, as it was officially called. He carefully took it out and handed it to me. Its attached ribbon was time-tattered, but the heavy medal gleamed in my palm. On its face, the medal announced, "To Rasmus S. Midgett, for Rescuing Single Handed Ten Men from the Wreck *Priscilla*, 1899." Around its perimeter, the inscription read, "In Testimony of Heroic Deeds in Saving Life from the Perils of the Sea."

"My mother was a Midgett," Ernie said, holding his hand three feet off the floor—an old joke that his heart wasn't quite in, but had to be got through. Hazel Midgett, wife to Ernal, mother to Ernie, was the great-granddaughter of Rasmus S. Midgett of the U.S. Lifesaving Service. Ernie reached over for the tattered book he'd also fetched. It was titled *Annual Report of the U.S. Life-Saving Service for the Fiscal Year June 30, 1900*, and was filled with official reports sent to Washington from the various lifesaving stations. The brief report on Rasmus Midgett and the *Priscilla* was a pretty dry read, even by the prose standards of a U.S. government report. It simply and bloodlessly recited the basic outline of the rescue: that one Rasmus Midgett did his appointed job by going through the surf and bringing to safety ten crewmen. Only a couple of times did the official prose show signs of a pulse. The narrator said that "the seas were running mountain high." The captain of the *Priscilla* was quoted as saying, "When we ran aground, I did not sound anymore. I knew that we were going ashore and passed the word forward for all hands to prepare to save themselves." Then the narrator summoned near-biblical prose to summarize the action: "Three times he [Midgett] descended the beach incline and each time dragged away a helpless man and bore him up and out of the angry waters to a place of safety. Ten lives were the priceless trophies of his valor."

The real experience, of course, had to have been much, much worse. It was August 1899, and this was the infamous San Ciriaco hurricane, a storm that sank more than fifty ships off the Outer Banks. Historian David Stick went through all the documents of San Ciriaco hurricane and the *Priscilla* tragedy. Here's a more human account of what happened. The *Priscilla*, a 643-ton barkentine, had left Baltimore bound for Rio de Janeiro. The cruise was more or less a family affair. The *Priscilla* carried a crew of twelve, including Captain Benjamin Springsteen, his wife, their twelve-year-old son, Elmer, and their older son, Mate William Springsteen. The *Priscilla* ran into hurricane San Ciriaco just north of Cape Hatteras and was so damaged by the encounter that she ran aground on Gull Shoal south of Chicamacomico —the present town of Rodanthe—and just north of Hatteras Village. She was driven nearly ashore by winds about three miles south of Gull Shoal Lifesaving Station. The huge surf began pounding the *Priscilla* to pieces. Captain Springsteen was on deck holding his young son in his arms while his older son tended to his mother and the young cabin boy, one Fitzhugh Goldsborough. Just at that moment, a huge comber broke over the *Priscilla*, ripping young Elmer from his father's arms and sweeping his wife and William and the cabin boy overboard. All drowned.

Surfman Rasmus Midgett was on patrol out of Gull Shoal Station at the time, riding his small beach pony when he heard the cries and saw the shattered ship. There was no time to return to the Gull Shoal Station for help. The *Priscilla* was rapidly breaking up beneath ten frightened souls. The ship finally split in two, the front portion drifting toward the beach. The stern end, with everyone on it, remained a hundred yards off shore. A hurricane surf cannot be imagined. It must be seen. And that was exactly what the diminutive, forty-eight-year-old Rasmus Midgett was staring into. He went into action, timing his dashes out toward the ship with the receding walls of water. He then swam the rest of the way. When he got as close as he could to the *Priscilla*, he yelled to the crew nearest him on the foredeck to slide down the ropes to him. One by one they did. Midgett made seven trips, dragged seven human beings through the surf to the firm, stinging sand of the beach. Three more men remained on the fractured deck of the ship, each badly wounded. One of them was Captain Springsteen. Somehow Midgett summoned the strength to dash again through the surf, swim out to the stern wreckage, pull himself hand-over-hand up the ship's ropes, hoist a man to his shoulder, jump back into the sea, and swim to shore with his burden. He did this three times. He then led his ten charges the three miles to Gull Shoal Station for warmth and first aid. Rasmus Midgett's salary at the time was forty dollars a month.

"See those two doors?" Ernie asked, pointing to a dark-stained pair, facing one another in a hallway just off the living room. I got up and examined them. Then the tumblers fell into place. These were almost identical to the bathroom door Ernie had donated to the Chicamacomico Lifesaving Museum in Rodanthe. The little sign in the museum said it was from the wreck of the *Priscilla*. So were these. I'd seen old photos of men squatting on her beached foredeck. There were pictures of the crew members Rasmus Midgett had saved standing amid the barrels and wood boxes and wreckage on the beach. There were pictures of the public vendue, or auction, of goods from the ship, taking place on the spot. Somehow the hero ended up with three cabin doors. It was a small, thin world out here.

Then Ernie said, "Lift up the table cloth." I looked puzzled. Lynne smiled and nodded her head. I looked. The dining room table was heavy oak with turned legs, each the size of an elephant's. It had a milky white patina.

"From another shipwreck," Ernie said. "We still need to get it refinished."

It was getting late. In our leavetaking, I hugged Lynne. She held me an extra beat and whispered she would pray for Mo. Ernie said, "You take good care of yourself now." I knew what he meant. A cupful of compassion. That was enough. More than enough.

────────────

I left early in the morning for my afternoon flight out of Norfolk. It was beautiful, sunny, but very windy, so I couldn't rue the irony of leaving on a perfect fishing day. It wasn't. Just north of Hatteras Village, I pulled over in a small parking lot across from the Canadian Hole recreation area on the sound side, and got out to take one last look at the sea and to smell the salt air full in the face. This was a different country in winter. For the most part, during the summer tourist season the Banks behave themselves. The seas sit down with hands in lap, and while the wind keeps up its gusty thrum, it whispers "kites" to the children, and across the road at the famous Canadian Hole, which is advertised, and probably rightly so, as "one of America's hottest windsurfing spots"—it shouts, "Sailboard!" Parasail!" The sun too can be counted on in the summer, and while an occasional thunderstorm blows through, it is almost always more a brief IMAX lightshow than anything else.

But after Labor Day, when the tourists have said their goodbyes and the three-month party is over, the Outer Banks, like a large dog finally let off its chain, reverts to its dramatically unpredictable behavior. The winds become erratic and moody, and are never without the faint scent of menace. The quality of light is changeable too, its range of expression more expansive, more fascinating, more temporary. This time of year the sun can warm you down to a T-shirt, or it can illuminate a chilling disaster. The sun shone no brighter than a few days back when we skidded and slid our way through Hatteras Inlet. Accounts are without number from the nineteenth and early twentieth centuries of lifesavers and citizens alike standing on the beach in the bright sun and biting air of the fall or winter, watching helplessly as men, women, and children, clinging to the twisted rigging of their sinking ships, dropped one by one to their deaths in the freezing sea. The sea: of all the elements in winter, it is the sea's moods that were the most varied and willful. In the few days I'd been here, we'd striper fished in shirt sleeves on a genial sea. Days later we were riding swells as tall as the house I live in.

The National Weather Service says, "On average, the Outer Banks will experience weather that has the potential to cause damage about three times a year. This includes northeasters and strong thunderstorms as well as hurricanes." Invariably the "three times" occur in the fall and winter when breathtaking beauty dances with grim danger. Beneath the sterile bureaucratic understatement of the National Weather Service prose lay the possibility of massive destruction and death. A northeaster next week could cut a new inlet through right where I was sitting, right where the banks narrow to a wrist. (Geologists have identified thirty distinct inlets cut through the Outer Banks since the early sixteenth century. Today there are seven). If one opened here, Hatteras Village would then become an island, a very small and very vulnerable island. Of course these days with satellite forecasting and clear evacuation routes, the odds of survival are improved. But forecasting isn't preventive. A generation ago, with forecasting still pretty much a guessing game—and without the Bonner Bridge to connect Hatteras Island to Bodie Island and the mainland—the odds were sometimes ominous. Ernie's father had his house up on blocks to let the water flow beneath it. As a further measure he drilled holes in the floor of the house to relieve water pressure in really bad storms and to keep the house from floating away. It worked, several times. How bad a storm was could be measured in the old Foster house by the waterlines on the living room wall, or how many steps the water had advanced toward the family huddled upstairs. In the memorable hurricane of 1933, water came in over the downstairs windowsills.

Despite the dangers of off-season on the Outer Banks, most residents prefer it to the crowds and confusion. Beginning in the fall, it was often the wind and the water—not greenhorn tourists—that determined what you did each day. Even so, no matter what the weather served up after Labor Day, you could usually find a way to whittle around it and get where you needed to go. It was also ironically when you could see more nature than in any other season—whales breaching in the inlet, great schools of baitfish almost in the surf, birds that would sit next to you on the beach, like pensioners, as seven sea gulls were doing right now. The unpredictable migration of great fish, the more predictable migration of waterfowl, deer tracks along the empty access ramps and salt sea ponds, the foraging signatures of raccoons and possums. And arching over all, the infinitely varied combinations of wind and water, sun and storm, light and shadow, and some nights a deep enough silence and more than enough stars to remind you gently of your humble place in the order of things.

What cannot be said
Will get wept.
—Sappho

CHAPTER ELEVEN

The Net House

MARCH. There was a cold sting in the air at first light, and by nine o'clock the triangular flags across the parking lot at the Hatteras Harbor office were snapping. Tall Bill stopped by my room at the Village Marina Motel behind the *Albatross* boats. He'd just tied up *Net Results* next to the *Albatross* office. He'd gone out to the sound early to set his nets, but the wind had kicked up badly, and he'd had to quit.

Bill's nose was red and running, but there was no disappointment in his voice. Weather queered things out here so regularly that you just rolled with it and went on to the next thing on your long list of chores. Bill said he was headed home. He'd do paperwork, and then maybe he'd go over and see if Michelle could have lunch with him. He already knew that Ernie and I had planned to go out today to Diamond Shoals for rockfish. That trip was off, he said. Ernie had just stopped by the dock as he was tying up and had told him so. Ernie had said too that he was going to work at the net house today. Bryan Mattingly was going to join him. Bill said Ernie was going to stop by soon and take me over to the net house with him.

We took our coffee outside and huddled up on the lee side of the motel so Bill could have a smoke. There were long pauses in the conversation, and finally Tall Bill said, "How are you doing?" It was the gently coded question. He had heard about Mo's fall, her broken hip back in January. He was inviting me to say what I needed to say. I kept it short and to the point without being dismissive. Compassion here on the Outer Banks did not require lengthy preambles. A simple telegram from the heart would suffice. The fact was Mo wasn't doing at all well, and I wasn't either for that matter. I told Bill that when she fell out of bed, her bones had shattered and "bayoneted"—her thigh bone lying painfully on top of the hip saddle. She was too weak for surgery, and besides she was in no mental state for any procedure; those cognitive seizures she'd been experiencing were getting more frequent and prolonged. So we'd opted for traction and hoped for the best. And it looked like we'd been bested. The traction wasn't working. Mo's hip was healing horribly; her right foot was turned 180 degrees to the left, and her other leg, the useless one, had begun contracting upward toward her chest. She was losing weight. There were bedsores. I didn't need to tell Bill what all this was doing to me. "Ahhh, it's tough," said Bill, staring across the highway at the Burrus Motel. Bill's response was enough for me. People who lived on a thin finger of sand forty miles out in the Atlantic were not expansive by nature.

Bill had another smoke, and then we shook hands, and he left. I'd barely taken myself and the coffee mugs back into room before Ernie showed up. Bryan was with him. We drove south through the village for only about a quarter mile and turned left and parked in the front of Ernie's net house. The net house was just off the road, partially hidden behind some scrub cedar and random bushes. It was a low, nondescript, shake shingle structure not much wider than a two-car garage but probably twice as deep. Like most everything else on Hatteras Island, the net house was raised off the sand a couple of feet. The right side of the building was being crowded by an abandoned mobile home. On this side it had a concrete ramp leading up to a set of double doors. Cars and boats could be rolled up and stored or worked on inside.

Ernie shouldered open the balky door, and we went in. It felt like a walk-in freezer. Ernie turned on the lights and lit the portable kerosene heater over near the long, narrow workbench. All around the dim recesses of the room was a double stack of wide wooden shelving, which was heaped high with old cotton nets. Overhead, countless fishing rods spanned the ceiling joists through drilled holes. The floor of the workshop was crowded with boxes and crates of old fishing gear, boat hardware, and assorted wood scraps. Over by the workbench a white-slatted fighting chair sat tipped on the floor. The floor itself looked like a gigantic Jackson Pollock painting. This was the Foster family net house. It was one of the few left in the village. Net houses

The Foster net house (Courtesy of Lynne Foster)

had been rendered unnecessary by nylon nets, which did not rot and therefore did not require careful drying and storage. Besides, real estate prices were getting to be such that keeping a net house, even as a workshop, had become a luxury. At one time not very long ago, net houses in a hundred villages like Hatteras along the North Carolina coast were the real and symbolic lifeblood of a community's work. Net houses were to fishing villages what barns were to farm towns: they were places where citizens stored and repaired what was vital to their lives and their livelihoods. They were also places where laboring men could meet and work and undertake the routine, daily maintenance of a community's fundamental bonds.

Bryan took off his insulated one-piece suit and entered the dusk at the back of the workshop. Ernie started cleaning off a section of the cluttered workbench near the fighting chair. He handed me a six-sided wooden spool, about eighteen inches long and wrapped with fishing line. "That's linen fishing line," he said, his back to me. "It was good stuff in its time. Trouble was, every two or three fishing trips, you had to take it off the reel and dry it on spools like that. Then you wound it back on the reel. It was a real nuisance."

He went on to give a well-organized lecture on linen line and the evolution of fishing line thereafter. There was much in Ernie's talk that reminded me of Tall Bill's lecture to that young couple a couple of years ago about the spawning cycle of striped bass and the variables that could alter it. It was unrehearsed but seamless and minus any wasteful rhetoric. Even without their teaching degrees, Tall Bill and Ernie were natural-born teachers. Ernie explained that linen was braided line, that each strand in the braid was the equivalent to three-pound test. Sixteen-thread braid was forty-eight-pound test; twenty-four-braid linen was seventy-two-pound test. Seventy-two-pound linen was the heaviest for a long time. Pretty much from the turn of the century to right after World War II, seventy-two-pound-test linen line had become the standard for offshore fishing. Linen line was replaced by nylon ("It had a lot of stretch in it—too much really, and it often 'blew up' on the reel"). Nylon was followed by Dacron and Dacron by monofilament and monofilament by spider wire and copolymers. Each had its own personality, its own advantages and disadvantages. They were all examined carefully. Ernie was very happy, puttering and lecturing.

Bryan scuffed back out of the shadows. He was carrying four big fishing reels cradled like melons at his beltline. They were gold anodized Penn reels ranging in model size from 50s to 80ts and 80tws. Ernie explained that the "T" stood for tournament. "Everything's a tournament!" he said with the mock enthusiasm of a camp counselor telling his charges that "Everyone's a winner!" The "W" had more meaning. "W" meant "wide." The spools, and therefore the reels on tw models were wider and held more line. That was a definite advantage, especially with a big fish on, but Ernie had discovered a countervailing shortcoming: "In a tw model, the reel handle is further from the center of the reel, and so it's harder to crank." Ernie's summary conclusion: despite the increased cranking difficulties of the wider reel, a Penn tw with eighty-pound-test line is sufficient to catch almost anything, except perhaps a bluefin tuna or a very large marlin.

Ernie's lecture moved steadily forward as he and Bryan worked on the reels, taking them apart, greasing them, checking the strike tension and the drag tension, and refitting the reel seats. They reassembled the reels. Bryan sat in the old fighting chair on the floor, and Ernie stood five feet away with a large plastic spool of new line that Bryan was carefully cranking onto the reel. As Ernie stood holding the spinning reel, his lecture took a historical turn, on the evolution of the drag system. The internal drag mechanism, the adjustable pressure on the line that slows and then carefully turns a running fish, was something that developed gradually, and is of great interest —and endless debate—among fishermen. The reels made by the Vom Hofe brothers in Brooklyn, New York, were among the finest made in the mid-nineteenth century. Yet they had only a "click" drag system that provided a very light—and very loud—resistance to the spool as it spun off line from a hooked fish. Increased pressure to slow down the spool could be applied by a "thumb stall" contraption or by a leather brake attached to one of the reel pillars. It was easy to bruise knuckles or break fingers with these devices.

By the 1920s Pflueger, Bronson, and Ocean City came out with star drags, the first adjustable, internal drag device. A spoked or star-shaped metal wheel behind the reel handle allowed the user to rotate it and adjust the tension on the line as it came off the reel. Then in 1932 the Penn Company was founded, and a new standard of excellence was created in reels. The star drag system became subtler and more responsive in its pressure gradations. The other internal workings enjoyed a similar leap forward thanks to more careful engineering and machining. Penn made the best reels, period. Even their spinning reels are unbeatable. But here too Ernie found room for a cautionary note. "Engineering isn't everything. Early on, Shimano reels were actually over-engineered—the drags would overheat and freeze up on you. They learned from their mistakes, though, and they came out with a simple hydraulic feature that would automatically adjust the drag pressure to compensate for the tensile change in the hot metal of the drag mechanism when you had a big fish on."

When they finished loading the line on the reels, Bryan got up from the wobbly fighting chair and disappeared once again into the dusk at the back of the workshop. He returned with two stout boat poles, each with a curved metal butt and each with a huge gold Penn reel, even bigger than the 50s and 80s. These were the big casinos, Ernie said—Penn 130s. The rods and reels had been given to Ernie by a friend. "Those reels alone cost around $1,100 apiece," Ernie said. I'd seen one of these. I'd used it back in November when I was out with Tall Bill and Bryan and I'd tied into that bluefin. I'd felt the weight of the fish, but not the rod and reel; it was set in the gimbal between my legs. Here in the net house, I tried to hold out the rod and reel at arm's length. I couldn't come close. While Bryan got to work on them, Ernie disappeared through a door by the workbench. I could hear him moving things around, boxes hissing on the floor. Finally he called for me.

"Know what this is?" he asked handing me a rod and reel. The rod was bamboo, about six feet long and had a handmade grip of wrapped and glued twine. The reel was black and tall and antique-looking, with bulbous

Charles Foster and grandson
Ernie mending nets, c. 1946
(Courtesy of Ernie Foster)

plastic grips on the reel handle. It was held onto the rod by two automobile hose clamps. My mind was riffling through files. Time was up. "That's the rod and reel that caught the world-record marlin." Ernie was pleased. It didn't seem possible. More than 800 pounds of fish on this outfit—if the quarry were an elephant, what I held in my hand would be a single-shot .22. It was cartoonishly inadequate. "See these line guides?" Ernie set the butt of the rod on the floor. They were thick metal guides, each a set of two guides actually, back-to-back on the rod, even the tip a double-guide arrangement. Each round guide hole had a movable agate collar in it which kept the line from cutting a groove in the metal. Ernie offered up another lesson, this one on rod physics. The over-and-under double-guide arrangement was there, he said, so that when the bamboo rod warped one way under the accumulated weight of heavy fish or from the pull of trolling heavy baits, you could simply turn the rod over, run the line through the underside guide and warp it back. Often, though, instead of warping back, rods simply split.

"And this," said Ernie reaching into the top cardboard box in a stack of boxes, "this is the bait that did it." Ernie held up an outsized trolling lure. This was the old Hawaiian Knucklehead, looking as goofy as its name with its red-and-white solid plastic head the size and shape of a beer can, its comic strip eyes, its tattered skirt, and dull tandem hooks. This was the contraption that a fisherman had given Ernal a week before they caught the world record. This was the lure whose hook had hung up and bent on the *Albatross* transom and had to be bent back shortly before the fish hit.

"And this," said Ernie, reaching into another box and handing me something less clunky and more classic Ferrari, "is one of those Pflueger Altapac reels old Tom Eaton gave to my father back in the 1930s. Tom Eaton built the first ice plant down here and changed everything."

The Foster net house, among other things, was a museum, and Ernie was half curator and half W. C. Fields in *The Bank Dick*, reaching surgically into a stuffed rolltop desk and magically tweezing out the requested document. Ernie now plunged his arms down behind some heaps of old net and came up with a neat little, lap-sized wooden box. "This was my father's sea chest," he said, opening its lid. He pulled out a small cylinder of thick cloth and unrolled it. Inside were a handful of wooden net needles. In the chest also was his father's net gauge, a smoothed wooden block less than six inches long that was used to make sure the net squares were of uniform size. Women did most of the net making, but grandfather Charles and father Ernal put in their time too. Both were very good at it.

We went back in the other room to see how Bryan was coming along. He needed another twenty minutes before he'd be ready for Ernie to help him put new line on the 130s. Ernie set to helping him at the workbench. When he'd finished the reel he was working on, he put down his vise grips and said, "Follow me. I want to show you something." We headed out the door of the ramshackle net house, took a right, between the net house and the neat white clapboard house Ernie had grown up in. We walked for a few hundred more feet. There before us lay the Foster family plot. Like so many other cemeteries in Hatteras Village and on the lower Banks in general, this one seemed oddly ad hoc and informally located—in adjoining backyards next to hammocks and lawn chairs and Weber Kettles. But unlike so many others I'd seen, including Buxton Cemetery, this one possessed a tended look and a tender beauty. Ancient live oaks—stunted out here like everything else by the salt air—formed an almost perfect canopy over the final destination of the Foster clan. Ernal was here next to his wife, Hazel. Brother Bill and his wife were here too, as was their father Charles and his wife. I asked Ernie about a non-Foster name on one of the small stones. "Oh. Well, that was a friend of my cousin's; he needed a place to stay so we put him here with our family."

I asked Ernie about another non-Foster name on a stone off to the side of the plot. It read

Thomas Vine Angell

1882–1937

From his friends of the

Gooseville Gun Club

He said, "Oh. That's Tom Angell. In his time he was the only black man on Hatteras Island. He lived in a house that used to be over there. He had life rights to the place." Ernie gestured to a newer two-story clapboard house whose backyard and the Fosters' backyard met at right angles to form the little cemetery we stood in.

The fragile memories of old villagers—Brittie Burrus, Luther Austin, Beaty Peele—differ on the details, but together they limn a quiet, unusual, decent life. Mr. and Mrs. Nelson Paul Angell "adopted" a young, homeless black boy when they were somewhere over on the mainland—New Bern, maybe Washington, N.C. They brought him to Hatteras Island, to Hatteras Village, to their cozy, two-story house, with its steep-pitched roof, its fancy Gothic windows, its fish-scale shingles high up on the gable ends, and its little porch facing south. Mr. Angell was in the lighthouse service. They had their own children, and they raised Tom right along with them. No one knows why they adopted him.

After Mr. Angell died, Mrs. Angell lived there with Tom. They had a peacock, which drew crowds to watch its tail fan out. And on weekends, in the little gazebo out back, Tom Angell would make homemade ice cream and give it away free. Tom was a cook at the Gooseville Gun Club. The club was near where the coast guard station is now. Before Mrs. Angell died, she arranged for Tom to stay in the house as long as he wanted. Tom kept the house up just the way it was when the Angells were alive. People remember him walking to and from the grocery store with his basket. On Saturdays and Sundays people came over to his place for his ice cream and chocolate cake. Miss Beaty Peele remembers when he died: "They had a big room in the house, and he was laid out in there. When it came time for the funeral, they took his coffin out of the house and put it on the walk before the door, in the yard, and all the people were standing around. There was a right good crowd at the funeral." Then they buried him out back under the live oaks. Tom Angell died in 1937, the same year old Ernal's original *Albatross* was built.

We stood in silence for a while. Just beyond the collection of stones, the thick island vegetation waited patiently to reclaim its own. "I suppose I'll be here someday," Ernie said, to no one in particular. As we started to leave Ernie pointed to the center of the little group of stones. There was a large pedestal; its bricks had shifted and twisted over the years. On top of that was an urn with no inscription. It was easily the tallest monument in the cemetery. "Know who that is?" Ernie asked with a smile. No. "A horse." He laughed and we walked back to the net house.

Back in the net house, Ernie and Bryan wound new 200-pound-test line

The Foster family plot. The headstone for Thomas Vine Angell is in the background. (Courtesy of Lynne Foster)

onto the Penn 130s, and then Bryan left to pick up his little girl. Ernie carried the new rods and reels back into the dusk. He came back and joined me on a crate near the floor heater. I was sitting in the fighting chair. It was getting colder. We talked some about our missed rockfish trip and when we might make it up. Forecasters were saying things were going to get worse before they got better. He asked me about Mo. I told him the depressing medical details I'd recited earlier for Tall Bill. The silence was cold and sharp. The heater held its one long note.

Finally, I felt compelled to say to Ernie what I'd left out of my account to Bill. I'd come down to Hatteras this time because I couldn't stay at home. It had simply gotten to be too much, and I needed to get out for a while. It was so painful to witness. For more than twenty years, Mo had refused to give in to the MS, even to give it a name, and now she seemed to be resigning herself, letting go of an iron resolve at her center. Her world was shrinking to the size of the room she was in; the world beyond that in the last few months had become an unwelcome muddle for her. These new habits of mind seemed to be obscuring her, erasing her vibrant colors, like a beautiful painting hung too long in the sunlight. She'd always been so alive in the world even when she couldn't walk through it anymore, and now she was developing what the medical literature called an "apparent indifference to things." The phrase caught in my throat. I had to gather myself. It wasn't just an "indifference to things." It was really "people, places, and things." The disease had become an improper noun, and the children and I were among the people to whom Mo was growing gradually indifferent. This woman who would talk quietly with her children for hours, until the phone bill was delivered by forklift, this woman now asked them the same questions two and three times in a row, and then had to go because *Wheel of Fortune* was coming on. Mo had always disliked television. *Wheel of Fortune* was a joke that came on after the news I was watching. And lately when I'd come home from my trips, down to Hatteras, or wherever, she no longer asked if I'd had a good time. She was too distracted, abstracted. It was the seizures, I knew—her "episodes" as she called them—but they were robbing her of the small gestures, the tender mercies that seam a marriage. I was frustrated and angry, and I grieved. I was tired of being brave. My God, how tired must she be? I was starting to think I wouldn't get her back.

I couldn't feel my feet. It had been a full moon tide, this answer to Ernie's simple question about my wife. It was probably the longest, uninterrupted statement I'd ever delivered to him. But he'd leaned in as I talked. Now I was sure he couldn't feel his feet either. He put his hand on my arm. Finally, he said, "Lynne would like to see you before you leave."

I got up out of the fighting chair with little grace. I walked over to the door. Ernie was bent over a box under the workbench. He stood up, holding a rag of some sort in front of him. He opened it up and spread it between us. It was a T-shirt, a very old and ratty T-shirt. "You know that wall with all the pictures inside the *Albatross* office? Well, there's one of my father as a young man. He's aboard the *Albatross* and he's wearing a T-shirt. It has three holes in the back of it." As he said this, he stuck his hand through the neck of the T-shirt and spread his fingers. "See? The same three holes. One hole on the right, two holes on the left. I came across it here the other day and I realized what it was. This was the T-shirt he was wearing in that old picture."

The next day before I headed up to the airport, I went into the *Albatross* office and looked. Sure enough. There was Ernal, his back to the camera and the three holes across his shoulder blades, sitting in the fighting chair.

Do you realize what it means
To the small folk drawn into the pattern of fate,
The small folk who live among small things,
. . . who stand to the doom of the house
. . . who stand to the doom of the world?
—T. S. Eliot, *Murder in the Cathedral*

CHAPTER TWELVE

Family and Floating Homes

On July 13, 2002, my wife died. My children and I were with her. Her family
—her mother and brothers and sisters—were just outside the room. The
slow anarchy of multiple sclerosis had finally grown impatient. Complica-
tions. She suffered a massive episode of internal bleeding. They could not
replenish the blood supply quickly enough, and so she lapsed into a coma,
a vegetative state. We held her hands and cried and cut locks of her hair.
She went away peacefully. We had trouble letting her go. She was the brav-
est person we had ever known. More than twenty-five years ago a beautiful,
model-thin Irish girl changed her children's diapers with numb hands and
tingling legs. She paid no attention to the unbidden guest whose shadow
had begun appearing across the floor of our lives. As a teacher at the Memphis College of Art, she had begun to teach sitting down, to subtly "wall
walk"—touching a wall to stabilize herself—as she went to and from class.
After that, she had used canes. She got ones that were colorfully painted.
She twirled them Chaplinesquely, laughed, and talked a good game about
them being fashion accessories, but even a child's eye could see the weight-
bearing job they performed. Then she used a walker. Then she was in and
out of a wheelchair. Then she was in a wheelchair. She had to give up her
job. Then she lost the use of her right hand. Then her right leg wouldn't

hold still. The faulty memory, the occasionally slurred speech. Through it all we raised our children; they went off to college, graduated, got jobs and moved to New York, San Francisco. We made social and domestic lives for ourselves, as best we could. Then the seizures began. The countless trips to doctors, specialists. The wagons circled closer around the fire. So.

I found that well-meaning friends, close and casual, tended to see grieving as linear, dissipating like radioactivity at a fixed rate over time. *It's been four weeks, six weeks. He should be better now. It's been six months . . . surely now . . .* I wasn't better, not consistently anyway. Grief wasn't linear at all; it wasn't some river that picked you up and swept you along, and then deposited you gently on a still, sandy shore. Grief was a storm surge. It swirled and eddied around you, higher and higher, until you believed you'd drown. Then it suddenly receded, and your clothes dried and your breathing returned. But then, ignoring all orderly tide charts, it would rush in again, angry, unexpected, wrapping around you, shooting up your legs, heading to your lungs, and you would panic again. Eventually, the moon halves, then quarters, and the tides become less pronounced. Or so they say. How long these tides would pitch and run I had no idea. But I did know I had to get out of Memphis for a while. I had settled the estate, mailed out death certificates to institutions to prove my wife was dead; I had spent Christmas day in a motel with my children because we couldn't face Christmas at home; I had sleepwalked through two semesters at the university, and realized I couldn't do it any longer. I announced my retirement. And now I absolutely had to get out for a while. That was in September.

SEPTEMBER. The pictures were horrific. They'd been taken before, during, and after by village residents and posted on a website. The befores I knew, I recognized. The durings were impressionistic, in a limited palette of grays and blacks and browns — sky, water, half-houses, roofs, crooked boats, parts of trucks, and all shot through lenses and windows speckled and spattered with rain and wind-whipped sea water. The after pictures required captions; there was little in them familiar to the eye. The problem was that parts had to stand for the whole, pieces for an entirety. There was the Sea Gull Motel, or at least part of it, and the there had changed locations. This stalwart 1950s mom-and-pop motel, the classic two-story in-line model was, at least a boxcar length of it, now angle-parked on Highway 12. You could see another section of it across the road in the leaning cedars. The motel's

After Isabel: a sea buoy on the beach (Courtesy of Lynne Foster)

ten-foot-high brick stairway had stayed behind and was reduced now to inviting people up into thin air.

Lovely Durant's Station Motel, near the Sea Gull and tucked, like it, behind the first dune line, was gone. Durant's signature gingerbread lifesaving station, nearly 100 years old, and which had given the motel its name, was now lost at sea. The Billy Mitchell Motel next door was now an aqua-pastel honeycomb, its office section ripped raggedly open, eviscerated to knotty pine paneling and pink insulation. The Cabanas' cabanas were scattered like brown LEGOS in the salt marshes back on the sound side. And the Village Marina Motel, closer into the village, twenty feet from Foster's Quay and Captain Ernie's boats, had sagged into a sinkhole where the boat ramp used to be. The room I had a reservation for now shared the deepest part of the hole with an Apache travel trailer.

I searched my computer screen in vain for the *Albatross* fleet behind the Village Marina and to the left. It seemed always just out of the frame. Other after-pictures showed the Sandbar Grill, where I'd spent many a pub-grub-and-beer night just north of the village. Or didn't show it; it was gone, shucked like an oyster from the concrete shell that remained, with the intact apartment over the saloon. It was al fresco now—see-through and drive-through.

After Isabel: the stairs of the Sea Gull Motel (Courtesy of Steve Earley, The *Virginian-Pilot*)

Next door, the Pelican's Roost was too. More after-storm pictures showed the huge beachfront homes down along Lighthouse Road shorn unevenly, roof and siding, window and latticework wrapping the stilts they stood on. Or no longer stood on. Some had fallen crazily, like spinning plates on a stick. Others had simply sat down on the ground. Other homes had taken French leave, offering a bouquet of skewed poles as the only evidence of their rude exit.

The precarious dune line that had shielded these from the sea was gone. And there on the scoured beach, huge black timbers prickly with metal, was the old shipwreck Ernie and I had looked in vain for a few years back when he had given me a tour of the village. And there on the website was an aerial shot of the breach, the new inlet cut though from ocean to Pamlico Sound at the Canadian Hole windsurfing area just above the village. Stilted houses marched up to its southern edge and stopped. It was actually three contiguous inlets separated by stepping stones of low, grass-covered dunes. Waves were breaking in its mouth. Where the ocean water raced in now and fanned out into the sound, you could see the roofs of submerged houses. A porpoise arced in the new sound water still brown from the blow.

Through a graceful act of engineering in 1964, Hatteras Island had been attached to the mainland by the Bonner Bridge. Now, almost forty years

The breach just north of Hatteras Village. For a few months, Hatteras Village was its own island. (Courtesy of Michael Halmanski)

later, nature had chosen to reverse the gesture. Not a bridge this time, but its opposite: to abridge, to cut off the lower part of Hatteras Island, the tip of the graceful, curving tail and by so doing to make this nether part an island once again, the village its only outpost, a single, compact capital. To abridge. So be it. Maybe Hurricane Isabel got to trace the new boundaries, to make the excision but, golly day, the Hatteras Islanders would reserve the right to name it. They would call it Little Hatteras Island henceforth. They even scrawled the moniker on a ragged piece of plywood (sign board was available everywhere on the sand), and stuck the new name in the rakish roadside frame that had held the old one.

There was silence from the island for about a week after the September 18 storm. Electricity, phone, water—everything was gone. Reports had the national guard and the Red Cross on the island. No one was allowed out there except permanent residents and rescue personnel. Boats ferried supplies and

A floating home (Courtesy of Lynne Foster)

people from up in Frisco and Buxton. Residents who'd fled were allowed back. Seasonal residents would have to wait. Then huge generators made for sporadic, round-robin power, and I got a return e-mail from Lynne and then Ernie. They were alright; they spoke of themselves as though they were a family of five; the three boats had made it through unscathed too. They'd been lucky. Ernie had moved the *Albatross II* and *III* from the slips at Foster's Quay to a location just fifty feet away — across the Hatteras Harbor Marina channel facing Foster's now, with their bows pointed into the oncoming storm winds. The original *Albatross* had been taken a quarter mile up the creek to the Hatteras Marlin Club slips where it roomed with cousin Willy Foster's *Ol' Salt*. Smart moves, as it turned out. The *II* and *III* had been silted in but were fine. The original was untouched and operable. They were using her as a village taxi. If Ernie had left the boats in their slips at Foster's Quay, they'd have been turned into flotsam or kindling.

The water, three or four or five feet of it, had roared over the dune line east of the village and covered everything in its westward rush to the sound. It raced under Ernie and Lynne's new house. In building it they'd decided at the last minute to add another twelve inches of clearance under it, to bring it to just over three feet. The water used every inch of clearance, coming so close to their ground floor that the sea tossed a starfish up onto the porch. The water raced on westward seeking out the low spots, which turned out to be where Slash Creek flowed into the sound at the south end of the town, and also the boat ramps, one of which was right next to Foster's Quay. The water became panicky at these spots, millions of gallons, and spilled down the concrete boat ramps and over the marina bulkheads at the sterns of yachts and charter boats worth millions of dollars. Pictures of the gray water streaming over the marina bulkheads gave the look of those low river dams beside New England textile mills. Finally, inexorably, the bulkheads got scoured out and gave way. Huge gray and tar timbers thrashed and clubbed at anything nearby as they made their angry way into the waters of the sound. The *Albatross* boats were out of harm's way, barely, but that's all it required to get lucky.

The next e-mail was from Ernie. It was brief but reflective; his father, he said, had foretold this, had predicted his son would experience one of these events. "He was right. This is mine." His father's "event" had been in '33. That was the one that had nearly killed him, had sent him fleeing a wall of water to the attic crawl space of a splintering building, had kept him under the roof joists, had humbled him into drinking water from the toilet tank, had made him watch a hunting dog float by on a table. "I've never seen anything like it," Ernie closed. Nor had any other residents. There had been the '33 hurricane, of course, and the one in '44. There was Hazel in 1954 and Emily in 1993—even the infamous Ash Wednesday storm in 1962 that had cut a new inlet just north of Buxton. But none came close to Isabel. Isabel was destructive beyond previous measure, but it had also been deceitful. When it came ashore, it was a category two storm on the Saffir-Simpson scale, with winds of 105 miles per hour.

For Outer Banks residents this wasn't so bad. Northeasters often exceeded those numbers. "For a lot of us out here," Ernie Foster observed, "the threshold is about 125 miles per hour. If they predict winds that high, we'll start thinking about evacuating." But Isabel didn't reach that threshold. And besides it was clearly weakening when it hit the coast of North Carolina. On September 8, ten days before it made landfall, Isabel had been a category four storm, with winds of 135 miles per hour. The winds kept going up, and on September 11, it became a category five with winds measuring 160 miles per hour. Isabel fluctuated between a category four and category five for the better part of week. On September 16 it seemed to calm down to a category two storm.

The problem forecasters underestimated had to do with that week Isabel spent at her strongest, her angriest. By persisting so long in the category of four and five, Isabel had churned the ocean around it to incredible heights.

And then when Isabel finally started moving northwest on a collision course with tiny Hatteras Village, it herded these angry seas ahead of it. Weather forecasters had ways of anticipating wind strength and storm surge; these had become fairly exact sciences. There were even wave models designed to predict the huge seas preceding a storm. These models, though, weren't so exact. Predicting wave action was iffy. The models that NOAA, the National Oceanic and Atmospheric Administration, had used on Isabel showed front-edge seas in the forty-five- to fifty-foot range. Officials couldn't believe it. This was way too high. Besides, just this past August when Fabian had hit Bermuda, the wave models had predicted this same range of waves, and the model was wrong. The forecasts hadn't panned out. They knew Fabian hadn't taken its time out in the Atlantic the way Isabel had. And they knew that Fabian had occurred at a higher latitude, which would flatten out the predictions a bit; still, Isabel couldn't clock in at the extreme high end of their modeling. But it did, and sneakily. On September 17, the day before Isabel made landfall, the NOAA buoy at Diamond Shoals fifteen miles from Hatteras Village was registering waves of sixteen to eighteen feet. By 9:00 P.M. the wave height was up to twenty-one feet. At 2:00 A.M. it was twenty-seven feet, and an hour later the buoy registered a 44.6-foot wave. Then it stopped reporting.

With a six-to-eight-foot storm surge, and waves of this magnitude, Isabel came ashore at Hatteras Village as a wall of water around twenty-five feet high. It shot up the beaches and through the breaches in the massive sand dunes. When there was more angry sea than breach to accommodate it, the water sheared off the dunes themselves, tore though the interdune swale, picking up vegetation, including old cedar trees and, further back, live oaks. When it hit the first line of homes, it didn't falter a step. It tore swimming pools and hot tubs out of the ground, took everything from beneath the high, stilted beach homes, and in many cases, snapped off the stilts and toppled the houses onto themselves and carried them along for the ride. Trucks went too, and cars, and trailer boats, refrigerators, freezers, air conditioners, hot water heaters, washers, dryers—all unused to a foot-race—lumbered and waddled to keep up. Like a horde of revolutionaries tearing up the cobblestoned streets of Paris, the sea raged forward, gathering up these items as weapons against those it encountered. Advance platoons raced ahead through the low spots. One such spot was at Teach's Lair Marina, where Highway 12 was furrowed out like a finger through icing and the marina building was obliterated. Luckily the boats in the bulkheaded oval had been moved. Another low spot was where Slash Creek headed back into the Pamlico Sound. This was at the west end of the village. A culvert had been put under Highway 12 to direct the Slash under the road and out to the sound. Many had argued for a bridge here, fearing a storm surge might create too much pressure on the culvert. Even these people didn't imagine what Isabel had in mind. In minutes, the culvert burst like a weakened artery; the road disappeared, and the bulkheads did likewise. The culvert pipe ended up a half mile away at the jettied entrance to Hatteras Harbor Marina, where the *Albatross* boats lay.

Another low spot was at the other end of the village, up where the Sea Gull, the Billy Mitchell, Hatteras Cabanas, and Durant's Station motels lay together. For days afterward, Marci Oden, couldn't talk about it without breaking down. She'd been on duty at the Sea Gull Motel when Isabel showed up. Her parents owned the Sea Gull, had for years, and she didn't want it left alone. It was midmorning on September 18, and she was already in trouble in the motel office. The water was up to her waist, and then the storm surge with its icing of waves burst through the office door and swept her into a connecting apartment. She called 911 on her cell phone, but they were helpless themselves. More waves and she was thrust into the garage. Her small pug dog floated by and she grabbed it by the tail and tossed it onto the roof of her nearby Jeep. She pulled herself up through a hole in the ceiling and watched for hour after hour as the water rose steadily to her. She was sure she'd be forced into a shrinking air pocket up near the ceiling joists, and then . . . "I gave my heart to God that night," she says, in a quavering voice. These people are stoic, not given to feelings of abject helplessness. There's always something you can do . . . Not always. And Marci Oden could do nothing but watch. Then in the swirling wash of debris and the dank wood smell, she saw the water slow its climb, and then stop. And then shortly after that, a banging outside, a human knock. Her father, Jeff Oden, was on the other side of the roof, on a surfboard. He'd paddled a long way. He grabbed his daughter, and they raced home.

Just down the road and across on the sound side of Highway 12, John and Judy Hardison had done some climbing of their own. They lived in Hatteras Estates, an enclave of larger homes. All day on the eighteenth, the Hardisons had watched the storm surge rise and bring with it wreckage from across the road where the four motels were, along with larger beachfront homes. Wreckage, including whole cabanas from Hatteras Cabanas, floated into their neighborhood and took out houses like bowling pins. Hatteras Estates was being destroyed by incoming debris. Judy Hardison was the manager at the Sea Gull Motel. She recognized its colors, its pieces, including furniture and room doors with numbers, as they bobbed by. She knew she was officially unemployed.

Then, around noon, their house began to crack and shift. It was separating from its platform. "We measured the water against the house next to us," Judy Hardison recalls; "it was twelve feet high at that point." The floor reeled drunkenly under their feet. They had to do something fast. Out on the deck they climbed over the railing and into a nearby tree. They climbed as high as they could. Both were in their fifties, and John had a bad knee and a heart condition. The water almost got him, but his wife pulled him up. The house lurched, hesitated for a moment, then spun loose from its foundations, and floated away. They were now in the tree, at the very top, and the water was up to their waists. But they weren't alone. "There was a snake up there with us," says Judy Hardison. They stared, one species at the other. And then they went back to the common task of surviving. "He was very reasonable," say the Hardisons; "he wanted to live too."

Not far away, Dave Chambers and his two roommates were in a similar jam. The house these three charter boat mates shared was deserting them. Dave Chambers led his friends outside to the second-floor deck. There was a live oak tree hanging over it. Like the Hardisons, they got up on the railing and into the tree. And just in time. It was daylight then, but darkness fell, and they had to stay put. Dave Chambers was a handsome, twenty-something black man. He was the only black man in Hatteras Village. He'd applied for the mating job over the phone, at the urging of his future roommates. He'd got a job offer from one of the boats over the phone. Everyone was surprised when he'd showed up and was black. His hard work and warm personality cleared up any confusion. Dave Chambers was part of the village family now. At the Captains' Banquet at the Channel Bass last November, he was conspicuous by the ring of laughter around him. Now they had survived, and Dave Chambers shook his head wrapped in Red Cross blankets, and said, "It's a good thing my ancestors spent a lot of time in trees . . ." Everyone laughed at the joke only Dave Chambers could tell.

Preliminary disaster estimates for Hatteras Island quickly reached $132 million. The tally for Hatteras Village alone was $110 million. It probably would have been easier for state disaster agencies to inventory what had not been touched in the village, but they chose to follow precedent. It read thus: "buildings suffering major damage: 126; buildings destroyed: 53; buildings uninhabitable: 58; buildings suffering significant but minor damage: 26. Total: 263." Structurally intact homes were crowded with multiple families; the community center had been flushed clean down to the studs, so most of

Hatteras's displaced citizens were eating meals in the cramped room behind the little public library where the Salvation Army had set up shop. Above the aluminum tables heaped with paper cups and plates and the fish coolers filled with chopped ice and jugs of iced tea, Caterpillar diesel engines roared by at frequent but irregular intervals outside the front of the library. On the library wall facing the stream of yellow earthmovers, the world-record marlin held vigil. The glass on the case holding it showed a water line about a third of the way up. The villagers laughed at how many people—and not just the children either—had asked if the marlin was alright.

"Just tell them you're coming over to Hatteras to help me rebuild my docks and bulkheads. You'll fall into the category of volunteer labor." Ernie was telling me this as I sat on the edge of my bed at the Falcon Motel in Buxton. It was October 11, three weeks after Isabel. Buxton and Frisco were the two little adjacent towns spanning Highway 12 just a handful of miles north of Hatteras Village. But with the new inlet recently cut through between them and Hatteras Village, Buxton and Frisco had become the end of the line for vehicles headed south on the Outer Banks. From here, you'd have to take one of the ad hoc ferries running to Hatteras out of the numerous little marinas and estuaries snaking out into the Pamlico Sound. This was a major staging area for the relief effort at Hatteras Village.

Buxton and Frisco, while very close to the village, had escaped relatively unscathed. The few motels here were filled with construction workers of various sorts who commuted daily over to Hatteras. The balance of rooms was taken by surf fishermen. There were no vacancies. Fishermen were like surfers: one man's weather tragedy was another's sporting opportunity. The locals resented neither group; in fact they took great comfort. It was a sign of some normal rhythm of things. The surfers were the free spirits of every community, its boisterous chorus, the surf fishermen its earnest pilgrims. And these were the high holy days. October, November: it was that time of year. The puppy drum were there, the big blues came and went frequently along the beaches, and the rockfish were due in any day. Frisco Fishing Pier had lost seventy-five feet off its end, and the beach ramp up to it was gone. But surf fishing off the beach was still good, and rumor had it if you parked and walked the mile south of Frisco down the beach to where the new inlet sliced through, you'd see birds working and baitfish schooling up. Baitfish meant big fish.

I fell into neither category—construction crew or surf fishermen. The group I came closest to was "journalists," and that, I knew, was something it wasn't wise to own up to, even if I was not writing a quick and dirty feature story but what I hoped was an honorable book about a local family and a village. In the wake of Isabel, news crews had thrown money at locals and commandeered their boats over to Hatteras Village to gather hasty visuals and clichéd sound bites. In a matter of a few days, they'd pretty much succeeded in annoying, even pissing off, just about everyone on the island. They'd tied up the handful of undamaged slips at Oden's Dock, had eaten out the dock store, drunk up all the bottled water, and generally been a plague. They were soon banished one and all. One news crew, a network one, had even worked its way down the Outer Banks as Isabel was coming ashore. They wanted the exclusive, no matter what. They'd made it to Pea Island Refuge at the northern end of Hatteras Island before the wind and water got them and their vehicle. Frantic cries for help on their cell phones sent volunteer rescue workers south in the tempest. The two-and-a-half-ton truck the rescue team was in was knocked over on its side by tide and wind. It had been a miracle no one had been swept away. The imperiled rescue crew had no way of knowing the news crew was safe and dry in someone's beach house. They hadn't bothered to call and tell anyone about their good fortune. Being a newsman, even a writer, on the Outer Banks in mid-October, was something best kept to yourself. Hence my story about volunteer labor for Ernie's *Albatross* docks.

Sunday morning was an astonishingly balmy, bluebird affair. In the parking lot at the west end of the Falcon Motel, the Pamlico Sound lay in unruffled calm. At the other end, Room 1 abutting Highway 12, you could see Cape Hatteras Lighthouse rising into the still blue wallpaper. I headed the four miles south to Frisco Cove Marina, where I would tell my little white lie and board the ferry for Hatteras Village. I wanted to get there in time to look around the village with Ernie and Lynne and then go to church. They thought I should see the church service. There was a brand-new minister, and it was pretty remarkable they said.

I parked just off the white-shell road snaking around the bulkheaded opening into the sound. I grabbed my gear and walked over to a large trailer that said, "Hatteras Island Rescue Squad." A stern but friendly volunteer sat just inside the trailer's open doors, at a little school desk. He had a ledger and a pencil. He wanted to know who I was and my purpose in going to Hatteras Village.

"To work with Ernie Foster and the *Albatross* fleet." Another man wandered up and listened in. Both clearly knew Ernie, but for some reason they wanted to more about the word "fleet."

"*Albatross* fleet?"

"Yes."

"What's a fleet?" Both men leaned in, but were expressionless.

I was confused. "Well, fleet . . . The *Albatross* fleet." I said it dumbly. I seemed to think if I used the word a second time, they would get it. It was the same dumb logic I'd used in yelling English at a foreigner, assuming that volume would make my request intelligible. There was a long silence. I stood there, not realizing I was wearing a hat with a leaping marlin logo, underneath of which it said, "*Albatross* Fleet."

I finally fumbled, "Well, uh, I guess 'fleet' is a way of saying Captain Ernie has three boats."

They managed a smile, barely, and surely at my expense. There was another long silence. It was just me there. No other passengers were waiting behind me. The silence grew. I stood there. I remembered twenty-five years ago, a canoe fishing trip my wife and I went on over in Arkansas. Out of Yellville, or maybe Flippin—one of those small towns, not even a town—just a huddle of buildings outside the Buffalo River National Park, where the river entered the wilderness and came out the other end three days and thirty miles later where they'd pick you up. Renting a canoe from a local who had more canoes than teeth, but not by much, and who made us sit on his cabin porch first on a musty floral couch and talk. He didn't talk much. The long silences were unsettling. My wife was from Minnesota, I from New Jersey. We were new to the South. Everything was so strange. A long silence. Then, "You people ain't gonna see nothin' for the next three days but yourselves and bojacks." Then more silence. Panicky now. What did he mean by that? Was it a naturalist tip? A warning? What were "bojacks"? I had flashes of *Deliverance*, which we'd seen not long ago: the dueling banjo scene, Burt Reynolds, Ned Beatty. Mostly Ned Beatty. But it turned out fine. The fishing was good, and bojacks turned out to be river people who were allowed to trap and fish and live in the parks because they were there first. Several bojacks had coffee with us at one of our camps. They were friendly. None said I had a pretty mouth.

The man behind the child-sized desk in the Hatteras Island Rescue Squad trailer was measuring the white lie I'd just told him. It didn't appear to be a strenuous process. I wasn't fooling anybody. But, finally, he had me sign the ledger and waved me onto the boat docked five feet away. The boat was a commercial affair—thirty-two feet, deep institutional blue all over, with a small cabin forward and an open rear deck with long benches port and starboard and an open lattice-work of pipe overhead. I recognized this as the dive boat from Hatteras Island. They took scuba diving groups out in the summer. It had become a taxi in the wake of Isabel. Though there were only twelve of us today (hence, no doubt, the leniency of the *Deliverance* boys), the boat could hold probably thirty people in the back and another ten in the little space below decks. But the boat was bow-heavy and we'd get wet every trip, even on this bluebird day. The boat set out promptly at 10:00 A.M. for the twenty-five-minute trip over to Little Hatteras Island. We swung west out into the deeper water of the sound, and then southwest toward Oden's Dock at Hatteras Village. No one talked much, even though those of us out on the rear deck all huddled on the port-side benches to avoid the regular spray soaking the starboard seats. After about fifteen minutes everyone quietly swiveled around to see the new inlet that Isabel had cut. People were referring to it as "the breach" and not "the new inlet" because a breach was something that required fixing, filling in, while a new inlet sounded too natural and permanent. If they called it a new inlet, the state and feds might not pony up the money to fix it. The breach was there, in the distance —three blue-green spaces separated by two bushy dots, flanked on either side by the long dashes of the Outer Banks. Just south of this new Morse code, a house floated gawkily in the sound.

As we approached Oden's Dock you could see evidence of Isabel's hand. The geometry of the rooflines along the sound side was amiss. Houses leaned, boathouses bowed down, boats were missiles pointed out to sea. The marina channels at the north end of the village were lined with furniture and appliances. At Oden's Dock, boats were filling up with fuel. The slips were full within the U-shaped hook coming out from the dock store. People stood in small groups under the wooden overhang of the store. In the bright sun just to the right of the store, a table was manned by official-looking men. People stood around talking. Many people leaned on bicycles as they talked. Lynne Foster was one of them. She waved, and I made my way along the U-shape to her. Ernie joined her from a group of men nearby. There was that same warm, understated welcome I'd always gotten, but this time without so many smiles. "Ernie and I were so sad to hear about your wife," Lynne said. Ernie nodded in agreement. We would talk about that soon enough. They asked how I was doing, about my summer spent in New York City, about my journey down here. Behind them were mountains of rubble piled along what people guessed had been the shoulder of Highway 12. Behind them their village lay in ruins—and they were asking me about my affairs. The curiosity was genuine. The selflessness was stunning. As absent as so many buildings in this village was self-pity. There was none in the village. People wept, but not from despair or anger. There wasn't time. It didn't solve anything. There was so much to do. At lunch, I heard a Salvation Army worker ladling spaghetti complain good-naturedly, "You people are doing most of our work for us. You're putting us out of business!"

We went into Oden's store to get some coffee. It was dark, and the shelves were thinned out. The glass-fronted coolers lacked color behind their frosted doors. But the table was there, the one with the depth-chart top. Mismatched chairs angled this way and that around it. The predawn coffee klatch. Ernie saw me looking that way.

"Yeah, the men are still meeting here. They didn't skip a beat. Day after the hurricane, they waded over and wanted coffee and lies. It was the first sign of normalcy we had in the village." Ernie went on to tell me about Spurgeon Stowe, one of the regulars. He didn't figure the fishermen and captains would meet after the disaster. He waited two days to show up and found he was late. He was very mad.

We got into Lynne's car and headed to the north end of the village for a quick tour before church. The Internet pictures had been accurate. There was almost no north end of the village. There was no road. Sand was heaped up like saffron snow on either side of us. Debris was everywhere. You had to connect the dots. Ernie and Lynne used the past tense a lot. My favorite little side-by-side restaurants were just as they were pictured. Gone. The new community center had been reduced to a croquet hoop of steel girders. The motels—Sea Gull, Billy Mitchell, Hatteras Cabanas, Durant's Station—were torn and heaped together and scattered apart. The new open-sided shed built recently to house the old *Jackie Fay* was gone. So was the *Jackie Fay.* "Finished," said Ernie. He didn't seem to have anything else to say. The *Albatross* boats had lost a brother. Up near the breach, we had to turn around on the sand path. Flagmen. Too much construction equipment. We backtracked and drove toward the ocean on Flambeau Road. Near the ragged dune line, we turned up Sea Scape Lane, a cul-de-sac that ended in a salt marsh. The houses here were modest, shingled, working class. They were almost all up on stilts, and they all had a dark line running at uniform height horizontally along their walls. It was as if a detailer had run a decorative pinstripe ten feet off the ground, the length of the street.

Ernie stopped the car. "Three-four weeks ago, right here, we'd be sitting under water." Lynne's was a tall SUV, but judging from the high-water line to our right and left, Ernie was right, by a good margin, too.

At the end of Sea Scape, fifty yards out into the salt marsh, a white Dodge Ram pickup stood on end like a candlestick holder in a sink half full of water.

"A bitter wine," Ernie said. He knew who owned it. The man had lost all three of his vehicles and had no one to help him retrieve his truck. Tow trucks were still tied up. "He's got nowhere to go anyway," Ernie observed by way of some vague consolation.

We drove back east on Sea Scape and turned left onto Lighthouse Road, which paralleled the beach. Along here the devastation was complete. From pieces of roof and flats of shingles gone to whole houses gone. The Internet was right again. Up at the north end of Lighthouse Road, we got out and walked up to a skewed collection of beach mansions. Their insides were outside everywhere, dining room sets, kitchen cabinets, refrigerators, light fixtures, exercise bicycles, mattresses. Decks that looked like pickup sticks, hot tubs naked and trailing plumbing. The houses themselves were stove in or peeled and pocked or slumped onto the sand, knocked off their pilings. Two identical four-story monsters, pastel pink and blue, seemed to have suffered the worst. They had fallen off their spiked perches and lay at angles on the sand, their French doors open, drapery waving out into the sunlight past the dented aluminum siding. These were houses you could find any-where, in any upscale subdivision in any part of the United States. There was nothing beachy about them. They were both owned by a televangelist. The dunes in front of them were gone. The only thing that stood between them and the Atlantic Ocean fifty yards away were two identical sets of chrome loops—the tops of chrome grab bars that led down the side of swimming pools now filled and buried under the sand. Swimming pools between you and the ocean: why swim in the ocean when you can paddle in a chlorinated body of water just like the one you would find at a Best Western in Iowa?

It reminded me of the FedEx Golf Tournament I'd covered some years ago. On the final day, high rollers sat at the second-story Clubhouse Bar watch-ing the TV coverage of the tournament. They could have swiveled around and seen the real thing—golfers finishing up on the eighteenth green a hundred feet on the other side of the bar's plate-glass windows—but they preferred to watch the TV version. At the Sea Gull Motel, brick stairs led up to thin air; here, a half mile away, two chrome ladders invited bathers into the sand.

We went back to Ernie's place so that he could put on a tie, and then we headed to church. The Hatteras United Methodist Church was in the modest heart of Hatteras Village next to the little public library and the Hatteras Volunteer Fire Company. It was the only functioning church on Little Hatteras Island, the Hatteras Assembly of God having succumbed to Isabel. Sunday was living up to its name; this Sunday in mid-October was about as perfect as you could get, warm in the sun and cool in the shade, shirtsleeve mild and windless. As we rounded the sandy bend where the Burrus Red-and-White sat and where Kohler Road stopped at Highway 12, the little island in the widened road across from the church was lit up with yellow mums. Lynne and Ernie stopped in the middle of what used to be Highway 12.

"Look at that!" Lynne said, "It looks like the sun itself."

"I'll bet I know who planted them," Ernie said. He recited a name. "Boy, it's nice to get a touch of color around here." Then he paused. "Where's the marlin sculpture?" The little four-foot-high leaping lawn ornament had been a fixture on what passed for the Hatteras Village Green for years. Recently it had gone under water. Lynne heard that it was in safe hands and would soon be returned to its spot. Ernie seemed satisfied.

Francis Asbury's Methodist outpost here in Hatteras Village was a modest red-brick affair. Without its steeple, it might have passed for a VFW Post, a professional building. In the tiny vestibule people stood talking. They greeted Ernie and Lynne as they came in. They greeted me too, though I had to supply a name. That seemed fine with them. Ernie and Lynne were held by the current at the back of the church. In a hallway to the left, a room was filled with cardboard boxes and household items. Clothes spilled out of the stack of boxes that tilted and toppled like the beach houses we had just inspected. I went over and sat in a pew. The church was one large, wood-clad room, with a vaulted wood ceiling and steel arches sheathed in wood holding everything up and open. Ernie whispered during announcements that as a boy he'd sit here and pray they'd figure out a way to turn this into a basketball court six days a week. They never did.

The windows were all open, and a lovely breeze came through all during the service. Two feet up the wall was the now-familiar water line. The windows were open partly because of the nice weather and partly in an attempt to dry out the wood floor and pews. Where the pews ended in front of me, a black piano angled off to the left. A lectern squarely faced the pews to the right. In between, on the wall, a plain wood cross hung next to a modest stained-glass window. It was past 11:30, but the minister was nowhere in sight. Here and there in the pews in front of me, people clustered and talked. The group to my right was excited about the prospect of a Christian surfers' group coming over to cook for them. Children ran up and down the aisle, laughing and shouting. There was no shushing. In the pew right in front of me, a teenager, shoeless and in cutoffs, lay asleep, his head on a couple of red hymnals. In the back, people came in and stopped to visit. Some walked with clothes over their arms from the clothing room. Ernie was the only one wearing a tie. In the last pew back there, a row of stuffed laundry bags sat fat and neat, like town burghers at a Rotary dinner. The parishioners had brought in their dirty laundry. It would be taken off by boat after the service: the people of Frisco and Buxton had volunteered to wash it and fold it and send it back to the village.

Here was a town assembling to pray and to try to knit itself back together. Fiercely independent people who probably hadn't been able to visit since back in the spring before the summer tourist onslaught now fumbled handshakes and hugged awkwardly and then warmed to the necessary task and talked intimately and cried and choked up when the minister asked for a roll call of those in need. This was the American church in its finest — and oldest — sense, as both a house of worship and a place for civic peace and coming together. This is precisely what the earliest public meeting houses in New England were built for. The large structures on the old town squares were literally and symbolically the hub of each small community. Here, beginning in the early seventeenth century, townspeople came to worship their God as well as to discuss their taxes and settle their boundary disputes. A town meeting was simply the congregation reconvened to discuss civil affairs. So it was that early on, with only one public building in the community, the separation of church and state was a fine and delicate one — less a matter for philosophers than scheduling secretaries. The early New England meeting house was our first church and the cradle of our democracy. And here in Hatteras Village, Hurricane Isabel had effected the same marriage of functions. People were here to pray and sing and give thanks as well as to bring their problems and their laundry and their offers of help.

Today's service would be nondenominational because the Reverend Charles Moseley's was for the foreseeable future the only church in town. But it was hard to tell what was nondenominational in a typical Methodist church. There was a method to much small town Methodism. It knew its audience. Here among hard-working, practical, and thoroughly decent people, Methodism eased up on the fire-and-brimstone rhetoric and taught instead the virtues of uncomplicated faith and simple piety. It was an ongoing sermon grounded as much in the wisdom of Poor Richard ("A penny saved . . .") as in Holy Writ. I was raised in the bosom of small-town Presbyterianism. We were told that Methodists were just Presbyterians who hadn't learned to read. The joke aside, it seemed to me back then that we—Presbyterians and Methodists—were pretty much cut from the same sturdy and practical cloth. Going from my Boy Scout meeting to the Presbyterian youth group gathering in the church annex was a seamless trip. And in like manner Methodism and the Outer Banks proved a perfect fit. And in the ruinous aftermath of Isabel, Methodism proved the finest minister. No pomp, little ceremony. No electricity required. There was even room for a used-clothing exchange, dirty laundry, and dreams of playing basketball.

Finally, there was extra stirring in the back of the church. The minister and his wife had apparently arrived. The knot of people grew to a double bowline and then untied itself between a break in the laundry bags and spilled the minister and his wife down the center aisle. The Reverend Charles Moseley was in rain gear and no particular hurry. He took off his green slicker and made his way down toward the lectern, visiting as he went. His wife did likewise. At the front, Peggy Moseley headed over toward the piano and Reverend Moseley toward the squared lectern. He was smiling quietly. The Reverend Charles Moseley was a large man, ample of middle, with a warm, smiling spoon face framed by thinning brown hair and a neatly edged short beard. People settled themselves as the minister hitched up his pants and straightened his tie.

"I've got salt crust in my beard, and the top of my tie is wet!" he announced, clearly pleased. He explained that he'd conducted services over at Buxton at 9:00 A.M. and at Frisco at 10:00, and then jumped in a small skiff and just minutes ago arrived back at his own church. "Odd business for a country boy." Reverend Moseley had a deep southern twang from the Piedmont region of western North Carolina. He was mountain people, and so was his wife. They had been assigned this church back in June and were just settling in when Isabel appeared in the Atlantic. As the storm bore down on the village, authorities and parishioners encouraged the Moseleys to take inland refuge. No sense risking anything, and besides they had a thirteen-year-old with severe diabetes. He needed four to five shots a day. If they got stuck out here without his medicine . . .

But they chose to stay. It was likely one of the best decisions the Moseleys

The Reverend Charles Moseley leading a church service in the wake of Isabel
(Courtesy of Steve Earley, The *Virginian-Pilot*)

ever made. By doing so, they had passed the test. They had been initiated, baptized. They had ridden out the storm, had borne their losses with everyone else in their church. And they were talked about for it. It had cemented the bond. And now Reverend Moseley could speak with knowing authority.

There was a long silence following his opening quip. The minister looked as though he were in prayer. Peggy Moseley sat at the piano. More silence. Then . . .

"Who died?" he asked as his head rose. Another long pause.

"Who died?" It came again.

"No one." That was the minister's answer to his own question. Yet another silence. "Life is good, friends. It's a gift." And we were allowed to let that sink in. It had indeed been a miracle. We'd all talked about it earlier, everyone had. No one had died in the hurricane. Half the village was gone, but somehow no one had died.

Reverend Moseley went on to discuss the meaning of riches. He talked about the rich man's entering Heaven, the camel and the eye of the needle. He even told the parable of Jack Benny—the skit where Benny is held up. "Your money or your life," he's told. A long, Benny pause. "Your money or your life!" more angrily. "I'm thinking! I'm thinking!" Benny replies. Most everyone knew the bit, but everyone laughed anyway. Then we sang, "Take my silver, take my gold." Reverend Moseley talked some more, but he knew that these days out here, bodies and not just souls needed his attention. One more hymn. He chose one, but there were groans. He seemed surprised, then bemused.

Someone said, "Oh, not that one. We don't know that one."

"Well, what one would y'all like?" he asked.

"'Amazing Grace,'" the same voice said, and there was general assent. "Amazing Grace" it was. There were tears around. The family in front of us with the sleepy teenager couldn't go on. They just bowed their heads. The boy's mother sobbed. In the aftermath of this fraught moment, many stood in stricken silence hoping the minister could somehow move them forward, somewhere. Reverend Moseley wisely opened the floor to people who wished to talk. And they did. This was the third church service since Isabel, and people still wanted to talk about what had happened—to them, their neighbors, their village. They still wanted to tell their stories. And they wanted to give thanks for family deliverance. And then there were requests that help be given to shut-ins (their names were recited, and everyone nodded), to families particularly hard hit. There was an inventory of goods available at the free relief store set up over by the docks. The lunch being served by the Salvation Army next door was announced. Reverend Moseley spoke up and said the time would come soon when the good Methodists of Hatteras Village would have them a real church feed, and he went on to describe it in mouth-watering detail. He pointed out that such feeds are also nondenominational and in fact were in the natural order of things: "Any time church folks get together, chickens and pigs must die." Everyone laughed.

There was a collection, and then, as a special treat, the minister said, tongue in cheek, he would play the banjo—unless they wanted to take up another collection to make him stop. The service ended with Peggy playing piano and Charles picking the banjo—very well—and everyone singing "I'll Fly Away." As we filed out for the lunch, next door, behind the library, someone quipped, "It should have been 'I'll Float Away.'"

Very like a whale.
—William Shakespeare, *Hamlet*

CHAPTER THIRTEEN

Fate Midgett

"Please go out fishing with Ernie. He really needs this. He really wants it, but he won't say so. He really needs to get back to work, to go fishing offshore." This was Lynne. Ernie was upstairs changing out of his church clothes. I'd been wanting to go out, of course, but I saw how much work everyone was faced with, and so I was trying to stay out of the way. But fishing was work, I was being told, the good kind, and so I agreed we'd go out Tuesday. Our old friend Mike Scott would mate for us.

On Tuesday morning, in the half-dark, I met Mike at his boatyard, and we drove together down to a little dock behind Frisco Rod and Gun. In minutes Ernie came burbling up out of the scrub oak estuary to pick us up. He'd borrowed a small center-console skiff as a ferry. In the morning fog, we wound our way out the tangled creek to the sound. The swampy backyards of fishermen's houses were cluttered with old boats, pickups, nets draped over bushes, staring dogs.

As soon as we reached the open water of the sound, Ernie opened the throttle, and we got on plane for the trip to Hatteras Village. I huddled on a pile of orange life vests in the bow. Half my coffee went in me, half on me. As we approached Oden's Dock, we could see the *Miss Hatteras* lumbering up to Frisco. We were close enough to see the children—a lot of them—running around on deck. Spurgeon Stowe's bottom-fishing boat was now the village school bus. It would bring the kids back at 4:00. Children with extracurricular activities could come later on a twenty-five-seat pontoon boat. Spurgeon was the subject of considerable conversation these days in the village. He was getting paid a little over $2,000 a day to be the village school bus driver. His position on the matter had to do with liability and responsibility not to mention the danger of messing up the drive train wrestling the *Miss Hatteras* up and back in the shallow waters of the Pamlico Sound. Some people thought Spurgeon was taking advantage, gouging. Others like Ernie smiled and said little. They seemed to think, *Get it while you can. Hell, everything out here is on a feast or famine cycle. Commercial fishing, charter fishing is boom or bust. Heavy nets, tight lines—then the next day, nothing.* So why shouldn't Spurgeon get it while he can?

We slowed near the village and came in on the Back Creek, a finger of estuary that cut the corner requiring boats to swing out and into the entrance to the Hatteras Harbor Marina in front of Oden's Dock. This way, too, we could see the damage to the private homes and the Hatteras Marlin Club. Idling along, we passed a small Carolina Skiff headed out into the sound. Ernie waved to the two men. He shouted, "Did you see your dog's picture in the paper?" They laughed and gave a thumb's up. Their newsworthy dog just stared.

The dock was busy, but not with the normal commercial and sportfishing activity. There were coast guard boats, small ones, and black dredge tugs. Men in uniforms and camouflage milled around. Other men with white Sheetrock buckets brimming with tools were headed off the docks toward the village. Women with bags and bundles were arriving or waiting for a boat ride up to Frisco. We were gassed up, so all we had to do was fill the fish box with ice and we were headed southwest toward Hatteras Inlet. Ernie cut the dockside visiting to a minimum. He seemed anxious to go offshore. It had been awhile for all of us. For him, it must have seemed a lifetime.

In twenty minutes we were aboard the *Albatross III* and near the mouth of the inlet. There were the giant dredges that had arrived a week or so ago, one just off to our port inside the finger of sand that made the north side of the inlet. Another huge, black-and-maroon smokestacked dredge was over on the Ocracoke side of the inlet. Across its black-and-maroon chest, it said, "Great Lakes Dredge and Dock Company."

Tiny men stood suspended in its black tracery. They looked like scraps of sheet tin. A huge rusty dredge pipe, some four feet in diameter, floated on pontoons and snaked out from the dredge, took a sharp right onto land and disappeared into the tangled undergrowth. We knew where it went; it lumbered through the vegetation and came out on the ocean beach on the east side of the sand spit and then undulated northward along the surf line. It ran by us two days ago when we were standing by the televangelist's interred swimming pools and busted-up beach houses. The pipe stopped when it reached the new breach. Sand from the old Hatteras Inlet would be pumped up to fill in the new one. Two birds with one stone.

Except old Hatteras Inlet didn't exactly need pumping out right now. We'd been up here yesterday on the original *Albatross* fishing for blues. The inlet was twice, really almost three times the width it had been before Isabel. And it was plenty deep, even though the coast guard had to reset the buoys to mark the new primary channel. The black pilings of the long-gone coast guard station were still in the water on the south side of the inlet. They were further out now, another hundred yards or so, off the tip of Ocracoke Island. Despite nature's generous gesture, the authorities decided they'd deepen the inlet anyway. It made more sense to pump sand out of the inlet than anywhere else. The old inlet was gone. The eye took in a newer, broader Hatteras Inlet, and this new one would remain only until the next big storm. The old sand fingers flanking the inlet were gone forever too. The dancing line of sand dunes on the north side was almost leveled now, and the green pine and scrub and stunted live oaks were no longer green. The vegetation was rusted, like the dredge pipe running through it, having been burned by the fierce salt-laden winds of Isabel. This would change too. The rust would eventually yield to fresh growth. The resident eye on the Outer Banks learns not to invest in long-term relationships. Photographs out here are less fixed memories than points of comparison.

We swung east into the mouth of the new inlet. Like our Sunday church day, yesterday out here had been a perfect, sunny, windless day. A fall football day, Ernie had said. We had brought Reverend Moseley and his wife out with us. They had not been fishing yet, had never done any saltwater fishing, and by their own admission had never caught anything bigger than a bream. In short order they had pulled in more than forty good-sized bluefish. They'd be distributed to the parishioners. For another day at least, pigs and chickens would live. Ernie had worked hard to keep the minister and his wife on the fish. Clouds of screaming gulls dove on schools of silversides. Pelicans and cormorants joined in the feeding frenzy. Large numbers of skimmers, more than we'd seen in recent memory, wheeled in unison above the shoreline a hundred yards north. The blues were busting up the baitfish from below, leaving tasty chunks and wounded fish for the birds to pick up. Despite the heavy presence of blues, Ernie fussed and muttered up on the bridge.

"Damn. The fish keep going right were we've been." It did seem that way. We'd get to where they were, and then they'd appear behind us. "Damn!" Ernie would put the *Albatross* in another slow pivot. "Water this calm, the boat moves the fish. Choppier water doesn't spook them." Then another turn. "Damn! It's so calm I can't even find the shoal water!" Ernie was very happy. So was everyone. Reverend and Peggy Moseley returned to Oden's with aching arms and fish for the flock.

Now, a day later, and the inlet was in a gray mood. A good chop was on the water, and we had to wear gear against the heavy mist blowing in. Far outside, northeast off our bow, sunny spots appeared and disappeared in the gray wool skies. It looked as though someone were turning on a ceiling light in an adjoining room. Off, on. Off and then on for a long while. Then off. Ernie was happy again today, but it wasn't like yesterday's happiness. Yesterday, Ernie's good mood was tied to his desire to please the minister and his wife. He'd worked hard to get them fish and had even violated a cardinal tenet his father had taught him — "You don't leave fish to go find fish" — but that's exactly what we had done: pulled in our lines in mid-bite and gone up to Diamond Shoals to see if the stripers were there. Of course, Ernie had wanted to show his guests the new inlet, the shoreline destruction, and the famous Diamond Shoals and its always angry water. A little fishing, a little sightseeing.

But, today, Ernie's happiness seemed more insular, more pensive — more his alone. He hadn't been offshore in a while, too long. It was like letting out a hunting dog for the first time in a fortnight. Before the animated joy there were those moments of quiet reacquaintance, of getting bearings, locating landmarks, a nose testing the air, the mind's hand running slowly over a familiar surface and nodding yes. Ernie squinted into the mist, his glasses glazed, his yellow slicker slick.

"We've got the whole ocean to ourselves," he said quietly. "Just like the old days." Ernie was just about right. Two boats would show up later in the morning on the radio — *Sushi* and *Hatteras Blue* — but that was it. We'd ride for the next hour and a half with the radio on. The only voices would be the occasional shrimpers talking to each other far off somewhere over the arc of the earth. What must it have been like for his father out here, literally the only boat, out of sight of land, with no radio, or later if you had one, with no one to talk to? Out here alone, an old flathead six car engine push-ing you forward and if you cut it off, nothing. Absolutely no trace of man, and none expected. No charter boats, no commercial boats, no freight-ers in the shipping lanes. Nothing. An endless prairie of scudding clouds, swells, and blinking whitecaps. If it was solitary, it certainly wasn't solitary confinement. This kind of aloneness didn't work on the mind, erode the soul. There might be no people out here, but out here it was as busy as a Christmas kitchen. Everything was alive, everything was moving, so many variables to take into account—wind, water, weather—so much to mea-sure and to weigh against your purpose out here, against your chances of survival. If you lapse into a reverie out here, fine, but you'd better come back soon to the matter at hand. A thin cupping of wood between you and your own mortality is enough to refocus the eyes and clear the head. A banal death amid such beauty would be the final irony of a life defined by irony on the unpredictable, brutal, and gorgeous Outer Banks.

Today we were headed out to the Rock Pile about twenty-one nautical miles southeast of Hatteras Inlet. The Rock Pile was actually some rock out-croppings on the bottom, about 200 feet down under the Gulf Stream and right at the edge where the continental shelf dropped off. The Rock Pile at-tracted fish and stirred up the rich nutrient soup over its head. It had been a consistently productive area for years—marlin, sailfish, tuna, wahoo, and other pelagics riding the warm Gulf Stream north.

Ten miles short of the Rock Pile, Ernie called down to Mike Scott to put out the spread. We'd be fishing seven rods, two short-riggers, two long-riggers, two flat lines (one with a planer), and a final shotgun rod in a holder up on the bridge behind Ernie. Our baits would be skirted and naked bal-lyhoo. It wasn't long before we were pulling in small bonito. Then at 10:15, a small blackfin. A little football. We could see birds to the south and west of us. They dove in the blinking room lights, dark here, brilliant there. On and off, and on again. Ernie was on the radio with the *Sushi*. We couldn't see him, but the captain was somewhere on the other side of the birds. It started raining hard. The radio was saying, "Chasing down some birds here. It's seventy-four degrees on the inside edge. The bite is under the birds." We were fishing the inside edge too, right where the warm Gulf Stream water met the cooler southbound current.

Today, more than any other time I'd fished off Hatteras, you could clearly see the color contrast between the blue water of the Gulf Stream and the green water outside it. The blue water this time of year ran up to eighty degrees, while the green water a few feet away was fifteen to twenty degrees cooler. A distinct linear demarcation. The edge of the Gulf Stream. It was right here where the action was. Here too, because of the peculiar chafing physics of the water, a line of amber seaweed could be found. The "Yellow Brick Road" captains called it because underneath that floating weed fish often hovered and fed, especially dorado or dolphin or mahimahi, or whatever you chose to call them. They were that snoutless, electric, blue-yellow species, so wonderfully sporting, so delicious.

We stayed edged up for about fifteen minutes more and then one of the flat line poles went off. A nice dorado. I held him behind the boat about twenty feet out while Ernie and Mike grabbed the light spinning rods and baited them with ballyhoo chunks. Every so often Mike tossed some cut-up ballyhoo behind the boat to keep the fish interested. You could see dorado flashing all around their hooked brother, darting after the ballyhoo. We got the spinning rods baited and free-spooled them back toward the hooked dorado. The water came alive. We couldn't catch them fast enough. We hoisted five, six, seven, then eight, and finally nine into the fish box. Then it was over, just like that.

I brought the attractor dorado in on the flat line, and we were off looking for more. The rain had reverted to that fine mist again. We trolled on, mostly in silence. Even the radio was dead. Charter fishing, in almost all places in the world, has the rhythm of a hook and ladder company. Long, long periods of inactivity, filled up with quiet chatting, policing equipment, dozing, reading, followed by brief moments of frantic, often heart-pounding activity. We entered the library. Water dripped from the outriggers, from the bridge railing, from the cabin roof, the boat rocked and jingled and clacked, the Cummins diesel thrummed its two notes. I sat on the bridge with Ernie. We enjoyed the muffled soundtrack, the gentle back and forth of the quartering *Albatross*. After a while, I asked Ernie how long he planned to do this, to go on running the *Albatross* fleet. It was obviously something he'd been thinking about—no doubt in part because Isabel recently had almost answered the question for him. But it was also because he was within shouting distance of sixty, and his kids were off and wanted nothing to do with the business. And this summer business had been off by about a quarter—for everyone, not just the *Albatross* fleet. People had vacation money but not the $800 to $1,000 it took for blue-water fishing. Ernie's answer came soon.

"Well, I'm not as agile as I used to be. I've been noticing that lately, just hopping on and off the boats. And . . ." His mind was working. He had a schoolboy's habit of chewing on his tongue when he was thinking. "You know, I've been watching these nature programs on TV, maybe that's it, and, of course, our trip to Africa not long ago, me and Lynne, all that amazing stuff we saw. Animals in these incredible struggles to survive . . . Day after day. I guess it's struck me lately that . . . , well, life is that struggle. Life isn't something you achieve after the struggle. Life is the struggle itself." Ernie was seldom embarrassed by such insights, such pronouncements, and he wasn't now. He seemed perfectly comfortable in the long silence that followed. In fact he wasn't finished answering the question.

"No, I'm not as agile, and my mind isn't as agile either. I find myself saying to people 'Give me time. I'll remember that guy's name or the name of that boat.' It comes eventually, but there's that hesitation . . . So I don't know. Maybe three or four more years. I might sell a couple of the boats, or keep one and put one on display . . ." It was hard to imagine a couple of the *Albatross*es turned into commercial fishers, another sitting in a shed along Highway 12, as the *Jackie Fay* had until a few weeks ago when Isabel came and got her. It was hard to tell if Ernie accepted this fate or was simply resigned to it. Whichever, he certainly was not inveighing against the gods for their banal script.

Down below Mike knocked on the ladder. Ernie and I came back around and looked out. All around us, in the gray-green chop were porpoises, hundreds of them loping along singly and in small groups. Eight to ten of them flanked our bow, close in. I'd seen almost this many when we'd watched them mating up near Diamond Shoals, but never this far out at sea. As we looked, one porpoise came up about twenty feet to port, came all the way out of the water horizontally and very animatedly whacked the side of its head on the surface of the sea. It made a loud noise. I counted; he did this eight times in rapid succession and then disappeared. Ernie was smiling. "You don't see them do that particular trick very often. He was just playing. Maybe he was just missing the boats not being out here. Maybe he's glad to see us."

Soon the porpoises were gone. A light rain continued to fall. I glanced at my damp watch. It was almost exactly noon. Just then the planer rod bent over and the reel began to sizzle. I scrambled down the wet ladder and got into the fighting chair. The fish had that frantic wahoo anger about it. It made two nice runs and then came in, exhausted. It was a twenty-plus-pounder, a good-sized fish, and it had been rambunctious enough that it tangled up with another flat line and shortrigger. With him still banging in the fish box, Mike and I hunched over the lines to untangle them. Ernie came down from the bridge and stood watching us. He was going to grab his lunch. We bent back to our work.

Then Ernie moved suddenly, almost knocking Mike off stride. We both looked up, and we saw what Ernie was staring at. It came out of the water a second time just as the porpoise had done twenty minutes earlier, arced out horizontally headed in the same direction as the *Albatross III*. The sailfish was out further, maybe twenty-five yards, and it didn't bang its head on the water. It shook it back and forth, and then went down again. "It's on the line!" Ernie shouted. We, all three of us, looked around frantically to see which rod had the hook-up. It was the bridge rod. I dropped my knife and headed for the ladder. Ernie shouted "NO! Stay here!" and he scrambled up. I came to my senses and waited. Ernie handed the rod down to me, and I slid over to the fighting chair. Mike hooked up the harnesses. I braced my legs on the footrest and just then the sailfish came out of the water, close in. It shimmied on its tail for longer than physics seemed to allow, and it lit up an electric neon blue, dark blue with lighter stripes. I had read about this phenomenon of billfish lighting up and then switching off next to the boat. Ernie had talked about it every so often, but I had never seen it firsthand. In the light rain and the flat gray background, the effect was stunning. The fish was a large, illuminated letter on an old manuscript. It crashed back into the water and then, almost immediately, was up again on another long tail-walk.

I was mesmerized. I remember saying, out loud, "I think that's the most beautiful thing I've ever seen." I had the presence of mind to keep a tight line, but not much more than that. I remember Ernie putting his hand on my shoulder and saying, "Well, bring him in then!" Ernie was running the boat from the controls behind me, backing it down, keeping the line as straight over the stern as he could. The sail would stay down now, except maybe for a half-appearance near the boat as he came in. I pumped and reeled, pumped and reeled. It took out line several times. But I knew I would bring this fish to the boat. I don't know why. It's not a feeling you often have as a fisherman, especially in mid-fight. You're too busy in the moment, and even if you had time, you wouldn't want to gum it up, to jinx yourself with any two-bit prescience. But I remember thinking I would see this fish close up, and the really odd thing is, I remember thinking this thought while standing up behind me in the fighting chair. I witnessed this encounter with a magnificent sailfish from a point just behind myself. I had dreamed my whole life of catching a billfish, and now for some reason

I was catching one and at the same time I was watching myself catch one. That was me there in the fighting chair and that was the sailfish out there. It was as close as I've come to an out-of-body experience, yet it didn't seem extraordinary at the time, nor does it seem particularly mystical now. It was as though the narrative of my life simply switched its point of view from first person to third person. I'm not attracted to the occult, nor am I even mildly interested in dreams and the meanings of dreams. Neither am I quick to climb on some psychoanalytic explanation tethered conveniently nearby—something like "a dissociative experience brought on by stress or general suggestibility"—and ride that nag to the dance in town. Whatever I experienced is what I experienced. Its mystery shall remain intact, and for my money that's how it should be. Sometimes, to explain is to diminish.

The fish showed itself clearly once close into the transom, and then I was on my feet feeding the leader into Mike's gloved hand. Ernie was standing up on the fish box taking pictures with my camera. I couldn't take my eye off the fish. Or he me. Its great unblinking black eye seemed fixed on me. I could see the hook in the roof of its mouth, the three-inch tear it had made during its struggle. And I noted the muddy stripe down its body where magnificent moments before it had been blazing blue.

"Do you want to keep it?" Mike asked.

I remember laughing at the thought. "No."

I put the rod in the holder and reached over the side and took hold of the fish's bill, below where Mike held it. The fish planed beside the moving boat, still staring at me. I could feel the life at play in its length. It was well over six feet. And then we let it go.

Ten years ago, maybe less, this sailfish would be hanging back at the dock with me standing beside it for pictures. Now that was the last thing I had wanted, and I was very happy. Seeing it, touching it had been enough. I climbed back up to the bridge. Ernie was subdued but happy. He apologized for yelling at me when the fish got on. It was fine.

After a while, I reflected on the moment. "You know," I said, "catching this sailfish just goes to show, if you think too much about something, if you want it too badly, it probably won't come to pass." I felt myself warming up, striding toward some large, profound finish. "Today," I said, "we hadn't even talked about billfish. Hell, the season is really almost over"—I wasn't sure about this, but no matter—"and what happens? We catch one." Now I appeared ready to add the homily: "If we could just relax and accept our fates," I intoned, "then our fates would happen." There was a long pause.

Captain Ernie stared out at the sea ahead of him. The mist blew in on us through the open plastic curtain. Then, without turning his head, he said, "I once had an uncle named Fate. Fate Midgett."

We trolled on through the early afternoon. We caught a stray wahoo, a bookend to the one we'd caught just before noon, and then around 2:00 P.M. the planer rod came alive, very alive. I got in the fighting chair and held on. The line hissed off the reel, hissed without break or hesitation. One hundreds yards, 150 yards, 175, then SNAP! Gone.

"Now that was a nice fish," Ernie called down from the bridge. "Probably a yellowfin." My arms were still tingling. In football and NASCAR racing, they talk about teams, drivers, winning going away. That fish just won going away, literally. It reminded me of that bluefin I'd hooked when I had been out with Tall Bill a year ago November, except we'd gotten a peek at that one. This one was simply disembodied force. The mystery of this fish would remain too.

It seemed the right moment to head back. Besides, the wind was picking up, and the rain was following suit. I helped Mike bring in the lines and stow the rods. Then he got out the short hose and the mop, so I got out of the way, up the ladder to Ernie. Ernie throttled up the *III*, and we swung back to the northwest and Hatteras Inlet. It was easy to talk above the engine up on the bridge. Ernie teased me about the sailfish.

"You know, you caught that fish, but you didn't hook it. Now if they ask about it, you're going to have to tell them who hooked it."

"Who was that?" I asked.

"Rodney Holder."

"Rodney Holder?" I was at a loss.

"Yup. Rodney Holder." His face was still.

Rodney Holder. Rodney Holder. Oh, rod holder. The rod was in the holder when the fish hit. OK. Fate Midgett. Rodney Holder: I would accept my hazing, my comeuppance like a man.

Then we talked for a while about engines. I was curious about costs. The *Albatross III* had a Cummins 250-horse diesel. On a typical offshore charter, the *III* would burn fifty to fifty-five gallons of diesel. A boat I had always thought of in contrast to the *Albatross* fleet was the *Big Easy*. The *Big Easy* was down at the Hatteras Landing Marina. It was a new fifty-seven-foot, state-of-the-art Briggs with every bell and whistle, every amenity for customer comfort. It also sported twin 660-horse Caterpillar diesels.

Ernie said, "Captain Parker easily burns more than twice what I do on an offshore charter. Of course, he gets there faster than I do, but at $1.40

a gallon for diesel, he's paying upwards of $200 a trip for fuel." And so we chatted on until the silences asserted themselves, and we enjoyed the ride and the breeze, now dried out.

An hour went by, punctuated by an idle comment here and there. I had a thousand questions I wanted to ask Ernie, but this was more pleasant, more appropriate. The day had started in still reflection, quiet friendship, and it seemed to want to end that way too. Fine. It was better now to feel rather than think. And this felt good. I wasn't sure when I'd be able to visit Hatteras again, to ride out on the *Albatross* boats with Ernie. Ernie had so much to do to recover from Isabel — rebuild his docks, the bulkheads, refurbish the boats. It might well take most of the three years or so he felt he had left in the business. And who knew if they'd be willing or able to fill in the new inlet, reconnect Hatteras with the mainland, run Highway 12 back down to the village. And if they did, over half the motels in the village were gone. Three remained. Where would the fishermen stay?

And for my part too, life was changing. Loss takes many forms. Ernie was facing his loss; I was here seeking respite from mine. Except three hours ago I had a sailfish on, and I remember thinking, "I can't wait to tell Mo . . ." The heart has a mind of its own. In getting Ernie to talk about his loss, part of me was trying to avoid dealing with my own. Yet in talking about his loss, Ernie was forcing me to face mine. It was all connected. I sensed that the day I came over to the ravaged island, even before I set foot on the splintered dock — the roofs floating in the sound, the houseless stilts sticking up along the water, the rubble choking the inlets. I sensed the connection when Reverend Moseley paused at the beginning of the sermon and asked his beleaguered parishioners, "Who died?" On this long fishing day together, Ernie never brought up Mo's death. But, of course, he had. We'd been talking about it all along, even in the silences.

Maybe the sight of land stirred Ernie. When that familiar dark strip appeared way off our port bow, Ernie spoke. I wondered if he were talking to me. He seemed to have been talking to himself because he began in mid-conversation.

"It really makes this feel different. Better. Isabel did this. It's really better in a strange way."

I said nothing. He went on. "The day after the storm, I knew the village was ruined. It came ashore the day before, during the day, so we could watch what was happening. We saw what it was doing. It was what my father predicted would happen. Once in everyone's lifetime, he said. And this was mine."

We passed the inlet buoy. "I woke up the morning after the hurricane. It was a beautiful, sunny morning. The bedroom window was up, and just as I opened my eyes, I heard a bird chirping. It seemed like the most amazing thing to me. I put on some clothes and walked downstairs and out into the front yard. The street was buried under a layer of sand. There were big timbers scattered all over the place. I could see what the water had done down the way over by my boats. But what really caught my eye was this little spider in a bush right next to where I was standing. I looked close, and it was building its web. It had somehow survived this terrible storm, and here it was rebuilding its web. I watched it for a long time."

A noiseless, patient spider. Ernie drew a breath and started again. "I wanted to start in helping everyone out, there was so much work to do, but I really couldn't. It was strange. I had this feeling that we were all in this thing together, and I somehow wanted to express that, I wanted to do something big, but I didn't know what. I just walked around all morning in this kind of detached state. I guess the big thing I did was just marvel at everything around me. It was really strange."

It wasn't long before we entered Hatteras Inlet. The rain had picked up once again and we zipped the plastic curtain flap shut. Big rain thrummed off our translucent tent up on the bridge. The sailfish flag snapped briskly off the outrigger just behind us. It was upside down to indicate a release. By the time we reached Oden's Dock, the rain had turned petulant, insisting on the attention of everyone in it. We tied up out by the diesel pumps on the outside hook of the wooden dock. Mike and I loaded up the plastic garbage can with our dolphin and small tuna and two big wahoo. We toted it up under the eaves in front of the dock store, right next to the cleaning tables. It was pouring. The only other boat moving around was that blue dive boat the islanders were using as a taxi. It was idling out where we'd tied up the *Albatross III*. Two hooded figures stood in the rain on its open back deck. Ernie was over talking to a group of men. I took out the two wahoo and stood them stiffly on their noses, holding one in each hand just below the black forked tails, which came up almost to my shoulders. Ernie came over. He looked at his watch. It was minutes from 5:00.

"Look, the dive boat's leaving in a few minutes for Buxton. The next one's at 6:00. It's the last one of the day. And these guys are saying it'll be packed with rescue personnel and construction workers. So maybe you and Mike better grab that boat," nodding out behind us. "Here give me those," Ernie said of the two wahoo flanking me. Mike and I looked at each other and nodded assent. I thanked Ernie hastily. I couldn't shake his hand because of the fish he was holding. It was all inadequate, and I was leaving the next day. What would be adequate? Not anything I could imagine. I'd borne witness to their lives and the life of their village changing forever, had gone to church with them, had gone out with Ernie on his first blue-water trip since the hurricane, had caught a magnificent sailfish.

Mike and I turned and jogged out into the rain out to the dive boat. Mike went down below. I stayed outside. The boat must have been waiting for us. It swung away from Oden's Dock almost immediately. Ernie stood there, a dark triptych—two vertical fish held at arm's length, canted outward slightly from a central human form, spraddled and still. A tin silhouette —Ernie looked like a yard sign you might find for sale at Robinson's Store over by the wind chimes and whirligigs. "Greetings from the Outer Banks."

It didn't seem possible, but it was raining even harder. I wanted to stay out in the elements. My foul weather gear was doing its job though my deck shoes were soaked and my rubberized pockets were full of water. One young man with a full brown beard, a felt hat, and a bucket of tools stood next to me in the rain. His black-and-brown mutt sat at his feet shivering and look-ing up at him often. The only other person out here was an older, heavy-set woman in white shrimper's boots. She sat on the windward side of the boat crouched on the bench behind an umbrella. She was using it as a shield. The waves flew up from the bow of the boat and rattled onto her umbrella, one after the other. It looked like some crazy vaudeville skit—someone offstage throwing buckets of water on this huddled person who would peek out every so often, her eyes twinkling, and smile at us and duck back under. She seemed happy where she was. I couldn't understand why she didn't move.

———

The following day was sunny and almost hot. A small breeze came up from the southwest and stirred the canopy of live oaks across the motel park-ing lot. It was just after sunup when I walked from my room and across Highway 12 to the Lighthouse Restaurant. I had arranged to meet Tall Bill for coffee before I left to catch my flight up in Norfolk. Half the tables were filled already with fishermen on their way to the beach and construction workers grabbing some bacon and eggs and coffee before catching the ferry over to Hatteras. Bill was over at a corner table by the huge wall aquarium, his long legs twined and his ratty *Net Results* hat bobbing as he talked with a couple of fishermen at the next table.

Bill loved to talk almost as much as he loved to fish. Because of his accent probably, it always struck me as that special kind of New Jersey garrulousness I'd grown up listening to at my parents' little restaurant on the boardwalk. Bathers, but more typically the fishermen and the locals who came for coffee and talk in the spring before Memorial Day and after Labor Day when the tourists went home: they were the ones who talked like Bill. The discourse had its own special rhythm and cadence, its own steady insistence and tone like the signature sound of a boat going through the water. It was very sure of itself, what it had to say, and it most often was rendered in a tone of incredulity or resignation at the recalcitrance of the life it was describing or the stupidity of people in it. The unspoken coda of these conversations was "Can you believe that?" Bill had taught science in public high school and so knew the intricate physics of a world where the land met the sea. He had also been forced to acquaint himself with government bureaucracy. He had grudging respect for the former and unalloyed contempt for the latter. If the inlet pass shoaled up overnight and he ran aground in familiar water, or if the Fish and Game people came up with illogical commercial fishing quotas, Bill's steady conversation made a beeline for the identical coordinates: "Can you believe that?"

Bill swung around when I walked up and gave a big smile and a handshake. He was in very good spirits. Bill was still seeing that woman we had met at the Captains' Banquet. Ernie claimed it had transformed Bill. He was right. Surely for the first time in our several-years-now friendship Bill did not open up on the topic of fishing or our mutual connection to the Jersey Shore. And surely too for the first time that morning in the Lighthouse Restaurant, a conversation didn't start on the subject of Hurricane Isabel. No, this man was in love. It was in the air around him as surely as the fatback odor was from his haul yesterday. Tall Bill wanted to talk about Michelle and he did, like one of his old high school students. It was nice to see. There was something in it too that was intimate, maybe as intimate as Tall Bill allowed himself to get. We had a special bond now. We'd both recently lost our wives, and the shape of our grieving matched. Embedded in his tale of new courtship was a respectful acknowledgment of our old bond.

I had a lot of questions for Bill about commercial fishing on the Outer Banks, and we sat a long time, occasionally walking outside so Bill could smoke a cigarette. After an hour and a half, I told Bill something else that was on my mind. Before I left around 2:00 P.M. for the airport, I really wanted to find the grave site of Benjamin B. Daily. I told Bill about Daily's exploits as an early lifesaver, about his gold lifesaving medals, his reputation. I told him too about my earlier attempt to find Daily's grave on Cemetery

Road just north of Hatteras School. I didn't tell him why I was looking for Daily because I really wasn't quite sure myself. I had read about Benjamin B. Daily, and, on a blowday a few years back, I had gone looking for him. Now, for some reason, it seemed an important loose end, and I wanted to connect it to something.

Bill thought for a moment.

"Yeah, the Dailys. Well, they're all over the place here. Above ground, underground. Everyone knows the Daily family. They've been here a long time. Hard to swing a dead cat without hitting one. Let's see . . . Let's see. You know, if anyone would know where Benjamin Daily is buried it would be Lisa Midgett. Yeah, she'd know. Here, you wait here." And Bill got up and went off to find a phone. He was back in no time.

"Well, sure enough. She said she knew. She says it's down Highway 12, down by Hatteras School, but it's not that Cemetery Road you were talking about. She says it's on the other side of the road, right across from the baseball diamond by the school. You can almost see it from the road. I think I know where she means. There's so many cemetery plots around here, I'll bet there's one in that patch of brush across from the school." We were in Bill's pickup heading south before I knew it. Bill smoked and talked, mostly about the new docking arrangements he'd had to make for the *Net Results* up in Frisco since Isabel. He wasn't sure when the fish houses in Hatteras Village would be able to open again, so he was selling fatback and such directly to the bait stores in Frisco and Buxton.

Soon we were by the baseball diamond. We parked on the shoulder and walked across the road and up a little incline thick with tangled brush. Pricker bushes had their way with us, and our socks were soon covered with annoying burrs. We saw the top of a low chain-link fence marking off a square area about half the size of a tennis court. Leg-sized trees crowded the fence and pushed through it. Others had died and fallen on it. It was only thirty feet off Highway 12, but it was slow going. We inched around the tangled perimeter until we found the gate. Inside was a scattering of stones, some old and lichen covered, some pinkish and newer. There in front, in the bow of this little lifeboat bound for eternity, was the tombstone of Benjamin B. Daily. Its inscription was plain and reticent and clear like the people on the Banks. A name, a birth date and date of death, the standard factual bookends of a life lived. The only hint of the remarkable nature of this particular life was a small bas-relief of a lifesaving medal with two oars crossed above it. Under the medal it said, "A Testimony of Heroic Deeds in Saving Life from the Perils of the Sea."

Benjamin B. Daily grave site
(Courtesy of Lynne Foster)

In *Moby-Dick* Captain Ahab nailed a gold coin to the mainmast of the *Pequod* and told the crew that the first man to spot the white whale could claim it. In their idle moments they wandered up to the coin, examined its cabalistic signs (a mountain, a sun, a crowing cock) and wondered at the narrative it contained. Here too, it seemed, a stranger could only stand in a tangle of brush and vines and ankle-deep dry leaves and wonder at the story contained in the indistinct details of the medal. I had read about, and so I knew, some of the hidden details. Benjamin B. Daily, captain of the Creed's Hill Lifesaving Station; in 1881 the near-impossible rescue of eleven doomed souls aboard the *A. B. Goodman*; it looked so bad that Daily and his crew had written out their own wills before they hauled their wood boat through the howling wind to the edge of the sea. Later he was captain of the Cape Hatteras Station further down the Banks. And then the rescue of another boatload of souls from the *Ephraim Williams*. That was in 1884. That was just a handful of facts, the tarred ribs sticking up through the sand. How many hearts were allowed to beat on unbroken, how many great-great-grandchildren were born and alive today because of one man's astounding ability to weave a wooden boat through a monstrous surf, to steer it through sleet and angry shoal water, and deposit a sodden human cargo onto a beach with blankets and bonfire?

Out here on the Outer Banks, so much tangible history—houses, vehicles, boats, beloved heirlooms, family albums, even buried coffins—is carried off

forever in the blinking of a hurricane's eye. Is the irony that the less material things like memory, lore, legend—those things more wind resistant and
weatherproof—fare better here? Maybe this medal was a mute reminder that
the good this man did was not interred with his bones. Here I was, after all,
running my fingers over its bas-relief topography. I looked over at Tall Bill.
He was squatted down, smoking. His knees stuck up like two oars as he read
the inscription on another stone further back toward the stern of the plot.
Then I thought of Ernie in the little family plot behind his father's net house,
how comfortable, how pleased he seemed to be there, how proud even.

Bill had to go meet Michelle, and I had to check out of the Falcon Motel,
so we headed back up Highway 12. We said our goodbyes, and we wished
each other well. There was the usual awkwardness, but we looked each
other in the eye and said what we really meant to say.

I still had an hour or so before I had to begin the drive north to the airport, so when I pulled out of the Falcon lot, I found myself turning south
on Highway 12. Off to my left was the road into the Hatteras Lighthouse
Park. I turned in. There were no cars on the access road headed east to the
lighthouse and the beach. One of the park ranger access roads angled off to
the left into the thicket of trees and brush. The chain across its mouth was
on the ground. I drove in and was soon all by myself. I got out of the car
and walked back for some way into the dry tangle of growth. I'm not sure
why I was doing anything I was doing on this last day on the Outer Banks.
At the time, I don't recall motive being an issue. I had just paid my respects
to the dead in that little cemetery plot with Tall Bill, and now I was alone in
the vibrant tangle of Buxton Woods in the shadow of the lighthouse. The
3,000 remaining acres of this maritime forest ecosystem were the sole living survivors of the land-clearing predations undertaken by generations of
settlers in the eighteenth and nineteenth centuries and by developers today.
Faulkner had marveled at the resilience of his beloved forests in Yoknapa-
tawpha County, Mississippi, a parcel of land that, in his wonderful Faulk-
nerese, he described as "a wilderness . . . an epitome and apotheosis of the
old wild life which little puny humans swarmed and hacked at in a fury of
abhorrence and fear like pygmies about the ankles of a drowsing elephant."
Well, here I stood, astride the drowsing elephant of the Outer Banks, still
threatened by man, but still very much alive.

Not only that. These remaining highland woods just north of Hatteras
Village gave continual life to those very forces that threatened it with clear-
cutting extinction; Buxton Woods contains the huge but delicate freshwater
aquifer that has made life on the Outer Banks possible. The fresh water sits

Young Ernie Foster (Courtesy of Ernie Foster)

—floats, really—like a giant contact lens atop a substrate of salt water (fresh water is lighter than its salty cousin, hence its ability to float atop it). Without this thin, convex, life-giving liquid shell, there would be no seven little villages from Rodanthe to Hatteras on the south Banks. There would be no drawing boards filled with developers' dreams, no motels, no thyroidic mansions, few boats, no *Albatross* fleet, no Fosters, no Midgetts, no Benjamin B. Dailys. Nature not only forgives those who trespass against her out here; she gives them the gift of life. Buxton Woods was the beating heart of the Outer Banks. And a uniquely chambered heart it was, too. Many species of flora and fauna in this 5,000-year-old forest are found nowhere else. Scientists call them "isolated disjuncts"—evolutionarily unique species, different in identifiable ways to their mainland counterparts. Buxton Woods was also famous for what ecologists and scientists call the "Line"—that is, a point of demarcation where two distinct ecosystems meet. And all who study it agree with writers and naturalists James Lazell and John Alexander that the Buxton Woods "Line" is "certainly one of the clearest edges visible in ecology, evolutionary biology, and biogeography." An examination of the photograph of the Outer Banks taken by Apollo 9 in 1969, or simply standing on the sandy Frisco Campground Road and looking west, allows you to see a dramatic change: a cascade of dark green vegetation, trees and shrubbery simply coming to halt at an area of sand and grass that continues south. This is the line between a northern ecosystem and a hotter, drier biota called the Intercapes Zone. Crossing from north to south is to leave behind essentially northern species like loblolly pine, blue beech, and hornbeam and to encounter more distinctly southern palmetto, live oak, and red cedar. Even though the "Line" has been tampered with by man, the Buxton Woods demarcation zone remains historically unique in its continuing clarity.

And so, having just respected the dead at that tiny, dessicated cemetery, I tried here in Buxton Woods to celebrate life and its unique persistence and generosity. Death and life, endings and continual beginnings, I thought of young Ernal Foster Sr. curing the juniper planking that would make his boat and define his life. And his son, Ernie, tending his father's beloved boat and his grave too, out behind the net house. I thought of my lovely wife forced so slowly to give up her bounty to the dead. I thought of my vibrant children at the start of their sailings. And I thought of that pale morning moon behind us in Hatteras Inlet and the orange wafer of sun rising above the *Albatross* bow.

Bibliography

Alexander, John, and James Lazell. *Ribbon of Sand: The Amazing Convergence of the Ocean and the Outer Banks.* Chapel Hill: University of North Carolina Press, 2000.

Bailey, Anthony. *The Outer Banks.* New York: Farrar, Straus and Giroux, 1989.

Ballance, Alton. *Ocracokers.* Chapel Hill: University of North Carolina Press, 1989.

Barfield, Rodney. *Seasoned by Salt: A Historical Album of the Outer Banks.* Chapel Hill: University of North Carolina Press, 1995.

Booker, Mike, and Lin Ezell. *Out of Harm's Way: Moving America's Lighthouse.* Gambrills, Md.: Eastwind Publishing, 2001.

Cleveland, John M. *The Albatross Fleet.* Coatesville, Pa.: Jerome W. Klein Printing, 1984.

DeBlieu, Jan. *Hatteras Journal.* Winston-Salem: John F. Blair, 1998.

———. *Wind.* Boston: Houghton Mifflin, 1999.

Frankenberg, Dirk. *The Nature of North Carolina's Southern Coast: Barrier Islands, Coastal Waters, and Wetlands.* Chapel Hill: University of North Carolina Press, 1997.

———. *The Nature of the Outer Banks.* Chapel Hill: University of North Carolina Press, 1995.

MacNeill, Ben Dixon. *The Hatterasman.* Winston-Salem: John F. Blair, 1958.

Meyer, Peter. *Nature Guide to the Carolina Coast.* Wilmington: Avian-Cetacean Press, 2000.

Peffer, Randall S. *Watermen.* Baltimore: Johns Hopkins University Press, 1979.

Shelton-Roberts, Cheryl, ed. *Hatteras Keepers: Oral and Family Histories.* Morehead City: Lighthouse Society, 2001.

Stick, David. *The Graveyard of the Atlantic.* Chapel Hill: University of North Carolina Press, 1952.

———. *The Outer Banks of North Carolina, 1584–1958.* Chapel Hill: University of North Carolina Press, 1958.

———, ed. *An Outer Banks Reader.* Chapel Hill: University of North Carolina Press, 1998.

West, Susan, and Barbara J. Garrity-Blake. *Fish House Opera.* Mystic, Conn.: Mystic Seaport, 2003.

Wright, David, and David Zoby. *Fire on the Beach: Recovering the Lost Story of Richard Etheridge and the Pea Island Lifesavers.* New York: Scribner, 2001.